Bug Proofing Visual Basic: A Guide to Error Handling and Prevention

Rod Stephens

WILEY COMPUTER PUBLISHING

John Wiley & Sons, Inc.

New York • Chichester • Weinheim • Brisbane • Singapore • Toronto

Publisher: Robert Ipsen
Editor: Carol A. Long
Managing Editor: Frank Grazioli
Text Design & Composition: Benchmark Productions, Inc.

Designations used by companies to distinguish their products are often claimed as trademarks. In all instances where John Wiley & Sons, Inc., is aware of a claim, the product names appear in initial capital or ALL CAPITAL LETTERS. Readers, however, should contact the appropriate companies for more complete information regarding trademarks and registration.

This publication is designed to provide accurate and authoritative information in regard to the subject matter covered. It is sold with the understanding that the publisher is not engaged in professional services. If professional advice or other expert assistance is required, the services of a competent professional person should be sought.

Library of Congress Cataloging-in-Publication Data:
Stephens, Rod
  Bug proofing Visual Basic : a guide to error handling and
prevention / Rod Stephens.
    p. cm
  "Wiley Computer Publishing"
  Includes index.
    ISBN 0-471-32351-9 (pbk. : alk. paper)
    1. Microsoft Visual BASIC. 2. Debugging in computer science.
  I. Title.
  QA76.73.B3S8333   1998
  005.26'8–dc21   98-37208
                                                                   CIP

Printed in the United States of America.

10 9 8 7 6 5 4 3 2 1

CONTENTS

Every program more than 10 lines long contains at least one bug.

While the preceding statement may not be provable, it is generally a good assumption. Removing absolutely every bug from any nontrivial program is an extremely difficult task. Proving every bug has been removed is even harder. To prove a program contains a bug, you need only demonstrate the bug. To prove that a program has no bugs is much more difficult.

In fact, some software development models assume that all complex programs have bugs and that they can never be completely removed. The goal is not to remove all of the bugs from the application, but to remove so many that those remaining appear only very rarely to the end users.

Visual Basic provides an environment for writing applications while minimizing bugs that is unmatched by other languages. Visual Basic's runtime libraries handle many of the messier details of Windows programming, removing a huge source of potential bugs. By automatically freeing objects that are not referenced, Visual Basic eliminates a wide assortment of memory handling errors that are quite troublesome in other languages.

Unless you have programmed extensively in Delphi, C++, or some other more powerful and flexible language, you cannot fully appreciate how many bugs Visual Basic prevents before they arise. It only takes a few hours tracking an obscure pointer problem in C++ to make you appreciate the fact that Visual Basic does not have pointers. More powerful and flexible languages let you do many things that are difficult in Visual Basic, but one of those things is to write bugs that are really hard to fix.

For other kinds of errors, Visual Basic's family of On Error statements allows a program to anticipate errors and take action to recover from them. The Err object allows a program to simulate errors for testing, or to generate new errors of its own.

Finally, Visual Basic's integrated development environment includes excellent debugging features. It allows you to step through your program, set breakpoints on specific lines of code, examine and modify values, set watches to monitor values as they change, change the program's point of execution, and even interactively modify the source code without interfering with the running program.

While Visual Basic provides all these potent tools, it is up to you to take advantage of them. The programming environment alone cannot guard against every possible kind of bug. If your program sets a variable to the value 17 when it should have the value 7, Visual Basic cannot know this is an error. You must detect this bug and use the development environment to find and fix the problem.

Many Visual Basic books mention bugs in passing. Most describe Visual Basic's On Error statements, but they cover On Error only briefly. The On Error statement itself cannot prevent, identify, or remove bugs, however. It merely allows the program to keep running in spite of them.

Bug Proofing Visual Basic explains bug prevention, detection, and eradication in Visual Basic. It tells how to design and implement code that prevents bugs from occurring in the first place. It explains techniques you can use to make your code expose bugs instead of hiding them. It shows how to test code so you can catch and fix bugs as quickly as possible. Finally, it explains how to bugproof Visual Basic programs so they can continue to run even if a bug slips through the design and testing process and is shipped to a user.

What This Book Provides

Bug Proofing Visual Basic has three goals: to explain how to code to prevent bugs from occurring, to show how to handle unexpected bugs that do occur, and to explain how to locate and fix those bugs. This book explains how to

- Code proactively to prevent bugs before they start
- Use coding and naming conventions to prevent bugs
- Write code that exposes bugs instead of hiding them
- Catch bugs quickly before they do serious harm
- Find bugs using tools like the debugger and code profiler
- Use debug and runtime versions of a program to make debugging easier
- Use On Error statements to handle unexpected conditions
- Record information automatically so you can fix bugs after users encounter them

Intended Audience

Before reading *Bug Proofing Visual Basic*, you should have some familiarity with Visual Basic, but you do need not be an expert. The book does not require any advanced knowledge of Visual Basic. If you have read any introduction to Visual Basic programming, you will have no trouble reading this book.

It can even be argued that it is more important for beginners to read *Bug Proofing Visual Basic* than for advanced programmers. After years of experience, many advanced programmers have learned some of the topics presented here the hard way, through trial and error. By reading this book, a beginner can learn these tricks and techniques quickly and easily without suffering the same pain and aggravation. The beginner can also develop sound programming practices before acquiring bad habits that will be hard to break.

Visual Basic Version Compatibility

The best programming techniques depend on fundamental programming concepts, not the idiosyncrasies of a particular version of a programming language. In fact, many apply in any programming language, not just Visual Basic. Much of what you learn from this book applies equally to Visual Basic versions 3, 4, 5, 6, or even Delphi and C++.

Most of the examples presented here are written in Visual Basic 4 and they run in Visual Basic 4, 5, and 6. The majority of the principles apply to any version of the language, although the details may be slightly different. The three main exceptions to this are Debug.Assert, classes, and the Visual Basic Code Profiler VBCP.

The Debug.Assert statement was not introduced to the language until Visual Basic 5 so you cannot use it if you are running an earlier version of Visual Basic. The Debug.Assert statement is quite useful for detecting bugs. This book explains how to use the statement and how to achieve similar effects in earlier versions of Visual Basic.

Classes were introduced to the language in Visual Basic 4. If you have Visual Basic 3 or some older version, you cannot create classes so you can ignore the parts of this book that deal with classes and objects.

Finally, the Visual Basic Code Profiler VBCP is provided with the Professional and Enterprise editions of Visual Basic. If you own one of the more restrictive editions, you cannot use the profiler so you can skip the chapter that discusses it.

Programs that do not work in Visual Basic 4 include the following:

Chapter 5, program Circles5. This program uses default values and optional parameters that are not variants. These features work only in Visual Basic 5 and 6.

Chapter 11, programs Bad11 and Good11. This chapter discusses optimizations that apply to compiled native code executables. Since Visual Basic 4 does allow you to create a native code executable, these programs only make sense in Visual Basic 5 and 6.

Chapter 13, programs Showerr. This program uses the vbMsgBoxHelpButton constant to make a message box present a help button. That constant was introduced by Visual Basic 5, so this program only runs in Visual Basic 5 and 6. However, if you remove this button, you can make the program run in Visual Basic 4 as well.

Programming languages often grow, but they rarely shrink. It is unlikely that Microsoft will remove the On Error GoTo statement or Debug.Assert in future versions of Visual Basic. That means the techniques explained in this book should be useful for many years to come. If any changes are necessary, they will be posted at this book's Web site at www.vb-helper.com/err.htm.

Chapter Overviews

Bug Proofing Visual Basic is divided into five parts that cover major topics in bug prevention, detection, and removal. The parts generally follow the sequence of events in an application's development cycle. They progress from code creation topics to error handling, testing, and debugging.

While the parts are arranged in roughly chronological order, there is a lot of overlap between topics in a typical project. For example, when a developer finds a bug during testing, he switches into debugging mode to find the bug. He then switches into development mode to fix the bug using good coding techniques that, hopefully, will not cause another bug. He then switches back into test mode to test the bug fix, and finally returns to the original task of testing the application as a whole.

The chapters in this book are relatively independent so you can read them in any order, even jumping from part to part if you wish. In fact, you may find it more interesting to skip around a little. If you grow tired of the development chapters, jump ahead to the testing chapters for a while.

A few topics are repeated in similar forms in different chapters. These topics affect development in multiple ways. For instance, Chapter 6, "Being Obvious," and Chapter 9, "Design," both mention declaring parameters with the ByVal keyword because you should think about ByVal during design and coding.

The parts of the book and their chapters are:

Part One. Work Environment

This may seem like a strange place to begin. After all, a good developer can program at any time and in any place. However, environmental factors can have a huge impact on the number of bugs you introduce. A distracting or tense environment may make you program quickly and sloppily to meet scheduled deadlines. That adds bugs to the code.

The chapters in this part of the book discuss environmental issues you should consider in your quest to produce high-quality code.

1. **Programming Philosophy.** In bug prevention, attitude is everything. This chapter describes the proper mindset for preventing and removing bugs quickly and easily.
2. **Work Habits.** This chapter discusses more specific techniques that can make bug management easier. Little things, like keeping a list of bugs you have encountered, can make identifying and fixing similar bugs easier in the future.

Part Two. Coding Style

This part of the book discusses specific Visual Basic coding style conventions you can use to make code easier to read and maintain. These chapters read like a list of commandments: do this, do that, do not do the other. In most of these suggestions, consistency is more important than the exact details. If you do not like a rule, change it. It does not really matter how you capitalize global variable names, as long as everyone on your project does it the same way.

3. **Variables.** This chapter describes methods for declaring and using variables to minimize the chances of introducing bugs.
4. **Constants and Enums.** Constants and enumerated values are important resources for reducing bug counts. This chapter explains how to use them to make code more readable and maintainable.
5. **Exposing Bugs.** Many programming practices considered safe actually hide bugs. This chapter shows how to write code that exposes bugs instead of hiding them.
6. **Being Obvious.** Program code should not be mysterious to programmers who read it. This chapter explains ways you can write code that is obvious to others.
7. **Comments.** Comments help bridge the gap between a program written for a computer to execute and humans trying to understand the code. This chapter

shows how to use comments to help readers understand the code so they do not add bugs to it later.

8. **Gotchas.** This chapter describes some bugs that are common in Visual Basic programs and tells how to avoid them. Some are rather subtle and can waste a lot of your time if you have never seen them before. They have certainly wasted a lot of *my* time.

Part Three. Development

Part Three deals mostly with development issues at a higher level than Part Two does. These include application and subroutine design issues, and optimization.

9. **Design.** Design decisions can have a large impact on the bugginess and maintainability of an application. This chapter gives some tips on designing maintainable applications.

10. **Encapsulation.** Encapsulation is both an old and new idea. Many object-oriented programmers treat encapsulation as a new concept invented by object-oriented languages. Actually, many programming constructs provide some degree of encapsulation. This chapter explains how to use variables, classes, subroutines, and other programming devices to encapsulate complex functionality and make it more bugproof.

11. **Optimization.** Optimization and bugproofing are often contradictory goals. Optimizing code often makes it harder to understand. On the other hand, bugproofing requires that the code be as easy to understand as possible. This chapter explains how and when to optimize while keeping the program reasonably bugproof.

Part Four. Error Handling

Even if you do your work properly, use good coding style, and follow practices to prevent bugs, errors will still occur. Inevitably, some bugs will slip through despite your best efforts. Other unexpected situations, like the user opening the floppy drive door or deleting a critical file, can still happen.

The chapters in Part Four explain how to handle these unexpected situations. They show how to build error handlers that allow a program to continue execution even when the unforeseen occurs.

12. **Error Handling Fundamentals.** This chapter describes Visual Basic's error handling mechanism: the family of On Error statements. A program can use On Error statements to prepare for almost any eventuality.

13. **Standard Error Handlers.** Many programs perform the same sorts of actions when they encounter errors. For example, they might log error information to a file to help developers find the bug later. This chapter describes several standard error handlers you can use to log errors for later analysis.

Part Five. Post-Coding Activities

Many developers believe their job is to simply write a bunch of code. After they write a piece of code, they rush on to something else. Occasionally, a bug might materialize and require attention, but in the meantime, the developer concentrates on something else.

Writing the code is not the final step. The developer must still test, debug, profile, and optimize the code. Then an independent tester must test the code to see if the developer missed anything, and the components of the system must be tested together. Finally, after the product is certified and released to end users, the development team should carry out a project postmortem to see if they can learn from their mistakes.

The chapters in this part of the book discuss activities developers should perform after writing code.

14. **Testing.** Many programmers consider testing to be a necessary evil that occurs at the end of a project. In fact, testing must occur during all stages of the project. This chapter describes testing habits and techniques you can use to prevent unwanted surprises from ambushing the project in its final stages.

15. **Profiling.** The code profiler that comes with the Professional and Enterprise editions of Visual Basic allows you to generate coverage and performance statistics for an application. Using these statistics, you can identify code that needs optimization or that may contain bugs. This chapter describes the profiler and explains how to use it to look for bugs.

16. **Debugging Habits.** Just as good habits can make coding and testing easier and more effective, good debugging habits can help you find and fix bugs more effectively. This chapter describes debugging habits that will help you make your debugging sessions more productive.

Appendices

Appendix A. This appendix contains an explanation of the self-test code presented in each chapter. It describes the bad points demonstrated by example programs and provides an improved implementation.

Appendix B. This appendix contains blank header comments you can use as templates in your programs. These templates are described in Chapter 7, "Comments," and are available electronically on the book's Web site at www.vb-helper.com/err.htm.

Writing Style

As you read this book, you will notice that it takes a rather authoritarian approach. It may seem as if it is saying, "Do this, do that, and don't do the other." Do not interpret these statements as dictatorial pronouncements from some programming hack with an inflated sense of his own importance. I do not pretend to know everything there is to know about programming.

The suggestions in this book are meant as advice only, not as unwavering rules. It was just much easier to write the suggestions as rules rather than filling the text with the phrases "you might consider..." and "a technique that is often useful is . . ."

Over the years I have spent hundreds of hours chasing bugs caused by myself and others. My goal with this book is to let you painlessly learn some of the lessons I learned through trial and error. If this book saves you more than the time it takes you to read it, I consider it a success.

If one of the suggestions does not fit in with your development environment, modify or ignore it. In many cases, it is more important that your programming team be consistent than that you follow the rules presented here exactly. For example, it does not really matter whether you declare global variables with LeadingCapitals, firstWordLowercase, or With_Underscores, as long as you all follow the same practice. Consistency is the key. Modify the specifics of the rules to suit your project's style.

A Note on Creativity

These suggestions may also seem like an attempt to stifle your creativity as a programmer. Some programmers become emotionally attached to their coding style and resent attempts to coerce them into following standard style guidelines.

The intent of this book is not to strangle creativity. Programming is an extremely creative process. It takes great skill and imagination to decide how to implement a certain behavior in a program. Joining together the pieces of code built by a team of different developers can be challenging and rewarding. Removing creativity from application development would make it impossible.

On the other hand, many programmers use their creativity in unproductive ways. They spend extra effort naming variables after pets or characters in Monty Python movies so they can get a chuckle when the variables come together in a certain line of code. Creativity belongs in the design, not in the implementation. Turning a detailed design into source code should be a straightforward, mechanical process. The code should be uncomplicated enough for another programmer to easily read and understand it. Interesting surprises and plot twists belong in fiction, not in program source code. This is one place where dull is beautiful. Make your application seen by the user be the work of art, not the source code seen by the programmer.

Common Sense

Rules that are common sense are easy to follow. Common sense tells you not to pass a police officer at 75 mph when the speed limit is 25 mph. This is a reasonably obvious rule that it is easy to remember and follow.

Unfortunately, computers have little to do with common sense. Until you understand all their strange little quirks and peccadilloes, the things they do can seem odd. You need to understand the strange ways in which the computer sometimes interprets seemingly ordinary commands.

Many of the suggestions in this book are common sense when you think about them properly. If you adjust your mindset, you can turn almost all of them into common sense. As you work through the book, you will learn new ways to think about programming. These new ways of thinking will mean the difference between just following a bunch of rules by rote and generalizing the rules to cover new situations.

After you learn to place ease of maintenance over conciseness, readability over execution speed, and bug identification over bug avoidance, the rest of the guidelines will seem obvious. Hopefully, by the time you have finished, you will be able to sum this book up in three words: Use common sense.

How to Use This Book

The chapters in this book are reasonably independent so you can read them in any order. You can even jump from one part of the book to another. In fact, you may find it more interesting to skip around a little. If you grow tired of the chapters on coding style, jump ahead to the testing chapter for a while.

Each chapter includes a "Self-Test" section that lets you make use of the concepts described in the chapter. Many of these sections include source code that disobeys the suggestions made in the chapter. You can examine the code and identify changes you could make to improve the code and make it more bugproof.

Each chapter also contains a "Bug Stopper" section that lists the key points covered by that chapter.

Appendix A, "Self-Test Solutions," contains improved solutions and answers. Note that there are as many possible solutions as there are programming styles. Appendix A shows one possible improved solution, but not necessarily the only one. Your solution may be different from the one in Appendix A but it may be equally correct. As suggested implementations are modified and when other examples are developed, they will be posted at the book's Web site at www.vb-helper.com/err.htm.

Updates and Feedback

Updates to this book will be posted at the book's Web site at www.vb-helper.com/err.htm. These will include new techniques for managing error handling in future versions of Visual Basic. They will also include useful techniques submitted by readers.

If you have questions, comments, or suggestions, or if you want to share your bug prevention, detection, and eradication techniques with others, send email to the author at RodStephens@vb-helper.com.

What's Next?

Time to get started! Turn the page or, if you feel daring, jump to the middle of the book and start reading. Examine the suggestions and work through the self-tests.

Then make the techniques described here your own. Take notes. Scribble in the margins. Cross things out and write in modifications to suit your project's style. Use sticky notes to mark things you want to discuss with other project members.

Finally, and most importantly, apply them. You will not get the full benefit of this book until its guidelines become habits. Then you will be able to spend less time finding and fixing bugs and more time doing what you really wanted to do when you became a programmer: programming.

PART ONE

Work Environment

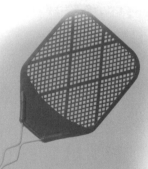

This may seem like a strange place to begin. It may seem at first glance as if work environment has nothing to do with programming or programming ability. I have known programmers who worked best between 10:00 P.M. and midnight, and others who worked best between 7:00 A.M. and 9:00 A.M. I have known some who wore faded jeans and T-shirts, and others who wore suits and ties every day.

While time of day and attire may have little to do with a specific programmer's effectiveness, other environmental factors and work habits can have a huge impact. A distracting or tense environment can give developers a self-fulfilling attitude of defeat. Poor work habits can ruin a programmer's productivity.

For example, consider a programmer who codes when tired, rushes through tasks to meet scheduled deadlines, and releases code without testing it first. Now consider another programmer who codes only when alert, carefully designs routines before implementing them, and would rather release code a day late than release it without testing. Which programmer is more likely to introduce bugs?

The chapters in this part of the book explain attitudes and work habits you should develop to ensure that you produce code that is as bug free as possible the first time. If the code you write is correct, you will not need to fix it later. It may take a little longer to do things right the first time, but the time you will save in debugging will repay you many times over.

A Reminder

Remember, the guidelines presented in this book are not intended to be unalterable rules carved in stone. They are just suggestions that will hopefully guide you past some of the pitfalls that have wasted my time over the years. They were just easier to phrase as rules instead of filling them with expressions like "you might benefit from…" and "I have sometimes found…" If something does not fit your project's style, by all means, change it.

CHAPTER 1

Programming Philosophy

Programming is a mental task, yet many programmers work with no mental discipline. In bug prevention, detection, and removal, mental attitude is crucial. If you assume that bugs are unavoidable, you will create bugs. If you assume the bugs can be fixed during final testing, you may find so many bugs at the end of the project that you can never finish. If you release your code before you test it, you are guaranteed someone else will find your bugs before you do.

This chapter explains how certain ways of thinking naturally lead to bugs while others prevent them. Some of these concepts may seem strange at first. After a while, they will become as straightforward as asking yourself, "Do I want a bug here, or not?"

Manage Properly

Managers rarely write the majority of the code on a project, so it might seem odd to have a section about management. There are several reasons this section is here. First, even if you are not a manager, you may be a senior developer who provides guidance to others. Even if you are a junior programmer or the only person working on a project, you at least manage yourself. You may have little other control over your environment, but you should try to manage your own efforts properly.

Finally, if you are suffering from bad management, the following sections will help you understand what is happening and why. You may be able to improve your situation by discussing it with your boss or by leaving an anonymous copy of this book on his desk with certain key pages marked. At worst, you can decide for yourself whether bad management has destroyed any chance of success and it is time to update your resume.

You might think management would have little impact on the number and kinds of bugs in the code. Actually, both good and bad management can have a tremendous impact on developer productivity. By maintaining the right atmosphere, a good manager can help programmers produce more code with fewer bugs. By developing the wrong atmosphere, a bad manager can demoralize the team and make them produce less code containing more bugs.

The following sections explain attitudes you should have as a developer. They are also attitudes you should foster in others as a manager. If all of the team members share these attitudes, they can reduce the time wasted on bug chasing and spend more time writing code.

Fight Bugs Every Step of the Way

Think of bugs in a manic-depressive way. Be optimistic that all bugs can and will be found as quickly as possible. Be pessimistic about the chances of actually finding every last bug.

Bugs can and must be stopped before they enter working code. You cannot release code to other team members without thoroughly testing it first. The longer a bug remains undetected, the harder it is to fix. By testing new code immediately, you can stop bugs as soon as they are created and before they contaminate other developers' code. It must be your goal to never affect another programmer or user by releasing code that contains a bug. This goal is ambitious, but realistic.

On the other hand, you must realize that some bugs will slip into the project no matter how careful you are. This means you must ruthlessly hunt for bugs throughout the entire project, from the initial requirements analysis phase to the final testing and documentation phases.

Bugs are not a force of nature that must be tolerated. They are something you can predict, hunt, corner, and kill. A bug is not some natural phenomenon that spontaneously appears in finished software just in time for demonstrations to corporate vice presidents.

Catch Bugs Early

Application development is sometimes portrayed in pyramid form as shown in Figure 1.1. The design at the bottom provides a solid foundation for the coding and testing that follow. Actually, the process is usually much more complicated. Figure 1.1 omits many of the details, including requirements analysis, definition of objectives, system behavior specification, test objective analysis, and so forth.

In a pyramid made of stone, the broad base spreads the weight of the stone at the top. If the base contains a weak brick, the others share the load so the pyramid does not crumble.

Unfortunately, the situation is somewhat reversed in software development. If a bug enters the project during the design phase, it will influence later development. Even if later code is implemented perfectly, it may still be wrong because it relies on incorrect assumptions in the earlier stages. A flaw at the bottom of the pyramid can spread through the later stages of development, as illustrated in Figure 1.2, until the entire structure crumbles.

To prevent later disaster, you must catch bugs as quickly as possible. It is worth spending extra time during the early phases of the project to make sure bugs do not contaminate the whole effort.

Stay in Control

One of the most sweeping things you can do to protect your productivity is to create an atmosphere of control. If you feel pressured to meet deadlines, the quality of your code suffers. You will not properly design routines before coding them and you will not spend enough time testing routines afterward. This introduces bugs into the code. Later, you will find the bugs and, in trying to fix them hastily, make more mistakes.

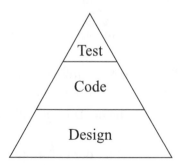

Figure 1.1   A traditional development pyramid.

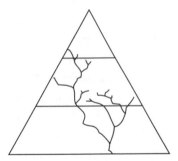

Figure 1.2 Flaws in early stages of a project may spread throughout later stages.

Bugs breed bugs. One routine may compensate for the incorrect behavior of another. When the original bug is fixed, the compensating routine may break. With larger mistakes, you may write correct code based on faulty assumptions. When the assumptions are corrected, the code fails. Hastily repaired code becomes a fragile collection of dubious assumptions and exceptions instead of an elegant model of program behavior.

As you spend more time chasing and fixing these bugs that should never have occurred in the first place, morale sags. You soon become trapped in a vicious circle. You do not have time to do your job properly. You rush to finish new code and chase old bugs. Your haste creates more bugs that take even more of your dwindling time later. At this point, the bugs control you, not the other way around.

Breaking this cycle is not as difficult as you might think. All you need to do is avoid the bugs in the first place. That means performing adequate design before coding and adequate testing afterward. This reduces the number of bugs introduced during all stages of the project. You waste less time fixing avoidable bugs so you can spend more time on careful design, coding, and testing.

Pressure to meet deadlines and produce code more quickly can make you lose control again. Use these techniques to prevent backsliding:

Give design higher priority than deadlines. Plan carefully so you do not create bugs in the first place.

Give testing higher priority than deadlines. Take time to test your code as soon as it is written so you can catch bugs before they affect other programmers.

Use methodical care, not haste and carelessness. Do not make sloppy mistakes by working hastily.

Fix bugs as soon as you find them. Bugs only get harder to fix later.

Once you are in control, you can easily stay in control. You just need to force yourself to take the time needed to do your job properly. After some practice, good design and testing techniques become second nature, and staying in control is easy.

Intercept Unnecessary Work

If you manage other programmers, you can help them stay in control by intercepting unnecessary work. Do not make the team members waste their time on progress reports, executive summaries, and other administrative busy work. Take on as much of this as possible and leave the developers to their development tasks.

If you are not a manager, do not pass work on to other developers. If you are faced with a simple task that you can perform quickly and easily, do it. If you pass the job to someone else, you waste the time it takes you to tell them what to do and the time it takes them to understand what needs to be done.

Keep an eye on your time and make sure you are not doing unnecessary work. If you are losing a lot of time each day to tasks that do not help your project, try to eliminate some of your tasks. For example, in one project, I provided operating system and language support for the other project members. Occasionally, people outside the group would ask questions and I was happy to help. Over time, however, the outside demands grew. Eventually, I could barely keep up with my own tasks because I was spending so much time helping others. At that point I decided to answer outside questions only after 4:00 P.M. The outsiders stopped asking their simpler questions and I was able to regain control of my own work.

Sharing resources, even among different project teams, is a good thing. In this case, however, too much of a good thing could have jeopardized the project.

Set Priorities

Programming is full of tradeoffs. One of the most common tradeoffs is speed versus size. Many programs can be made faster by using more memory. For example, suppose you have a function that calculates the shortest distance between two points in a street network. You could make the program much faster if you precompute the shortest distance between every pair of points in the network and then store the results in a table. Now instead of using the function whenever you need a value, you can look the value up in the table. This makes the program faster, but takes a lot of memory. If the street network connects 10,000 points, the table will contain 100 million entries.

There are several other tradeoffs you make while writing code. For instance, you implicitly decide

- How fast the code is
- How much memory the code uses
- How understandable the code is
- How likely the code is to contain bugs
- How much the code looks for errors
- How hard the code is to test
- How robust the code is
- How soon the code will be finished

For instance, you might use a state-of-the-art algorithm taken from the latest research journals. That code will probably be very fast and may use very little memory. However, because it is state-of-the-art you cannot have had much prior experience with it. That means it is more likely to contain bugs than a simpler algorithm you may have been using for several years. Unless you are very careful and you have a thorough understanding of the literature, the code may be less understandable, too. Whether the code is robust and how well it performs error checking depends on your specific implementation.

You should discuss these tradeoffs with other project members so everyone has the same priorities. If one programmer places speed above all else and another places robustness first, they may be working against each other. Each may make unnecessary changes to code to try to meet these conflicting goals. Agree on the team's priorities so everyone has the same objectives.

Change Priorities

Different stages in product development address different needs. The purpose of the initial development phase is to produce working code, and priorities should reflect that goal. You should place great emphasis on producing code that is understandable, maintainable, and less likely to contain bugs.

During the final stages of application development, you need to optimize the code. The goal is to improve the performance of those parts of the application that need it the most. Because the goals have changed, your priorities should change to match. At this point, it may be more important to produce fast code than code that is easy to read.

This does not mean you should start giving variables incomprehensible names, drop indentation that shows program structure, and stop using comments. It simply means you can use more complicated algorithms that you might have avoided earlier out of fear of complexity.

As the application matures, realign priorities accordingly.

Defer Optimization

Many programmers concentrate only on speed and memory usage. Unfortunately, these are usually far less important than readability, maintainability, and robustness, at least during the early stages of the project.

Typically, 90 percent of a program's time is spent in 10 percent of the code. Similarly, most of a program's memory use is often localized in a small number of routines and data structures. If you go to great lengths to optimize speed and memory use in every part of the program, 90 percent of your work is spent on code that does not need the extra effort.

Even worse, optimizing every part of the program makes much of the code more complicated, less understandable, and more likely to contain bugs. Not only does 90 percent of your work fail to make the application significantly faster or smaller, but it also makes matters worse by generating more bugs.

Initially, you should concentrate on making code bug free, understandable, testable, and maintainable. Later, when the project is almost finished, you can run tests to determine which code needs optimization. After you find the 10 percent of the code that takes 90 percent of the time, you can concentrate on improving only that code. You do not waste your time optimizing the other 90 percent of the code and you avoid all the bugs that premature optimization would have caused.

Deferring optimization also means that bugs created during optimization are introduced late in the project. The longer a bug remains hidden before it is detected, the harder it is to find and fix. Because the optimization bugs are introduced late in the project, you cannot have written a lot of code that depends on these bugs. That makes the bugs easier to find and repair.

Don't Optimize

For many years after their invention, computers were extremely expensive. A computer that was powerful enough to be useful cost millions of dollars. In comparison, programmers were cheap.

Today, computers are relatively cheap and programmers are very expensive. If a program is not fast enough, installing new memory or buying a faster computer are reasonable options. Unless the program will be used on hundreds of computers, it will be cheaper to buy more hardware than to make a programmer spend more than a few hours optimizing the program's code.

If an application's performance is adequate, do not optimize it. You will save not only the unnecessary optimization time, but also the time to fix the bugs optimization causes.

Get It Working First

High-quality code makes scheduling much easier. Suppose you have a project in which 90 percent of the code is written but riddled with bugs. Guessing when the last bug will be fixed is impossible. You cannot predict when the code will be working, which features will be working first, and when the finished application will be ready for release.

Contrast that with a project in which 50 percent of the code is written but it is very high quality and has almost no bugs. In that case you can predict with some confidence that the coding phase is about halfway finished. Since the team writes high-quality code, you know from your schedule which features will be working first. You may even be able to rearrange the schedule somewhat to change the order in which items are finished. After you include enough time for adequate testing, you can predict when the finished application will be ready for release.

A partial implementation that works is also better than a complete implementation that is full of bugs. Suppose one application is nearly complete but it crashes every five minutes. Another application is only half-functional, but that half is flawless. Menu items and buttons for features that are not yet implemented are disabled. People will perceive the second as the better, more professional application. If you doubt that, think about which you would rather demonstrate to your company's president.

Get the application working properly first. Then optimize it. Make sure each piece is working before you move on to the next.

Be Steady and Thorough

A programming adage states, "There's never time to do it right, but there's always time to do it again." If you rush through development to meet deadlines, you may do shoddy work. You make mistakes you would have avoided had you spent enough time to properly design, code, and test the program. Instead of finishing the project a little late, you may finish on time with a program so full of bugs it is worthless. You then need to rework the code again and again until you fix enough bugs so that the program is usable.

Be steady and thorough, not fast and careless. In programming, even more than in many other occupations, haste makes waste. Build a routine, test it thoroughly, and move on to something else. Do not rush frantically from task to task, trying to get as much done as possible as quickly as possible. If you take the time to ensure that your routines are bug-free when you write them, you will not need to debug them later.

On the other hand, unlike the tortoise in the fable "The Tortoise and the Hare," you do not need to be slow and steady. It is fine to be fast, as long as you are thorough. Design a routine, implement it, test it thoroughly, and then move on to the next task.

Code Offensively

For many years, programmers have been taught to code defensively. Defensive coding means writing a routine so it can handle a wide variety of possible strange or incorrect inputs without crashing. For instance, consider the following implementation of the factorial function:

```
Public Function Factorial(num As Integer)
    If num = 0 Then
        Factorial = 1
    Else
        Factorial = num * Factorial(num - 1)
    End If
End Function
```

This routine enters an infinite recursion if its parameter num is less than 0. If the parameter is –1, the program calls Factorial(–1), which calls Factorial(–2), which calls Factorial(–3), and so forth until the program exhausts the system stack and crashes.

The traditional defensive version of this routine uses an inequality test to catch cases where the parameter is less than 0.

```
Public Function Factorial(num As Integer)
    If num <= 0 Then
        Factorial = 1
    Else
        Factorial = num * Factorial(num - 1)
    End If
End Function
```

This defensive version allows the Factorial function to continue running when it receives an invalid input. Unfortunately, it also silently hides a probable bug. Factorials are not defined for numbers less than 0. If the calling routine executes Factorial(–1), it probably contains a bug. The defensive version of the Factorial function hides the bug by continuing to execute as if the parameter were valid.

Instead of hiding the bug, the function should draw attention to it. It should explicitly check its arguments to verify that they make sense. If not, the routine should make the bug obvious by stopping or by raising an exception.

For example, in Visual Basic 5 and 6, the program can use the Debug.Assert statement to verify that the argument is at least 0. Debug.Assert takes a Boolean expression as an argument. If the expression is false, Visual Basic halts execution at the Assert statement. The developer can then examine the code to find the problem.

When it compiles the application, Visual Basic removes the Debug.Assert statement from the code. If the compiled program encounters this bug, it cannot stop because the Debug.Assert statement is missing. To allow the program to continue if an unexpected error occurs and the Debug.Assert statement has been removed by the compiler, the code can use defensive programming techniques.

```
Public Function Factorial(num As Integer)
    ' Validate parameters.
    Debug.Assert num >= 0

    If num <= 0 Then
        Factorial = 1
    Else
        Factorial = num * Factorial(num - 1)
    End If
End Function
```

Take the offensive and catch bugs before they catch you. Chapter 5, "Exposing Bugs," has a lot more to say about writing code that makes bugs obvious instead of hiding them.

Write for Others

Program as if someone else is going to read your code later; someone almost certainly will. Even when you read the code later, it may be far enough in the future that you may as well be someone else. By the time you read the code again, you may not remember any of the routine's finer details.

Assume the person reading your code is not the brightest programmer in the world and will misunderstand the code if possible. In many companies, maintenance programmers are often the least experienced so this may be close to the truth.

On the other hand, this person is a programmer and has at least some programming knowledge, so you do not need to explain every little detail about how Visual Basic works. You need to explain what the code is trying to do, not what the ReDim statement does.

The person may be trying to understand your code, or he may be trying to find a bug. The bug may be in your routine, or it may be in another routine that calls yours. To make it easy for this person to understand what your code is doing, keep the code as straightforward as possible. Remember that this later person may be you—the time you save may be your own.

Write for Humans

Computers execute programs but you need to write code for *people*. The computer does not care whether the code contains comments, proper indentation, and variables with meaningful names. It does not care if the code is written in Visual Basic, Delphi, or machine code. In fact, it does not care if the code does what it is supposed to do. The computer will not locate and fix bugs. It will not even notice a bug unless the program tries to do something illegal like divide by 0.

Only a programmer can examine the code and decide whether it is operating correctly. Only a human can find and correct a bug. Always remember that you write code for other people, not for the computer.

Code for the Ages

Do not use quick and sloppy techniques, expecting to clean the code up later. Chances are good that no one will have time. Assume your code will remain in use exactly as you write it for the next 30 years. Later, if you do have the free time, you can consider rewriting it. Of course, that may introduce new bugs. It is better to get the code right the first time and not rewrite it.

Do not expect to fix code in a future release. That may happen and it may not. There are probably trillions of lines of code still in use that were written 10, 20, or even 30 years ago. The programmers who wrote that code probably thought it would be rewritten a few years later. Had they been correct, there would never have been a year 2000 problem.

I once worked with a huge mainframe application that included code written over a span of more than 20 years. I am certain the programmers who started the project had no idea it would still be running decades after they finished the initial release. Over the years, the program had become a conglomeration of code written in several different programming languages. It included data that was compiled into the code. This is the equivalent of putting assignment statements directly into a Visual Basic program instead of loading the data from a database. Whenever the business rules changed, the program had to be recompiled. The company grew to depend on the program until it was absolutely essential to operations. The program cost more than $100 million per year to run, but it could not be rewritten because, after decades of uncoordinated changes, the code had grown too incoherent for anyone to understand.

Write as if your code will be used for many years to come. Chances are good it will be.

Code without Ego

Many programmers become emotionally attached to their code. That is only natural. If you spend a lot of time and effort building something, it is natural that you will become attached to it.

Unfortunately, code sometimes needs to be rewritten. It may need to be rebuilt to implement a better algorithm. After too many bugs have been found in one routine, it may be better to rewrite it from scratch rather than patch it further. Sometimes it may be completely thrown away and replaced with a different method.

You must be ready to let go of your code so it can be rewritten, replaced, or discarded.

Do not feel your code is a reflection of yourself. A bug in your code does not mean you are any less of a person. If you feel that a bug is a stain on your reputation, you will not look as hard as you should for bugs because you will not really want to find any. You will also not be receptive to others testing your code and reporting or fixing bugs.

Many programmers learn these lessons only after years of experience. Some developers never learn. They remain hostile to changes in their code no matter how obvious it is that the changes are improvements.

Remember that the goal is to build the best solution possible, not to stick with the original code until it is an incoherent mass of bug fixes and patches. Do not let ego and attachment stand in the way of improving the code.

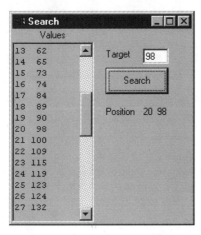

Figure 1.3 Program Bad1 displaying the average of a list of random numbers.

Self-Test

Many of the ideas presented in this chapter cannot be easily demonstrated by example code. Pointing to a piece of code and saying it is the result of hasty work or too much emphasis on speed is difficult.

Program Bad1 violates several of the more easily demonstrated guidelines presented in this chapter. The program, shown in Figure 1.3, generates a random list of numbers. When you enter a value in the Target field and click the Search button, the program uses a binary search to locate the item you entered in the list.

The following code shows how program Bad1 works. Assume that this code has just been written near the beginning of the project, and that it has been accepted into the project's code library. You should be able to make several improvements. Appendix A, "Self-Test Solutions," contains a revised version of this code with some suggested changes.

```
Option Explicit

Private Values(1 To 50) As Integer

Private Sub Form_Load()
    Ready
End Sub

Private Sub Ready()
Dim i As Integer
Dim txt As String
```

```
        Randomize
        Values(1) = Int(Rnd * 10 + 1)
        For i = 2 To 50
            Values(i) = Values(i - 1) + Int(10 * Rnd + 1)
        Next i
        For i = 1 To 50
            txt = txt & Format$(i, "@@") & _
                Format$(Values(i), "@@@@") & vbCrLf
        Next i
        txtValues.Text = txt
    End Sub

    Private Sub CmdSearch_Click()
    Dim i As Integer

        i = BinarySearch(Values, CInt(txtTarget.Text))
        lblPosition.Caption = Format$(i, "@@") & _
                Format$(Values(i), "@@@@") & vbCrLf
    End Sub

    Public Function BinarySearch(list() As Integer, _
        target As Integer) As Integer
    Dim a As Integer
    Dim b As Integer
    Dim c As Integer

        a = 1
        c = 50
        Do While a <= c
            b = (c + a) / 2
            If target = list(b) Then
                BinarySearch = b
                Exit Function
            ElseIf target < list(b) Then
                c = b - 1
            Else
                a = b + 1
            End If
        Loop
        BinarySearch = 0
    End Function
```

Summary

Mental discipline is critical for effective programming. The following Bug Stoppers summarize concepts that are helpful for maintaining a bug-free attitude. Attitude is everything. Without the proper mindset, you may write thousands of lines of code very quickly, only to waste months of extra time debugging them.

By coding more carefully, you can produce more working code in less time. You can control the code and not let deadlines and bugs control you.

BUG STOPPERS: Programming Philosophy

Manage properly, even if you are the only developer.

Fight bugs every step of the way.

Catch bugs early.

Stay in control.

Intercept unnecessary work.

Set consistent priorities.

Change priorities as the project matures.

Defer optimization.

Don't optimize unless necessary.

Get it working first, then optimize if necessary.

Be steady and thorough, not fast and sloppy.

Code offensively to expose bugs, not hide them.

Write for others, not for yourself.

Write for people, not for the computer.

Code for the ages.

Code without attachment or ego.

Work Habits

This chapter discusses specific work habits and programming techniques you can use to make bug management easier. Simple practices, like keeping a bug log and working when you are most alert, can reduce the number of bugs in your code and allow you to find and repair the bugs that do occur more easily.

Keep a Notebook

As much as some managers might wish to believe programming is a simple construction task like building a brick wall, it is not. Programming is an experimental laboratory science. It includes plenty of theoretical research, too, but real programs must work in the real world, not just in theory. Programs are carefully designed using the latest tools and techniques, but in the end, trial and error plays an important role in all but the simplest applications.

Scientists in other experimental fields keep laboratory notebooks and programmers should too. Things you should put in the notebook include

- Decisions made at project meetings
- Other meeting notes
- Phone numbers of customers, vendors, etc.
- Notes made during phone calls

- Initial doodlings while you think about programming ideas
- Diagrams and flow charts of algorithms you may need
- References to journals and books in which you find something useful
- Timing results when you test different algorithms
- Bug descriptions and fixes
- Lists of things to do later

When I start a new major project, I start a new notebook. Usually I take 50 to 100 pages of notes during the course of the project, not including notes I keep online in the form of email and other electronic documentation. After I write something down, I almost never need to look at it again. A few times each month, however, I need to look up some little detail that I have forgotten. This is particularly helpful with obscure bugs that I only rarely encounter. The notebook lets me look up the bug and its solution in just minutes, instead of wasting hours trying to recreate the solution.

Physical and online notebooks each have their advantages. You can take physical notebooks to meetings, draw freehand flow charts and data flow diagrams in them, and tape journal articles in them. Online notebooks can be searched, are easy to cut and paste into documentation, and are easy to email to other developers.

I usually use a combination of both systems. If something is easy to enter online, like a bug description, I email it to myself and store it in a special project email folder. If it is hard to store electronically, like diagrams or meeting notes, I put it in my notebook.

Keep a Bug Log

A bug log is one of the most important parts of your notebook. Quickly finding information about previously encountered bugs can save you hours of effort.

One useful technique is to email bug information to yourself. Put descriptive information in the message's subject so you can search for the report later. File the message in a bugs mail folder. In the message, you should note

Description. What is the bug?

Cause. What caused the bug? Is this a symptom of a larger bug?

Symptoms. How can you tell if the bug is present?

Cure. How did you fix this bug?

Prevention. How could this bug have been prevented?

Detection. How can similar bugs be detected automatically?

If your project uses a shared bug log, you can learn from errors found by other developers. To create a shared bug repository, create a special user named Bugs. When you send yourself a bug note, send a copy to Bugs. Later, if you need to find a bug report, you can log on as Bugs and search everyone's bug messages.

Analyze the Bug Log

When your project is finished, analyze the bug log to learn from past mistakes. See which bugs caused the greatest trouble for the most developers and focus on them. Discuss new methods that the team can use to detect and correct bugs earlier than they did in this project.

Pay particular attention to bugs that remained undetected for a long time. Those bugs tend to cause the most mischief so it is worth some extra effort to prevent them in the future. Determine when each bug was introduced and spend additional time discussing ways to avoid bugs that occur early in the development cycle.

Note which phases may need improvement. If many bugs were introduced during the program's high-level design phase, you should probably spend more time on that phase in future projects.

It is also worth noting which developers created the most errors and during which phases of the project. Be careful that this does not become a hunt for scapegoats, but it may indicate which developers could use extra training in a particular aspect of development. For example, you may find one programmer who introduced more than his share of bugs into the database management code. That programmer might benefit from some extra database management courses.

Save Everything

Save everything you receive that relates to the project, no matter how trivial it seems. Keep every email and memo you receive. Take notes during meetings, conversations, and phone calls. If important decisions are made, type the notes up and email them to yourself and to the others involved in the decision.

The amount of material you save will start to add up, but it should cost you very little to keep it until the end of the project. In some of the projects I have worked on, the amount of historical data added up to a few megabytes of disk space and a few thousand pages of printed text. It easily fit on one backup tape and in a single storage box.

You may never need to access most of this information, but once in a great while it can save you hours of frustration. In several of the projects I have worked on, a customer reopened an issue that had been closed earlier in the development process. By quickly retrieving the old memos and emails that had resolved the issue before, we were able to reevaluate the problem and get back to work on new issues with little wasted time.

In some projects we created an account named History. Every project member sent copies of meeting notes, conversation notes, and memos to this account. On those infrequent occasions when two developers disagreed on a customer request, they could refer to the history email to learn exactly what was said and when without bothering the customer over a closed issue.

Do It Now

If you think of something that needs to be done, do it. If you cannot do it right away, write it down or email it to yourself. Outline how you will do the work if the task is complicated. Do not assume you will remember to do it later. During the course of a large project, you will have thousands of chances to forget some small task, any one of which could prevent a bug.

If you cannot handle the task now, you will probably need to handle it later in any case. Do not ignore it hoping it will go away. If you do not have time for the task but it must be done, point it out to the project manager so someone else can handle it.

Fix It Now

It is a well-known fact that the longer a bug remains in the code, the harder it is to fix. Removing a bug is easiest when the code is fresh in your mind. If a long time has passed and you have worked on dozens of other routines since you wrote the original code, you must spend extra time reacquainting yourself with the routine before you can fix the bug.

In the meantime, other developers may have written subroutines that implicitly rely on your routine's buggy behavior. When you fix the bug, those other routines may stop working. The other developers will need to stop what they are doing to fix them. In the worst case, still other routines will break when those routines are fixed.

If you discover a bug, fix it right away. If the bug is not in your code, tell the code's author. Make sure the bug gets fixed as soon as possible. Do not let higher-priority tasks delay fixing the bug. There are no higher-priority tasks than removing bugs from the code. Remove bugs as quickly as possible to prevent their effects from spreading.

Test It Now

As soon as you write a routine, test it thoroughly. Execute every line of code in the debugger to make sure it does what it should. It is easiest to test code in this way when it is fresh in your mind. Do not wait until you have forgotten how the routine works.

The longer a bug remains in the code, the harder it is to find and remove. Catch the bugs right away before they make themselves comfortable and before someone else writes a routine that relies on this routine's buggy behavior.

This does not mean testing for this routine is over forever. You still need to perform module- and system-level testing later, but you can catch a huge number of bugs simply by stepping through the code right after you write it.

Make it your goal to never let a bug slip past this test. The few minutes you spend testing now will later be repaid many times over.

If It Works, Don't Fix It

Once you have written a routine that works, and you have tested it to make sure it works correctly, move on to something else. Do not waste endless hours puttering away at the code trying to reduce the routine's runtime by a few percent. Later, if the routine turns out to be a performance bottleneck, you can rewrite it.

When you look at someone else's code, or even code you wrote in the past, resist the temptation to change it. This can be particularly difficult if you are an accomplished developer reading a less-experienced programmer's code. You may be tempted to rewrite everything you see.

You could undoubtedly improve the code, but that would defeat the purpose of having more than one person working on the project. You must admit to yourself that you cannot personally write every line of code. If someone else's code works, leave it alone.

Review the other programmer's code. Test it if you think it has not been properly tested. If the code has problems, ask the original author to fix them. However, if the code works as it should, leave it alone and move on to something else.

Don't Fiddle

Leave working code alone. Do not rewrite it to clean it up, reformat it, or tighten a few loose loops here and there. Chances are your small improvements will make little difference to the complete application anyway.

Do not rewrite working code unless you have an extremely good reason to do so. Modifying code is more likely to introduce bugs than writing new code, so write some new code instead.

Even adding or removing comments can be risky. Many programmers think they do not need to completely understand a routine to change its comments. Then, while modifying the comments, they make just one or two trivial changes. If they do not understand the entire routine, there is no way they can know whether the changes will make a difference. While intending to change only comments, the programmer has broken a working routine.

Even worse, after changing only comments (and one or two things they think are inconsequential), many programmers will not retest the routine. If a bug has been introduced, it will be much harder to catch and fix later.

Many developers rewrite routines to make them more maintainable. That only makes sense when you personally have some knowledge about the routine that others who will maintain the code in the future do not have. If you wrote the routine and it is still fresh in your mind, and you are about to leave the company, and the person who is taking over for you is a junior programmer, it makes some sense to try to pass along your knowledge. In that case, try to restrict yourself to adding better comments to the code.

If someone else wrote the code, leave it alone. Rewriting it now when you do not need to will not make it any more maintainable than rewriting it later when you have a good reason to do so.

If the code isn't broken, don't fix it or it will soon be.

Design Before You Code

Many beginning programmers write down the purpose of a routine and a plan of attack before starting to code. They do this because they do not have the experience to know immediately what they need to do. Without at least a skeletal plan, a beginner can waste a huge amount of time typing, deleting, and retyping a single line of code until it works.

More experienced programmers sometimes grow lazy and start coding without any clear strategy. They just pull up an editor window and start typing.

Sometimes this works, but this strategy allows the developer to begin writing code without a complete plan for where it is going. As the code develops, the later code may conflict with code entered earlier. A really good programmer will notice the problem and go back to fix it. A less-experienced programmer may not notice the problem, particularly if the routine is long. The result may be some very subtle bugs.

Think first, then code. Do not touch finger to keyboard until you have a clear plan for the routine.

One fast and easy way to integrate design and coding is to generate the design as a series of comments. Start by writing a description of the problem. This should be no more than one or two sentences. If you cannot clearly state the routine's purpose in one sentence, it probably does not perform a single coherent task. In that case, you should break it into smaller routines, each having a well-defined purpose.

A sorting routine might have this purpose:

```
Sort an array of numbers.
```

Next, write a general description of the solution. Include statements to validate parameters and verify the result. This description should indicate in English how the routine will perform its duties.

The description should not involve any Visual Basic commands. It should be nonspecific enough that you could use it to implement the routine in another language like Delphi or C++.

```
Sort an array of numbers.
    Validate the parameters.

    For each position in the array:
        Find the smallest item not yet positioned:
        Swap the smallest item into the position we are considering.

    Verify the solution.
```

Now refine the solution by adding more detailed descriptions of the steps you need to take. Indent to show that a line is part of the previous line.

Again, the description should not invoke actual Visual Basic commands, though it will become increasingly obvious which commands are needed. For example, for one line, you may know that you will need to use a For loop.

Continue refining the description until it starts to look like an English form of Visual Basic.

```
Sort an array of numbers.
    Validate the parameters.
    Check that the array contains between 10 and 1000 entries.
    (Anything outside this range may indicate a bug)

    For each position in the array:
        Find the smallest item not yet positioned:
        Start with the item currently in the
            position we are considering.

        For each entry after this one:
            If an entry is smaller than the smallest so far:
                Save its value and index.

        Swap the smallest item into the position we are considering.

    Verify the solution.
    For each item after the first:
        Check that it is at least as big as the previous item.
```

Now put apostrophes to the left of each line of the description to turn them into comments.

```
' Sort an array of numbers.
    ' Validate the parameters.
    ' Check that the array contains between 10 and 1000 entries.
    ' (Anything outside this range may indicate a bug)

    ' For each position in the array:
        ' Find the smallest item not yet positioned:
        ' Start with the item currently in the
        '     position we are considering.

        ' For each entry after this one:
            ' If an entry is smaller than the smallest so far:
                ' Save its value and index.

        ' Swap the smallest item into the position we are considering.

    ' Verify the solution.
    ' For each item after the first:
        ' Check that it is at least as big as the previous item.
```

Next, insert the routine's declaration with any required parameters after the top-level description. Insert other Visual Basic code to implement the functionality described in the comments. The code should echo the comment before it. Add blank lines as needed to make the code easier to read.

The following code uses an #If statement to control program execution during design time and in the final compiled program. In this case, the compiler symbol DEBUG_MODE is defined during design time to verify the routine's solution. Before compiling the final program, the developer sets DEBUG_MODE to False so this code will be removed from the final version. This technique and several others for verifying program correctness are discussed in Chapter 5, "Exposing Bugs."

```
' Sort an array of numbers.
Public Sub SelectionSort(ByRef numbers() As Integer)
    ' Validate the parameters.
    ' Check that the array contains between 10 and 1000 entries.
    ' (Anything outside this range may indicate a bug)
    Debug.Assert (UBound(numbers) - LBound(numbers) + 1) >= 10
    Debug.Assert (UBound(numbers) - LBound(numbers) + 1) <= 1000

    ' For each position in the array:
    For i = LBound(numbers) To UBound(numbers)
        ' Find the smallest item not yet positioned:
        ' Start with the item currently in the
        '     position we are considering.
        smallest_value = numbers(i)
        smallest_index = i

        ' For each entry after this one:
        For j = i + 1 To UBound(numbers)
            ' If an entry is smaller than the smallest so far:
            If numbers(j) < smallest_value Then
                ' Save its value and index.
                smallest_value = numbers(j)
                smallest_index = j
            End If
        Next j

        ' Swap the smallest item into the position we are considering.
        numbers(smallest_index) = numbers(i)
        numbers(i) = smallest_value
    Next i

    ' Verify the solution.
    #If DEBUG_MODE Then
        ' For each item after the first:
        For i = LBound(numbers) + 1 To UBound(numbers)
            ' Check that it is at least as big as the previous item.
            If numbers(i) < numbers(i - 1) Then Stop
        Next i
    #End If
End Sub
```

Now look through the code and see what variables it uses. Declare them at the top of the routine. Explicitly declare each variable on a separate line.

```vb
' Sort an array of numbers.
Public Sub SelectionSort(ByRef numbers() As Integer)
Dim i As Integer
Dim j As Integer
Dim smallest_value As Integer
Dim smallest_index As Integer

    ' Validate the parameters.
    ' Check that the array contains between 10 and 1000 entries.
    ' (Anything outside this range may indicate a bug)
    Debug.Assert (UBound(numbers) - LBound(numbers) + 1) >= 10
    Debug.Assert (UBound(numbers) - LBound(numbers) + 1) <= 1000

    ' For each position in the array:
    For i = LBound(numbers) To UBound(numbers)
        ' Find the smallest item not yet positioned:
        ' Start with the item currently in the
        ' position we are considering.
        smallest_value = numbers(i)
        smallest_index = i

        ' For each entry after this one:
        For j = i + 1 To UBound(numbers)
            ' If an entry is smaller than the smallest so far:
            If numbers(j) < smallest_value Then
                ' Save its value and index.
                smallest_value = numbers(j)
                smallest_index = j
            End If
        Next j

        ' Swap the smallest item into the position we are considering.
        numbers(smallest_index) = numbers(i)
        numbers(i) = smallest_value
    Next i

    ' Verify the solution.
    #If DEBUG_MODE Then
        ' For each item after the first:
        For i = LBound(numbers) + 1 To UBound(numbers)
            ' Check that it is at least as big as the previous item.
            If numbers(i) < numbers(i - 1) Then Stop
        Next i
    #End If
End Sub
```

Finally, run the subroutine and test it thoroughly. Step through the code in the debugger to make sure it all runs. In particular, check that the verification code at the end actually runs. If the DEBUG_MODE compiler constant is not defined, this code will be skipped.

You may feel that all these extra steps waste time. Actually, they are steps you need to perform anyway. They are just being accomplished in a different order. You need to think the solution through completely one way or another. By refining the solution in English instead of Visual Basic, you can concentrate on the design without being distracted by Visual Basic syntax.

When you have finished refining the English version of the routine, you will have a conceptually integrated design that you can translate into Visual Basic quickly and easily. At this point, translation is almost purely mechanical. You have already debugged the design so you will not need to spend as much time writing and rewriting the code to make the routine work. The time you spend designing the routine in English saves you time while coding.

When all this is done, you have a completely commented subroutine. You can add a few extra comments to clarify any confusing issues, but the description you originally built should explain most of the routine. The time you spend in design not only saves you coding time, but it also saves you much of the time you would have spent commenting the code later.

Code When You Are Alert

Programming requires precision. If you code when you are inattentive, you are much more likely to introduce new bugs and overlook old ones than if you code when you are alert.

Different people are most alert and productive at different times of the day. For many, early morning, after lunch, and late afternoon can be dangerous times to code.

Figure out when you are not at your peak and do something that is less exacting during those times. Read your email, check newsgroups, fill out expense reports, and write progress reports. Later, when you are wide awake, go back to programming, testing, and debugging. Save the most productive hours of the day for precision tasks like coding and debugging.

I am most alert and creative during the early morning and mid-afternoon. Those are the times when I produce the highest-quality code. Right after lunch is when I am most sluggish, so that is when I try to read my email and perform administrative chores.

If you really need to get some programming done right away but you feel a bit drowsy, take a break. Walk around your building or close your office door and do some calisthenics. Get your blood flowing and then go back to work.

Code in Manageable Pieces

Code and test in intervals long enough to accomplish a single task. For example, design and implement a single subroutine in one sitting. Then take a break and do something else for a little while. Stretch, walk around, and clear your mind. Come back refreshed and ready to concentrate.

Try to perform related tasks together. If you need to write several printing routines, write and test them over a one- or two-day period. Your work will be faster and easier if you can keep shared concepts in mind while you work on them. Even then, break the tasks up into manageable subtasks. If you work continuously on the same code for too many hours, you will lose your edge. Stop, stretch, and start again refreshed. Do not code nonstop until you can barely keep your eyes open.

The computer industry is filled with stories of developers working 18 hours a day for weeks at a time to meet some critical deadline. There are two problems with this strategy. First, these developers have seriously messed up their schedule. There is no excuse for these kinds of hours. Either the developers let the project get away from them or the original schedule was unrealistic.

Second, working such ridiculously long hours increases the chances that developers will introduce bugs into the project. Finding and fixing those bugs will mean wasting more time than they would have if they had worked more carefully.

This does not mean developers must never work extra hours, but continuing the practice for days at a time leads to diminishing returns. Eventually, an additional hour spent programming may produce only 45 minutes of productive work. The rest of the hour is wasted chasing bugs that would not have been otherwise introduced.

Close Your Door

Effective programming and debugging requires deep concentration. You need to ensure that you have large blocks of uninterrupted time during which to work.

Remove as many distractions as you possibly can. Ignore your email. If possible, deactivate it so prompts like bells do not interrupt you when new mail arrives. Close your office door, unplug your phone, and draw the curtains. If you work in a cubicle with no door, face your monitor so you cannot see people walk by. If people still interrupt you constantly, hang up a "Do Not Disturb" sign.

Once others realize that you do not want to be bothered when your door is closed or when you are hunched over your terminal, they will probably respect your need for quiet.

If all else fails, hide. While working on one project, I was interrupted so frequently that I started spending three hours each day working on a terminal in a training room on the other side of the building. My most productive hours tend to be early in the morning, so on another project I came to work at 6:00 A.M. I usually got two or three hours of continuous work done before the interruptions began.

Near the end of several of the projects I worked on, the customers became increasingly intrusive. They wanted to be kept informed at all times so they started calling the project members more and more frequently. They requested weekly and even daily status reports. Eventually, the project leader told them to contact only him and that he would only answer email and return phone calls after 3:00 P.M. That gave all of the developers more uninterrupted time to do productive work. It also filtered the customers' calls. They no longer called unless they really thought it was important. They managed to answer many of their own questions when they tried.

Self-Test

Because this chapter deals with work habits rather than specific coding techniques, this section does not contain sample code. However, there is still an important exercise you can use to review the ideas discussed in this chapter.

First, get a notebook. Write down everything you do in a typical day. If you are not sure where your time goes, keep the notebook with you for a few days and take notes.

Next, identify the parts of the day during which you are alert and productive and those when you are not. Then match the tasks you perform each day to the time periods that are most appropriate. Consolidate tasks if you can. For example, if you read electronic mail a dozen times a day, group these sessions together and read your mail in one or two longer sessions.

Put tasks that require precision and attention to detail in your most-alert time slots. Put less-demanding tasks in less-productive slots. Follow the new schedule for a few days and see if you can improve your productivity. Appendix A, "Self-Test Solutions," describes the results I achieved when I tried this experiment.

Summary

The Bug Stoppers that follow summarize the key bug-preventing work habits described in this chapter. Some of these practices may seem awkward at first, but once you get used to them they become second nature. A few, like keeping a notebook, take a little extra work but can occasionally save you a tremendous amount of time. Others, like leaving working code alone, can save work now and prevent bugs that you will need to fix in the future.

BUG STOPPERS: Work Habits

Keep a notebook.

Keep a bug log.

Analyze the bug log.

Save everything.

Do it now.

Fix it now.

Test it now.

If it works, don't fix it.

Don't fiddle.

Design before you code.

Code when you are alert.

Code in manageable pieces.

Close your door.

PART TWO

Coding Style

Many of the coding guidelines in the following chapters are designed to steer developers away from buggy situations. Some make certain kinds of bugs less likely to occur. Others make bugs easier to find when they do occur.

Several of these suggestions forbid anachronistic syntax. Deftype statements, for instance, are a throwback to older versions of Basic and Fortran that allowed only very short variable names. When variables could only be six characters long, it made sense to use initial letters to indicate data type. For example, all variables with names starting with H, I, or J were integers.

Modern Visual Basic allows variable names to be much longer so this practice is no longer necessary. It can also cause confusion, so the guidelines that follow recommend that you do not use Deftype statements.

Other guidelines are meant to remove ambiguity from what might otherwise be confusing situations. At times these rules appear as arbitrary dictates that stifle creativity. Coding requires creativity, but reading code should not. If the code is hard to read, it will be harder for developers to find and remove bugs. It will also be more likely that bug fixes will introduce new bugs.

Standardizing certain naming conventions and coding practices can make reading the code easier. For example, if every developer names global variables with LeadingCapitals, you can easily tell whether a variable is global or not. This small reduction in artistic license can make the code much easier to understand.

With this type of suggestion, consistency is more important than the exact details. It does not matter whether you use LeadingCapitals, initialLowercaseAndCapitals, or Leading_Capitals_With_Underscores to represent global variables as long as every developer follows the same standards. If you do not like one of these stylistic rules, change it. Just make sure everyone agrees on the new style.

Variables

This chapter explains methods for declaring and using variables that can prevent bugs. Most of the rules are extremely simple. Once you have become accustomed to them, they are very easy to follow.

The exact details of some of these rules are unimportant as long as all developers follow the same practices. For example, Hungarian notation improves readability, but which characters you use to denote specific data types does not matter. You can use any combination of characters you like. In fact, when you create new classes and user-defined data types, you should invent new abbreviations to use with Hungarian notation.

The power of these guidelines comes from consistent use. Every member of the team must follow them at all times. Breaking the rules even occasionally can have disastrous consequences. For example, if most of the team avoids variant data types, they will come to expect certain kinds of behavior in expressions. If one programmer uses variants extensively, the others may be confused. They may expect a statement to behave one way when it actually does something else.

Explicitly Declare Variables

Explicitly declare all variables on separate lines. If you do not declare a variable, Visual Basic assumes it is a variant. If you leave off the variable's data type, Visual Basic also assumes it is a variant. For example, the following statement declares a variant named count.

```
Dim count
```

To avoid ambiguity, always declare variables with their data types, even if the variable is a variant.

```
Dim count As Variant
```

Declare each variable on a separate line. Many programmers, especially those experienced with another language, try to declare multiple variables on one line like this:

```
Dim A, B, C As Integer
```

In Visual Basic, the data type part of a declaration only applies to the immediately preceding variable. All the other variables are assigned the default data type variant. In this case, the code declares variable C as an integer, and variables A and B as variants.

Usually this declaration is a mistake and all of the variables are intended to be integers. The single-line declaration should be rewritten as

```
Dim A As Integer, B As Integer, C As Integer
```

If the author of the code understands the original declaration and really wants to create two variants and an integer, someone reading the code later may be confused. Even if he understands what the declaration actually does, he may not be sure the original author understood correctly. He may change the declaration into an incorrect one trying to fix a problem that is not there. Prevent this confusion by explicitly declaring all variables with their data types, even variants.

To make it easier for the reader to find all of the variable declarations, put each on a separate line. Place them all at the beginning of the routine or module in which they are declared.

```
Dim A As Variant
Dim B As Variant
Dim C As Integer
```

Use Option Explicit

Normally when Visual Basic sees a variable it does not recognize, it silently creates the variable. This allows the code to create variables as they are needed without explicitly declaring them. For example, the following code is a valid Visual Basic subroutine.

```
Private Sub CountTo10()
    For i = 1 To 10
        Debug.Print Format$(i)
    Next i
End Sub
```

One advantage to automatic variable creation is that variables that are not used are not created. For example, suppose a subroutine uses the variable tmp in an intermediate calculation. Suppose the routine is later modified so it does not use tmp anymore. If tmp is explicitly declared and the declaration is not removed, the routine still allocates memory for tmp even though it is unused. Implicit variable declaration prevents this problem.

Unfortunately, implicit variable declaration often causes some much more subtle problems. Consider the following function:

```
Public Function Factorial(num As Long) As Long
    factorial_value = 1
    For i = 1 To num
        factorial_value = i * factorial_valeu
    Next i
    Factorial = factorial_value
End Sub
```

When it reaches the first line in the function, Visual Basic sees the variable factorial_value. Since it has not seen this variable before, it automatically allocates memory for it. Initially, that variable is initialized with the value 0.

When the program reaches the third line, it sees the misspelling "factorial_valeu." Visual Basic has not seen this name before, so it assumes this is a new variable. It automatically allocates memory for factorial_valeu and initializes its value to 0. This variable is never assigned a new value, so it always remains 0.

The program then sets factorial_value equal to itself times factorial_valeu. Since factorial_valeu always equals 0, factorial_value is set to 0. Eventually, the function returns the value stored in factorial_value, which is always 0.

Finding the bug in this function could be very frustrating. The code looks fine to Visual Basic, so it will not report an error. The only way to solve the problem is to walk through the code and stare at it until you see the typographical error.

You can prevent this sort of error by starting all modules with the following statement:

```
Option Explicit
```

When a module begins with the Option Explicit statement, Visual Basic generates an error whenever it sees a variable that has not yet been declared. In the following code, Visual Basic immediately complains about the undeclared variable factorial_valeu. Instead of hiding the problem and causing an obscure bug, the system makes the problem obvious.

```
Option Explicit

Public Function Factorial(num As Long) As Long
Dim factorial_value As Long

    factorial_value = 1
    For i = 1 To num
        factorial_value = i * factorial_valeu
    Next i
    Factorial = factorial_value
End Sub
```

Note that Option Explicit does not require that you explicitly declare data types for variables. You still need to do that yourself. The following code is valid, although it would be better to explicitly declare factorial_value's data type as in the previous example.

```
Option Explicit

Public Function Factorial(num As Long) As Long
Dim factorial_value

    factorial_value = 1
    For i = 1 To num
        factorial_value = i * factorial_value
    Next i
    Factorial = factorial_value
End Sub
```

Don't Use Deftype Statements

In the following code, the first statement makes Visual Basic automatically allocate variables starting with the letters A through D as integers if their type is not explicitly given. Then the second line declares the variable data_points. Because the statement does not explicitly give the variable a data type, and because the variable's name begins with the letter d, Visual Basic makes the variable an integer.

```
DefInt A-D

Dim data_points
```

Visual Basic has other commands such as DefLng and DefBool to define other default data types.

These statements made sense in early versions of Basic and Fortran where variables had to have very short names. If names can only have six characters, starting all integer variables with I can make it easier to understand the purpose of a variable. For example, INOCHR might be an integer holding the number of characters used by a routine. If you follow this naming convention, DefInt I makes sense because all variables starting with I are integers by convention.

Modern Visual Basic's variables are not as restricted as those in ancient Basic and Fortran. Now you can name this variable num_characters to make its meaning clear. Because variables can have more descriptive names, the initial I is not needed (but see the following section on Hungarian notation).

Even if you use Deftype statements, an explicit declaration overrides the default data type. If every integer variable does not start with I and not every variable starting with I is an integer, DefInt I is misleading. In the following code, the variable individuals defaults to the integer data type but idiots is explicitly declared as a collection.

```
DefInt H-K

Dim individuals
Dim idiots As New Collection
```

These declarations can cause great confusion later in the code. If you know that all variables starting with the letters H through K are integers, you may misunderstand the meaning of the variable idiots. The following code could be quite confusing.

```
MsgBox idiots(individuals)
```

Deftype statements are anachronisms. Do not use them.

Use Hungarian Notation

Hungarian notation is an extension of the practice of using the first letter in a variable name to indicate its data type. Since Visual Basic's variables can have relatively long names, Hungarian notation can add several characters to indicate the variable's data type and scope.

Hungarian Specifics

Hungarian notation consists of several prefix characters identifying a variable's scope and data type, followed by the variable's name. The prefix characters are usually lowercase and the variable name usually begins with a capital letter as in cmdExit.

Table 3.1 lists the prefixes recommended by Microsoft to indicate a variable's scope. This prefix should be the first letter in the variable's name. Routine local variables have no scope letter in this system.

Table 3.2 lists some of the prefixes recommended by Microsoft to indicate a variable's data type. These three-letter codes come after the scope letter.

It is generally better not to use the udt value to indicate a generic user-defined type. Instead, invent a new three-letter abbreviation for the specific user-defined type. For example, for the user-defined type named Player, you might use the abbreviation plr.

Of course when you invent a new abbreviation, you must be certain all developers use the same value. It will be confusing if some programmers use plr and others use ply.

You can use three-letter prefixes to indicate the types of controls as well as variables. Table 3.3 gives Microsoft's prefix recommendations for the most common control types. For more complete lists of Microsoft's recommendations, see the Books Online that comes on the Visual Basic CD-ROM.

Table 3.1   Scope Prefixes

SCOPE	PREFIX
Application global	g
Module global	m
Routine local	

Table 3.2 Data Type Prefixes

DATA TYPE	PREFIX
Boolean	bln
Byte	byt
Collection	col
Currency	cur
Date/time	dtm
Double	dbl
Integer	int
Long	lng
Single	sng
String	str
Unspecified object	obj
User-defined type	udt
Variant	vnt

Because controls are always defined at a form level, control names usually do not include a scope prefix. For example, an Exit command button might be named cmdExit.

On the other hand, a variable reference declared within the code does have a meaningful scope so it can include a scope prefix. For example, suppose a form contains a group of option buttons. When the user clicks one, the following code saves a reference to that button in the form's moptSelection variable.

```
Private moptSelection As OptionButton

Private Sub optOpenFile_Click()
    set moptSelection = optOpenFile
End Sub

Private Sub optCloseFile_Click()
    set moptSelection = optCloseFile
End Sub
    :
```

You can also define your own prefixes for classes, related constants, and enumerated types. A group of constants that specify different user types might all have names beginning with usr.

Many programming groups redefine the prefixes shown in Tables 3.1, 3.2, and 3.3 to suit their own needs and preferences. For example, the Boolean prefix

Table 3.3 Control Type Prefixes

CONTROL TYPE	PREFIX
CheckBox	chk
ComboBox	cbo
CommandButton	cmd
CommonDialog	dlg
Data	dat
DirListBox	dir
DriveListBox	drv
FileListBox	fil
Form	frm
Frame	fra
HScrollBar	hsb
Image	img
Label	lbl
Line	lin
ListBox	lst
MDI Child Form	mdi
Menu	mnu
OptionButton	opt
PictureBox	pic
Shape	shp
TextBox	txt
Timer	tmr
VScrollBar	vsb
RichTextBox	rtf
Unspecified Control	ctr

bln is sometimes changed to bool and the variant prefix vnt is often changed to var. It does not matter what prefixes you use, as long as everyone on your project uses the same values.

Some developers use prefixes for subroutines and functions as well as variables and controls. For example, a function declared private within a module that returns the factorial of a number as a long integer might be named mlngFactorial.

Purpose

Hungarian notation provides additional information about a variable's scope and data type. When you see a variable named gdblFieldLength, you know it is a global variable declared as a double precision number.

Hungarian notation also prevents some kinds of name space conflicts. For instance, in the following code, the variable count is defined at the module level and within the subroutine. The definition of count inside the subroutine hides the module-level variable. Inside the subroutine, count refers to the local variable, not the module-level variable. Name collisions like this one can be confusing.

```
Private count As Integer

Private Sub DoSomething()
Dim count As integer

    For count = 1 To 100
        :
    Next count
End Sub
```

The best way to avoid this sort of name confusion is to not use the same name for multiple purposes. There would be no problem if the module-level variable was named control_count instead of count.

Hungarian notation also protects against this kind of name conflict. In this example, the module-level variable would be renamed mCount and there would be no conflict.

A particularly useful example of this protection is in naming controls. Controls and their data are logically related. A TextBox control and the text it contains are very similar in purpose. In fact, the TextBox control's default property is Text. That means a program can use Text1 and Text1.Text interchangeably.

If you use a control type prefix to name controls and data type prefixes to name variables that contain a control's value, you can give the control and its value similar names without confusion. For example, a TextBox containing a customer's name might be named txtCustomer. The program could store and manipulate the TextBox's value in the string variable strCustomer. The similarity between these two names makes their relationship clear while their prefixes make it obvious that they are not quite the same.

One drawback to Hungarian notation is that a variable name is tied to a specific implementation as well as the variable's purpose. For instance, the name mintNumEmployees is a module-level integer variable. During development, if you decide to change the variable to a long integer, you must rename the variable.

This is somewhat annoying because the meaning of the variable has not changed. Ideally, you should not need to rename a variable unless its meaning has changed. This is one of the prices you pay for using Hungarian notation.

A Word of Caution

You should use Hungarian notation with some discretion. A bad variable name with a fancy prefix is still a bad variable name. For instance, suppose you are reading the code in a clean room control program and you come across the variable gdblDHum. You can tell this is a global double precision variable, but that is all. You do not know what the variable means, how it is used, or where it is declared. Unless there is a useful comment nearby, you will have to search for Public gdblDHum and hope a comment near the variable's declaration can shed some light on the situation.

On the other hand, suppose the variable's name is DesiredHumidity. Now you have some idea of the variable's purpose and use. If you know a bit about the application, you may know or guess that the value is a floating-point number.

If the variable is named gdblDesiredHumidity, you know the scope, data type, and purpose of the variable.

Some developers think Hungarian notation is a magic solution that will make any program maintainable. Prefixes only help if the variables' base names are informative, too. Without a meaningful base name, knowing the variable's data type is worthless. If you have to pick between Hungarian notation and meaningful names, meaningful names are the right choice every time.

Use Meaningful Names

As mentioned in the previous section on Hungarian notation, meaningful variable names are more important than scope and data type prefixes. Make names descriptive enough that another programmer will have no trouble figuring out your variable's purpose.

Do not use obscure abbreviations. Do not abbreviate to save one or two characters. Instead of writing SpecTeamLdr, use SpecialTeamLeader. Even simple abbreviations take longer to understand than completely spelled phrases. The extra typing you save by abbreviating is not worth the added distraction you impose on the reader.

Some abbreviation is fine, but you should agree with the other team members on the abbreviations you will use. The code will be harder to read if different developers use different strategies. For example, you might agree that count variables should begin with Num as in NumEmployees. The code will be harder to read if it contains the variables NumEmployees, NoCustomers, Product-Count, and so forth.

Capitalize Consistently

The point of Hungarian notation is to make it easier to understand a variable's scope and data type. Another way to make scope clear is to use consistent capitalization. For example, you can write the names of global variables in Mixed-Case. Table 3.4 shows one possible capitalization scheme. Notice that this scheme does not differentiate between global and nonglobal constants.

This method indicates scope but not data type. You can add a Hungarian data type prefix, or make variable names descriptive enough that the data types are obvious.

This method also does not handle name conflicts. You cannot declare a module-global variable named Count and a subroutine variable named count. If you try, Visual Basic will change the capitalization of whichever variable you declare first so it matches the second variable's capitalization.

Avoid Name Conflicts

Visual Basic allows a program to have more than one variable with the same name at different levels of scope. For example, the following code uses variables named A declared with module-global and subroutine-local scope. If you execute this code, it will display the values 1, 2, 3, 1.

```
Private A As Integer            ' Module global scope.

Private Sub Print_Values
    A = 1
    Debug.Print A               ' Print the module global value.
    Print_2
    Print_3
```

Table 3.4 Capitalization Conventions

SCOPE	FORMAT
Constants	ALL_CAPS_WITH_UNDERSCORES
Application global	MixedCase
Module global	Mixed_Case_With_Underscores
Routine local	lower_case_with_underscores

```
    Debug.Print A              ' Print the module global value.
End Sub

Private Sub Print_2
Static A As Integer            ' Subroutine scope. Starts 0.

    A = 2
    Debug.Print A              ' Print the local value.
End Sub

Private Sub Print_3
Dim A As Integer               ' Subroutine scope. Starts 0.

    A = 3
    Debug.Print A              ' Print the local value.
End Sub
```

Multiple variables with the same names at different levels of scope can be confusing. Give these variables different names.

As mentioned in the section describing Hungarian notation, variables with different scopes always have different names if you give them scope prefixes. However, even if you use scope qualifiers, variables with similar names can cause a lot of confusion. If you are editing a program, it could be very difficult to decide whether the value you need to modify is mintFiles or intFiles. Even if you know which variable you need, you could easily mistake one for the other when reading the code quickly.

Avoid these difficulties entirely by giving different variables completely different names. In this case it would be better to name the variables NumOpenFiles and num_working_files.

Limit Scope

Give constants, variables, subroutines, functions, and other scoped items the most limited scope possible. Do not use a global variable if a module-global variable will work. Do not use a module-global variable when a subroutine variable will do.

Giving a variable greater scope than necessary increases the chances that some routine will modify the value incorrectly. It allows two routines to use the variable in ways that make them interfere with each other.

Limiting the scope of objects as much as possible hides them from other parts of the code. That means when you read those pieces of code, you do not need to be aware of the objects' existence. This reduces the number of things you need to think about while you read the code so it makes the code easier to understand.

Use Static Variables

If a subroutine needs to save a value between invocations, use a static variable, not a module global variable. For example, the following code uses a module-global variable to increment a value each time it executes the ShowCount subroutine.

```
Private the_count As Integer    ' Module-global variable.

Private Sub ShowCount()
    the_count = the_count + 1
    MsgBox "Count:" & Str$(the_count)
End Sub
```

This version uses a static variable instead of a module-global variable.

```
Private Sub ShowCount()
Static the_count As Integer     ' Static variable in the subroutine.

    the_count = the_count + 1
    MsgBox "Count:" & Str$(the_count)
End Sub
```

If you need to initialize a static variable to some value other than the default defined by Visual Basic, use another static variable named done_before to determine whether the variable has been initialized yet like this:

```
Private Sub ShowCount()
Static done_before As Boolean   ' Have we initialized the count?
Static the_count As Integer     ' The count variable.

    ' See if the count variable has been initialized yet.
    If Not done_before Then
        ' If has not. Initialize it now.
        the_count = 5            ' Start with a count of 5.
        done_before = True       ' Don't initialize next time.
    End If

    the_count = the_count + 1
    MsgBox "Count:" & Str$(the_count)
End Sub
```

Use module-level variables only when two routines within the module need to access the same value. Use global variables only when two routines in different modules must access the same value. If possible, avoid global variables by moving the two routines into the same module and using a module-level variable.

Use Specific Data Types

Use the most specific data type possible for a given situation. Do not declare variables of type Object, Control, or Form when you can be more definite.

For example, suppose you have defined a type of form named TaxForm. Suppose also that you have a global subroutine named SetTax that takes as a parameter a TaxForm. You could declare the parameter as a TaxForm, a Form, or an Object. If SetTax will always be passed a TaxForm and never some other kind of form or object, declare the parameter as type TaxForm.

```
Public Sub SetTax(frmSalesTax As Object)    ' Bad.
Public Sub SetTax(frmSalesTax As Form)      ' Better.
Public Sub SetTax(frmSalesTax As TaxForm)   ' Best.
```

Declaring the variable with the most specific data type gives Visual Basic more information about the object. That lets it resolve certain object references earlier than it could otherwise. For example, suppose TaxForm includes a TextBox named txtSubTotal and consider this code:

```
Public Sub SetTax(frmSalesTax As Object)
Dim sub_total As Single

    sub_total = CSng(frmSalesTax.txtSubTotal)
        :
End Sub
```

When the program is compiled, Visual Basic cannot tell what kind of object the program will pass to SetTax. It cannot know if the frmSalesTax object includes a control named txtSubTotal. For all Visual Basic knows, the program might pass SetTax a reference to a Printer object.

In the following code, on the other hand, Visual Basic knows that the frmSalesTax is a TaxForm object. Because all TaxForm objects contain a TextBox named txtSubTotal, the system knows more precisely how to access the value frmSalesText.txtSubTotal. This lets the program access the TextBox more efficiently. In some examples, the program can access a variable declared with a specific type in one-third the time it takes to access a generic Object variable.

```
Public Sub SetTax(frmSalesTax As TaxForm)
Dim sub_total As Single

    sub_total = CSng(frmSalesTax.txtSubTotal)
        :
End Sub
```

Using the most specific data type possible also makes certain kinds of mistakes immediately obvious. If you try to pass a form of type InventoryForm into the SetTax subroutine, Visual Basic will generate a type mismatch error when the code invokes SetTax. This error clearly indicates that the code is trying to pass CalculateTax the wrong kind of object. When you see this error message, the problem is easy to fix.

However, if the routine takes a generic object as a parameter, SetTax will run until it tries to access a property or method that is defined by TaxForm but is not defined by InventoryForm. If both forms define all of the values needed by the routine, SetTax might not generate an error at all. This could cause a very subtle bug. SetTax would look fine internally, but there would be a bug in how the routine was invoked.

Allowing a routine to take a parameter with a weakly defined type can also confuse those who read the code later. Instead of concentrating on a single type of argument, the reader must keep track of many parameter types. He must wonder what the routine will do when the parameter is a form, control, object defined by a class, printer, clipboard, recordset, Nothing, or any of a huge number of other possibilities.

Similar principles apply to variable declarations, function return types, property procedure return types, and any other place the code specifies a data type. The following code legally sets a variable of type Object to reference a new object of the Player class. It would be better to declare the variable to be of type Player.

```
Dim attacker As Object

    Set attacked = New Player
```

Keep things efficient and simple by declaring variables using the most specific data type possible.

Use TypeOf and TypeName

Sometimes you must declare an object using a nonspecific data type. For example, you might write a subroutine that must be able to take a parameter that is either a TaxForm or an InventoryForm. To allow the program to pass either type of form to the routine, you should declare the routine's argument to be of type Form.

Unfortunately, this also allows the program to pass any other kind of form to the routine. Under some circumstances, that might cause some very subtle bugs.

When you use nonspecific data types like this, use Visual Basic's TypeOf and TypeName statements to verify that the parameter actually has one of the types you expect. For example, the following subroutine ensures that its argument is either a TaxForm or an InventoryForm. If the program passes it any other kind of form, the subroutine raises an exception.

```
Public Const ERR_WRONG_FORM_TYPE = vbObjectError + 27

Public Sub ResetForm(frm As Form)
    ' See if frm is a TaxForm or an InventoryForm.
    If Not ((TypeOf frm Is TaxForm) Or _
            (TypeOf frm Is InventoryForm)) _
    Then
        Err.Raise ERR_WRONG_FORM_TYPE, _
            "MyProject.ResetForm", _
            "The parameter should be of type TaxForm or " & _
                "InventoryForm but it actually has type " & _
                TypeName(frm)
    End If
        :
End Sub
```

Avoid Variants

An extension of the previous rule, "Use Specific Data Types," is that you should not use variants. Variants are the least specific of the standard data types and they can contain almost any kind of data. Variants take more memory, are slower, and are often more confusing than other data types. They can lead to particularly confusing data conversion errors.

For example, consider the following subroutine that adds a value to a global total.

```
Public TotalValue As Variant

Public Sub AddToTotal(new_amount As Variant)
    TotalValue = TotalValue + new_amount
End Sub
```

Now consider the statements in the following code. The first passes the value 10 to AddToTotal. Because the subroutine expects a variant parameter but 10 is an integer, Visual Basic converts the argument into a variant containing an integer and passes that to AddToTotal. At this point, the variant TotalValue is not yet defined. Because the value being added to TotalValue is an integer, Visual Basic converts TotalValue into a variant holding an integer with default value 0. It adds the new value so TotalValue becomes an integer with value 10.

The second line passes the value 10.1 to AddToTotal. Because the subroutine expects a variant parameter but 10.1 is a floating-point value, Visual Basic converts the argument into a variant containing a double and passes that to AddTo-Total. Before it can add the parameter to TotalValue, Visual Basic must promote the values so they have the same data type. Because double precision variables can contain integer values but not vice versa, Visual Basic promotes TotalValue to a double. The program adds the two numbers and stores the result in Total-Value. The variable TotalValue is now a variant containing the double precision value 20.1.

The third line passes a string to AddToTotal. Visual Basic converts the string into a variant containing a string. AddToTotal then generates an error when it tries to add a string to a double precision value.

```
AddToTotal 10
AddToTotal 10.1
AddToTotal "Hello"
```

This is confusing, but other even stranger scenarios are possible. The following two lines set TotalValue equal to the string "10 days" with no error. When the code executes the first statement, it adds a variant containing the string "10" to the undefined variable TotalValue. The result is that TotalValue is a variant containing a string with value "10."

Then the second passes a variant containing the string "days" to AddToTotal. The routine concatenates the string "days" to TotalValue and TotalValue becomes a variant containing the string "10 days."

```
AddToTotal "10"
AddToTotal " days"
```

The situation is confusing enough that some programmers may even try to execute the following statement. Here the programmer probably thinks the program will add 3 to TotalValue. The actual result depends on TotalValue's current value. If it contains a string, the AddToTotal subroutine will concatenate the string "Three" to it. If TotalValue contains a numeric value, the program will generate an error when it tries to add a string value to a numeric value.

```
AddToTotal "Three"
```

All this confusion disappears if you declare the parameter passed to AddToTo-tal as an integer, double, string, or any other more specific data type. In every case, the proper behavior for the subroutine is much more obvious.

While variants have some big drawbacks, they do have a few advantages. First, they can have undefined values. For many database applications, it is useful to distinguish between no value and other values. For instance, in Visual Basic, integers are initialized to 0. It might be useful to distinguish between 0 and an uninitialized value. The following code shows how a routine can tell whether a variant has been initialized.

```
Private Sub MySub()
Static the_value As Variant

    If IsEmpty(the_value) Then
        ' Initialize the_value.
        the_value = 0
    End If
        :
End Sub
```

Variants can also contain arrays. Visual Basic's Array statement allows you to quickly create a variant array containing specific data values. This makes it roughly the equivalent to a DATA statement in standard Basic and Fortran. The following code fills a variant array with employee names.

```
Dim employees As Variant

    employees = Array("Amy", "Brent", "Julia", "Michelle", "Rod")
```

The entries in a variant array are variants themselves and they can also be arrays. This is convenient for creating irregular array-like data structures. The following code creates the equivalent of a two-dimensional array in which each row in the array contains a different number of elements. The MsgBox statement prints the value of item 1 in row number 2. Variant arrays are numbered so the first entry has index 0, so this item has value 25. Figure 3.1 shows the irregular array graphically.

```
Private Sub Form_Load()
Dim row0 As Variant
Dim row1 As Variant
Dim row2 As Variant
Dim array_2d As Variant

    row0 = Array(1, 4, 5, 3, 8, 7, 9)
    row1 = Array(17, 12, 15)
    row2 = Array(22, 25, 21, 29, 27, 25)
    array_2d = Array(row0, row1, row2)

    MsgBox array_2d(2)(1)
End Sub
```

Another advantage of variants is that they can be declared publicly in classes and forms. Visual Basic does not allow forms or classes to declare public variables

1	4	5	3	8	7	9
17	12	15				
22	25	21	29	27	25	

Figure 3.1 Variants allow a program to create the equivalent of an irregular two-dimensional array.

that are arrays. A program can work around this restriction by declaring a public variant variable that contains an array instead of declaring the array directly.

Finally, variants are used by Visual Basic to pass a variable number of arguments to a subroutine. The following function adds up the values of its parameters and returns the total.

```
Public Function AddItems(ParamArray values() As Variant)
Dim i As Long
Dim total As Double

    For i = LBound(values) To UBound(values)
        total = total + values(i)
    Next i
    AddItems = total
End Function


    :


Dim A As Integer
Dim B As Integer
Dim sub_total As Integer

    A = 101
    B = 2875
        :
    ' Add 13 to items A and B.
    sub_total = AddItems(13, A, B)
```

It is argued by some programmers that variants are the only data type a program should use. In fact, the World Wide Web scripting language VBScript, which is based on Visual Basic, only allows variant variables.

Despite their advantages, however, variants often add ambiguity to an otherwise simple situation. Use them only when you need their special features, like their ability to build irregular arrays or to implement public array members of a class.

Use Variant Subtype Functions

When you do use variants, use Visual Basic's variant subtype functions to determine the kind of variable you are examining. The following code shows a more robust version of the AddItems function from the previous section. It uses the IsNumeric function to ensure that its arguments are numeric.

```
Const ERR_ARGUMENT_NOT_NUMERIC = vbObjectError + 17

Public Function AddItems(ParamArray values() As Variant)
Dim i As Long
Dim total As Double

    ' Make sure the parameters are numeric.
    For i = LBound(values) To UBound(values)
        If Not IsNumeric(values(i)) Then
            Err.Raise ERR_ARGUMENT_NOT_NUMERIC, _
                "MyProject.TotalItems", _
                "Parameter" & Str$(i) & _
                " with value """ & i & _
                """ is not numeric."
        End If
    Next i

    ' Add the parameters.
    For i = LBound(values) To UBound(values)
        total = total + values(i)
    Next i
    AddItems = total
End Function
```

Now if the program executes the statement TotalItems(1, "cat", 3), Visual Basic generates a very specific error message instead of a less meaningful generic type mismatch.

This subroutine examines all of its arguments before it begins any calculations. Because the checks are at the beginning of the subroutine, it is easy for you to later look at the code and verify that the checks are performed. It is also easy to change the parameter validations later if the argument list changes.

If the routine checked the argument types as it was adding them together, these tests would be buried deeper in the code. In this example, it would still be easy to find and modify the tests. In a more complex example, scattering the tests throughout the code would make the code harder to read. Putting all the tests at the beginning of the routine makes the code easier to understand.

Table 3.5 lists Visual Basic's variant subtype functions that you can use to check variant data types.

Beware the One Form

When you define a form named MyForm, Visual Basic creates a template that you can use to make any number of forms of this type. For example, the following code creates and displays five instances of MyForm using the New statement.

```
Private Sub ShowFiveForms()
Dim i As Integer
Dim frm As MyForm

    For i = 1 To 5
        Set frm = New MyForm
        frm.Show
    Next i
End Sub
```

Visual Basic also creates a single special instance of the type MyForm that has the name MyForm. Many programmers confuse MyForm objects in general with this special form named MyForm. For example, the following code creates a new form. It then attempts to set the form's caption and display the form. Unfortunately, it sets the caption for the one instance named MyForm instead.

```
Private Sub ShowOneForm()
Dim frm As MyForm
```

Table 3.5   Functions for Determining Variant Types

FUNCTION	PURPOSE
IsArray	True if an array.
IsDate	True if a date or time.
IsEmpty	True if uninitialized.
IsError	True if an error value created by CVErr.
IsMissing	True if an optional parameter that is missing.
IsNull	True if null. This is not the same as uninitialized.
IsNumeric	True if a numeric value.
IsObject	True if an object.
VarType	Returns a constant indicating the variant's type.

```
    Set frm = New MyForm            ' Create a new MyForm.
    MyForm.Caption = "My Form"      ' Set the caption of the one MyForm.
    frm.Show                        ' Display the new MyForm.
End Sub
```

As if this were not confusing enough, this code has also realized two copies of the form: one referenced by the frm variable and the original form named MyForm. If you close all of the visible forms after running this code, the special form named MyForm will still be running, even though it was never displayed. While no forms are visible, the program will not stop because the special instance of MyForm is still loaded. Be aware of this sort of confusion.

Another way the one form can cause problems is if a form's code explicitly references its own type. For example, the following MyForm code attempts to set the form's height and width when it is loaded. Unfortunately, it references the one form named MyForm rather than itself. Instead of resizing itself, the form resizes the one form. When the form appears, it will not have the correct size. This code has also referred to the one form so that form is loaded, even though it is probably not visible. If you close all visible windows, the one form will still be loaded so the program will not stop.

```
Private Sub Form_Load()
    MyForm.Width = 6000
    MyForm.Height = 2880
End Sub
```

To avoid this problem, never refer to a form's type name within its own source code. Always refer to the current form implicitly as in this code:

```
Private Sub Form_Load()
    Width = 6000
    Height = 2880
End Sub
```

Better still, emphasize that the current form is the one you want to reference by using the Me keyword as in this code:

```
Private Sub Form_Load()
    Me.Width = 6000
    Me.Height = 2880
End Sub
```

Most programs either use the one form or they use only other forms created using New. If the program will only need one copy of the form, it can refer to the one form explicitly as in the following code:

```
UserNameForm.txtUserName = ""
UserNameForm.Show
```

If a program will need several copies of the form, it should not use the one form. It should create the new forms using New instead.

```
Dim frm As New MyForm

    frm.Show
```

You can make a form enforce these standards in its Form_Load event handler. Use the Is operator to see if the current form's Me variable refers to the same form as the special one form. If you do not want to use the special one form, raise an error if the two values match as in the following code:

```
Const ERR_ILLEGAL_ONE_FORM = vbObjectError + 1010

Private Sub Form_Load()
    ' Make sure this is a new form, not the "one form."
    If Me Is MyForm Then
        Err.Raise ERR_ILLEGAL_ONE_FORM, _
            "MyForm.Form_Load", _
            "The one form instance of MyForm was loaded. " & _
            "You must create new forms using New."
    End If
End Sub
```

Note that this test examines only the reference to the one form, not the form itself. That means it does not realize the one form so you do not need to worry about that form being loaded. In fact, using this technique, the one form can never be realized since the form's Load event handler will raise an error.

If you want to allow only the special one form and prohibit creating forms with the New statement, raise an error if the form's Me value does not match the one form's value as in this code:

```
Const ERR_ILLEGAL_NEW_FORM = vbObjectError + 1011

Private Sub Form_Load()
    ' Make sure this is the "one form," not a new form.
    If Not (Me Is MyForm) Then
        Err.Raise ERR_ILLEGAL_NEW_FORM, _
            "MyForm.Form_Load", _
            "The program created a new instance of MyForm " & _
            "using New. It should only use the one form named MyForm."
    End If
End Sub
```

The one form that has its own type as its name can cause confusion in several ways. Beware of the one form and the subtle bugs it can cause.

Self-Test

Program Bad3 violates several of the guidelines presented in this chapter. This program, which is shown in Figure 3.2, generates a list of random values and then calculates statistics for them. Click the Randomize button to make the program generate the numbers. Click the Total button to see the numbers' total. Click the Average button to see their average.

One possible improved version of this code is listed in Appendix A, "Self-Test Solutions." Note that this is not the only possible solution. You can download updated bad and good versions of this program from the Web at www.vb-helper.com/err.htm.

```
DefInt I-K

Dim NumTxt

Private Sub Command1_Click()
    ComputeTotal
End Sub

Private Sub Command2_Click()
    Average
End Sub

Private Sub Command3_Click()
    Prepare
End Sub

Public Sub Average()
Dim NumTxt

    For Each ctl In Form1.Controls
        If ctl.Name = "Text1" Then NumTxt = NumTxt + 1
    Next ctl
    For i = 0 To NumTxt - 1
        Total = Total + CInt(Text1(i).Text)
    Next i
    Text2.Text = Format$(Total / NumTxt)
End Sub

Public Sub ComputeTotal()
Dim box As Object
```

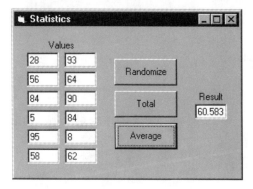

Figure 3.2 Program Bad3 displaying the average of a list of random numbers.

```
    If NumTxt = 0 Then
        For Each box In Form1.Controls
            If box.Name = "Text1" Then NumTxt = NumTxt + 1
        Next box
    End If
    For i = 0 To NumTxt - 1
        Total = Total + CInt(Text1(i).Text)
    Next i
    Text2.Text = Format$(Total)
End Sub

Public Sub Prepare()
Dim box As Object

    If NumTxt = 0 Then
        For Each box In Form1.Controls
            If box.Name = "Text1" Then NumTxt = NumTxt + 1
        Next box
    End If
    For i = 0 To NumTxt - 1
        Text1(i).Text = Format$(Int(100 * Rnd) + 1)
    Next i
End Sub
```

Summary

Declaring a variable may seem like a simple thing, but it sets the stage for how the variable is later interpreted. Giving the variable a descriptive name, limiting its scope, and using the most specific data type possible can reduce confusion later. Following these principles and the others summarized by the following Bug Stoppers makes the code easier to understand and can reduce the number of bugs in your project.

BUG STOPPERS: Variables

Explicitly declare variables on separate lines.

Use option explicit.

Don't use Deftype statements.

Use Hungarian notation.

Use meaningful names.

Capitalize consistently.

Avoid name conflicts.

Limit scope.

Use static variables.

Use specific data types.

Use TypeOf and TypeName.

Avoid variants.

Use variant subtype functions.

Beware the one form.

4

Constants and Enums

C onstants and enumerated types provide symbolic representation for numeric values. They let you use an understandable name for a value instead of a meaningless numeric quantity. Constants and enumerated types are very easy to use, so there is no excuse for using hard-coded numbers instead.

The following sections explain constants and enumerated types, and they discuss a few related topics that are not immediately obvious.

Use No Magic Numbers

When someone else reads your code later, hard-coded numbers like 12 and −32768 often seem mysterious. Because these numbers seem to have been picked out of thin air, they are sometimes called *magic numbers*.

In the following code, the InitializeColors routine and the declaration of the array BackgroundColors are in two different modules. If someone reads the InitializeColors code without having recently looked at the definition of the BackgroundColors array, the choice of the magic number 7 is puzzling.

```
Public BackgroundColors(0 To 7) As OLE_COLOR
```

In another module:

```
Private Sub InitializeColors()
Dim i As Integer

    ' Fill in the BackgroundColors array's entries.
    For i = 0 To 7
        BackgroundColors(i) = QBColor(i)
    Next i
End Sub
```

You can make the code clear by commenting every occurrence of the number 7.

```
Private Sub InitializeColors()
Dim i As Integer

    ' Fill in the BackgroundColors array's entries.
    ' They are indexed from 0 to 7.
    For i = 0 To 7
        BackgroundColors(i) = QBColor(i)
    Next i
End Sub
```

This helps, but it has a few drawbacks. It requires you to add a lot of comments to the code. It also makes it much harder to change the size of the array later. If you eventually decide the array should have bounds from 1 to 8, you need to search for every occurrence of the values 0 and 7 and change them to 1 and 8. You cannot simply perform an automatic search and replace because these values may be used for other things. If the program also contains a control array with controls indexed from 0 to 7, you do not want to replace occurrences of 7 that involve the control array.

Constants and enumerated values prevent all of these problems. Use meaningful names so the reader can tell what the constant represents. You can add extra comments where the values are defined to give the reader more detailed information.

Changing an array's bounds is easy if they are defined using constants. You can simply change the constants' definitions.

```
' We need 8 colors with indexes 0 through 7.
' At some point we will use the Mod operator to
' pick one.
Public Const MAX_COLOR = 7
Public BackgroundColors(0 To MAX_COLOR) As OLE_COLOR

' In another module:
Private Sub InitializeColors()
Dim i As Integer
```

```
    ' Fill in the BackgroundColors array's entries.
    For i = 0 To MAX_COLOR
        BackgroundColors(i) = QBColor(i)
    Next i
End Sub
```

To change the BackgroundColors array so it has 16 elements, all you need to do is change the definition of MAX_COLOR.

```
' We need 16 colors with indexes 0 through 15.
Public Const MAX_COLOR = 15
```

Dimension Arrays with Constants

When you dimension arrays, it is important that you use constants or enumerated values instead of hard-coded numbers. This makes it easy for you to later change the array bounds.

It is particularly important if you have several arrays that must have the same bounds. By changing one constant definition, you can change all of the array bounds without worrying about verifying that all the array declarations are kept synchronized.

```
Public Const NUM_EMPLOYEES = 100

Public EmployeeNames(1 To NUM_EMPLOYEES) As String
Public EmployeeIds(1 To NUM_EMPLOYEES) As Long
Public EmployeePhoneNumbers(1 To NUM_EMPLOYEES) As String
```

When you resize an array dynamically, use a constant, enumerated value, or variable. For example:

```
Public NumEmployees As Integer
Public EmployeeNames() As String
    :

    NumEmployees = NumEmployees + 1
    ReDim Preserve Employees(1 To NumEmployees)
```

These examples use constants, enumerated values, or variables to determine upper bounds for arrays, but they still hard code the lower bounds as 1. Many programs hard code lower array bounds when they are 0 or 1. Usually this is not confusing. However, if the program contains many arrays that have lower bound 0 and many others with lower bound 1, you may want to create constants for these values as well.

```
' We need 8 colors with indexes 0 through 7.
Public Const MIN_COLOR = 0
Public Const MAX_COLOR = 7
Public BackgroundColors(MIN_COLOR To MAX_COLOR) As OLE_COLOR

' In another module:
Private Sub InitializeColors()
Dim i As Integer

    ' Fill in the BackgroundColors array's entries.
    For i = MIN_COLOR To MAX_COLOR
        BackgroundColors(i) = QBColor(i)
    Next i
End Sub
```

Use NUM and MAX Constants

For arrays with lower bound 1, define the upper bound in terms of the number of items in the array. For arrays with lower bound 0, define the upper bound to be the maximum index in the array instead. For example, the following code defines a one-based array containing 100 items.

```
Public Const NUM_EMPLOYEES = 100
Public Employees(1 To NUM_EMPLOYEES) As EmployeeRecord
        :
    For i = 1 To NUM_EMPLOYEES
        :
    Next i
```

The following code defines a 0-based array with 100 employees.

```
Public Const MAX_EMPLOYEE = 99
Public Employees(0 To MAX_EMPLOYEE) As EmployeeRecord
        :
    For i = 0 To MAX_EMPLOYEE
        :
    Next i
```

If you define the upper bound for a 0-based array in terms of the number of items, For loops and other code that accesses the array are more confusing. Keeping track of which item is the last in the array is just one more thing that can cause confusion.

```
' This version is more confusing.
Public Const NUM_EMPLOYEES = 100
Public Employees(0 To NUM_EMPLOYEES - 1) As EmployeeRecord
```

```
    :
For i = 0 To NUM_EMPLOYEES - 1
    :
Next i
```

If for some reason you will frequently need to know the number of items in the array, create separate constants for the largest index and the number of items. Define one constant in terms of the other so you can change both by changing only the first.

```
Public Const NUM_EMPLOYEES = 100
Public Const MAX_EMPLOYEE = NUM_EMPLOYEES - 1
Public Employees(0 To MAX_EMPLOYEE) As EmployeeRecord
    :
For i = 0 To MAX_EMPLOYEE
    :
Next i
MsgBox "Processed" & Str$(NUM_EMPLOYEES) & " processed."
```

Use LBound and UBound

When the program needs to know an array's bounds, it should use the same constants that it used to dimension the array. Even better, it can use Visual Basic's LBound and UBound functions to learn the array's bounds. Now constants are unnecessary because the magic numbers appear only where the array is allocated.

```
' We need 8 colors with indexes 0 through 7.
Public BackgroundColors(0 To 7) As OLE_COLOR

' In another module:
Private Sub InitializeColors()
Dim i As Integer

    ' Fill in the BackgroundColors array's entries.
    For i = LBound(BackgroundColors) To UBound(BackgroundColors)
        BackgroundColors(i) = QBColor(i)
    Next i
End Sub
```

One time this does not work is if you need to declare several arrays that all have the same bounds. Array declarations require constant values for the array bounds, so they cannot use LBound and UBound. In this case, you can combine the two previous strategies. Use private constants to define the array bounds where the arrays are declared. Use LBound and UBound to find the array bounds in other places.

```
' We need 8 colors with indexes 0 through 7.
Private Const MIN_COLOR = 0
Private Const MAX_COLOR = 7
Public BackgroundColors(MIN_COLOR To MAX_COLOR) As OLE_COLOR
Public ForegroundColors(MIN_COLOR To MAX_COLOR) As OLE_COLOR

' In another module:
Private Sub InitializeColors()
Dim i As Integer

    ' Fill in the BackgroundColors array's entries.
    For i = LBound(BackgroundColors) To UBound(BackgroundColors)
        BackgroundColors(i) = QBColor(i)
    Next i
End Sub
```

It is a little known fact that control arrays have LBound and UBound properties you can use to find the minimum and maximum Index property values for the controls in the array. For example, the following code blanks the TextBoxes in the txtNames control array.

```
Dim i As Integer

    For i = txtNames.LBound To txtNames.UBound
        txtNames(i).Text =""
    Next i
```

Use the control array LBound and UBound properties whenever you need to create variable arrays that should have the same dimensions as a control array.

Note that control arrays are not guaranteed to hold a control with every index between the LBound and UBound values. For example, txtNames might have controls with indexes 0, 1, and 3. In that case, the program must protect itself against trying to access txtNames(2).

Give Related Values Related Names

Give related constants and enumerated values the same prefix so it is obvious that they are related.

For example, suppose the RotatingPicture ActiveX control rotates images. It uses numeric codes to indicate the direction of rotation. The following code defines rotation direction values using the prefix rotdir so it is obvious that they are related.

```
Public Enum rotpic_RotationDirection
    rotdir_Clockwise
    rotdir_CounterClockwise
    rotdir_None
End Enum
```

The RotatingPicture control might use the following property procedures to allow a program to get and set the rotation direction.

```
' The control's private, internal value.
Private mRotationDirection As rotpic_RotationDirection

' Return the current rotation direction.
Public Property Get RotationDirection() As rotpic_RotationDirection)
    RotationDirection = mRotationDirection
End Property

' Save a new rotation direction.
Public Property Let RotationDirection( _
    new_value As rotpic_RotationDirection)

    mRotationDirection = new_value
End Property
```

Add and Remove Values with Care

If the program uses a group of related constants or enumerated values in an If or Select statement, be careful when you add or remove values. For example, if you add a new value, it will not be included in Select statements that use the other values until you add it there as well.

The following code defines three filter constants. It then uses the value of the Filter variable to decide which kind of filter to build.

```
Private Const filter_PREWITT = 1
Private Const filter_HIGH_PASS = 2
Private Const filter_LOW_PASS = 3
    :
    Select Case Filter
        Case filter_PREWITT   ' Build a Prewitt filter.
            :
        Case filter_HIGH_PASS ' Build a high pass filter.
            :
        Case filter_LOW_PASS  ' Build a low pass filter.
            :
    End Select
```

If you later decide to add a new filter type, creating the new constant filter_LAPLACIAN is not enough. The Select statement does not include the new constant so it will fail if the program selects the new filter type. It will not find the new value in its list of cases so it will not build any filter.

To protect the program from this sort of bug, add a Case Else clause to the Select statement. If the Select statement reaches the Else code, the program should stop. Then if you define a new value and forget to add it to the Select statement's cases, the program will stop and make the mistake obvious instead of continuing as if nothing was wrong.

```
Select Case Filter
    Case filter_PREWITT    ' Build a Prewitt filter.
        :
    Case filter_HIGH_PASS ' Build a high pass filter.
        :
    Case filter_LOW_PASS  ' Build a low pass filter.
        :
    Case Else             ' This should not happen.
        Stop              ' Stop so we can find the problem.
End Select
```

Similarly, use an Else statement in a long series of If Then Else statements.

```
If Filter = filter_PREWITT Then
    :
ElseIf Filter = filter_HIGH_PASS Then
    :
ElseIf Filter = filter_LOW_PASS Then
    :
Else                    ' This should not happen.
    Stop                ' Stop so we can find the problem.
End If
```

Define Enumerated Values

Adding or removing a value from an enumerated type can change the meanings of the remaining values. Visual Basic assigns numeric values to enumerated types in the order in which they are defined. By default, Visual Basic gives the first the value 0. It gives subsequent symbols a value 1 greater than the previous value. In the following code, the comments indicate the values assigned by Visual Basic.

```
Public Enum btBorderType
    btNone                          ' 0
```

```
        btFancy                      ' 1
        btSingle                     ' 2
        btDouble                     ' 3
End Enum
```

If you later decide to remove the value btFancy, Visual Basic will renumber the other values so btSingle is 1 and btDouble is 2. If your program uses only these symbolic values, this does not matter. If you save the values in a file or database, however, the new numbering will not agree with the saved data.

If you save enumerated values to a file or database, explicitly assign numeric values to them. Then you can add, remove, or rearrange them without changing their values.

```
Public Enum btBorderType
    btNone = 0
    btFancy = 1
    btSingle = 2
    btDouble = 3
End Enum
```

Group Related Values

Place related constants and enumerated values in the same module so they are easy to find. Also put them next to each other within the module.

This does not mean you have to create a separate module for every set of constants. In fact, some developers put all constants in the same module whether or not they are related. Whether you define constants in one module or many, keep related values together.

Self-Test

Program Bad4 violates some of the guidelines described in this chapter. The program is shown in Figure 4.1 randomizing a list of user-entered values. Fill in the TextBoxes on the left and click the Randomize button. The program rearranges the items randomly and displays them in the labels on the right.

Appendix A, "Self-Test Solutions," contains one possible improved version of the following Bad4 code. Remember that this is not the only possible solution. You can download updated bad and good versions of this program from the Web at www.vb-helper.com/err.htm.

Figure 4.1 Program Bad4 randomizing a list of user-entered values.

```
Option Explicit

Private Values(0 To 9) As String

' Randomize the values entered by the user.
Private Sub cmdRandomize_Click()
    LoadValues Values, 0, 9
    RandomizeValues Values, 0, 9
    DisplayValues Values, 0, 9
End Sub

' Load the values from the txtInput TextBoxes.
Private Sub LoadValues(list() As String, _
    min As Integer, max As Integer)
Dim i As Integer

    For i = min To max
        list(i) = txtInput(i).Text
    Next i
End Sub

' Randomize the values in the array.
Private Sub RandomizeValues(list() As String, _
    min As Integer, max As Integer)
Dim i As Integer
Dim new_index As Integer
Dim temp_string As String

    Randomize
```

```
    For i = min To max - 1
        ' Randomly pick an entry with index between
        ' i and max to go in position i.
        new_index = Int((max - i + 1) * Rnd + i)

        ' Swap that entry with the one in position i.
        temp_string = Values(i)
        Values(i) = Values(new_index)
        Values(new_index) = temp_string
    Next i
End Sub

' Display the values in the lblOutput Labels.
Private Sub DisplayValues(list() As String, _
    min As Integer, max As Integer)
Dim i As Integer

    For i = min To max
        lblOutput(i).Caption = list(i)
    Next i
End Sub
```

Summary

Constants and enumerated types can make code easier to read, understand, and modify. Use them whenever possible. Many experienced developers believe that code should contain no hard-coded numbers except 0 and 1, and then only when they are used as lower array bounds. Other developers believe even lower bounds should be defined as constants.

The following Bug Stoppers restate the main concepts presented in this chapter.

 ## BUG STOPPERS: Constants and Enums

Never use magic numbers.

Dimension arrays with constants.

Define the number of items in a 1-based array. Define the maximum index for 0-based arrays.

Use LBound and UBound.

Give related values related names.

Check Select and If statements when you add or remove constant values.

If you save data, assign values to enumerated types.

Group related values together in the same module.

CHAPTER 5

Exposing Bugs

Chapter 1, "Programming Philosophy," mentioned that defensive programming sometimes hides bugs. By continuing to execute safely even when an error occurs, a defensive subroutine covers up an error that might be a symptom of an important bug.

This chapter explains methods for making bugs obvious. By aggressively exposing bugs and potentially incorrect behaviors whenever they occur, a program can make bug finding and repair quick and easy.

Verify Arguments

Many errors occur because one routine calls another incorrectly. The caller passes the wrong kinds of arguments to the other routine, or it passes values that do not make sense. If the caller does not understand the routine's arguments, it cannot use that routine correctly.

Even if it does receive a correct result while passing incorrect arguments to the routine, the caller is looking for trouble. Because the arguments are out of the normal range, the routine probably assumes the caller does not use those values. Another developer may later change the routine's behavior when it receives these parameters thinking it will not hurt calling routines. In that case, the caller will stop working correctly.

This kind of bug can be hard to catch. Sometimes the bug may not appear until long after the called routine was changed. Even if it is immediately obvious that something is wrong, it is not apparent where the bug lies. A change to one routine has caused a bug in another that used to work properly before. Unless you are intimately familiar with the way in which the caller works, you may need to perform an extensive search to find the problem. When you do look at the caller, you will be prejudiced toward thinking the routine cannot be broken because it worked before.

The best time to catch this kind of error is the instant the incorrect arguments are first passed to the called routine. If the routine immediately reports an error, you can fix the caller quickly and easily.

Routines should verify that their arguments are correct before they start calculating with them. During project design, the routine should stop execution if it encounters an invalid argument. This action lets developers quickly find the problem and fix it.

Use Debug.Assert

If you are using Visual Basic 5 or 6, you can stop execution using Debug.Assert. The Debug.Assert statement checks a condition you specify and stops execution if the condition is False. The following code shows how a subroutine might verify that its variant arguments are strings. For example, the first Debug.Assert statement stops execution if the Boolean value VarType(param1) = vbString is False.

```
' Make sure the parameters are strings.
Debug.Assert VarType(param1) = vbString
Debug.Assert VarType(param2) = vbString
Debug.Assert VarType(param3) = vbString
```

When you compile a program, all Debug statements including Debug.Assert statements are removed. The intent is to use these statements during development and testing, but then remove them before building the final application. Because the statements are not part of the compiled executable, the program can run faster.

Unfortunately, removing the Debug.Assert statements leaves the routine unprotected. If another subroutine passes incorrect arguments in the compiled executable, the program will try to continue executing. This may produce the wrong results.

Even worse, you probably have not tested the program thoroughly when incorrect arguments are passed into the routine because Debug.Assert usually stops them. There is no telling what the routine may do in that case.

Also Visual Basic 4 and earlier versions do not have a Debug.Assert statement. All of these facts conspire to make Debug.Assert a marginal solution.

Use Stop

You can obtain a result similar to a Debug.Assert statement using an If statement and the Stop command.

```
' Make sure the parameters are strings.
If Not (VarType(param1) = vbString) Then Stop
If Not (VarType(param2) = vbString) Then Stop
If Not (VarType(param3) = vbString) Then Stop
```

These statements work in Visual Basic 4 and earlier versions. They also work in the compiled executable program. Unfortunately, when this code is compiled, the Stop command displays the rather uninformative message "Stop statement encountered" and then the program halts. The message does not tell developers where the Stop statement was encountered, gives no useful information to the user, and does not allow the program to trap and handle the error. That makes Stop statements and Assert statements equally ineffective in compiled programs.

One solution is to use a conditional compilation constant to determine the action the program should take. If DEBUG_MODE is True, the program uses If and Stop statements to verify the argument's correctness. If DEBUG_MODE is False, the routine raises an error for the calling routine to handle if the argument is invalid.

```
' Set to False before compiling.
#Const DEBUG_MODE = True
    :

    ' Make sure the parameters are strings.
    If Not (VarType(param1) = vbString) Then
        #If DEBUG_MODE Then
            Stop
        #Else
            Err.Raise err_INVALID_PARAMETER, _
                "MyProgram.MySubroutine", _
                "Parameter must be a string"
        #End If
    End If
```

This method allows the program to handle the error properly whether or not it is compiled. It also allows you to examine the behavior of the program in both modes by simply changing the value of DEBUG_MODE. For example, you can set DEBUG_MODE to False and run the noncompiled version in the development environment to see how the program will behave when it is compiled. This can help you test the program's error handlers, a step often overlooked by developers.

This technique still has a few problems. First, it requires that you remember to change the value of DEBUG_MODE whenever you compile. This method is also quite verbose. It takes roughly nine times as much code to validate the parameters as the previous version.

The following code uses two techniques to address these issues. First, it uses the variable DebugMode instead of the constant DEBUG_MODE. The program sets the value of DebugMode when it starts and the variable is then available to the entire program.

To set DebugMode, the program uses a trick involving the compiler's behavior. If the program is compiled, it contains no Debug statements; in particular, it contains no Debug.Print statements. To determine whether is has been compiled or not, the program tries to execute the command Debug.Print 1 / 0. If the program has been compiled, this statement has been removed and the program continues. On the other hand, if the program is running in the development environment, it tries to display the value 1 / 0. This generates a divide by 0 error. The program uses an On Error statement to trap this error and set DebugMode to True.

The second technique the program uses is to move the argument verifying code into a subroutine. Subroutine VerifyVariantType checks that a variant argument is of the correct data type. This subroutine reduces the amount of duplicated code and shortens argument checking.

```
' True if we are in the development environment.
Public DebugMode As Boolean

' See if we are running in the development environment
' or a compiled program. Run this routine at startup.
Public Sub SetDebugMode()
    On Error GoTo CompiledVersion

    ' If the program is compiled, the following
    ' Debug statement has been removed so it will
    ' not generate an error.
    Debug.Print 1 / 0
    DebugMode = False
    Exit Sub

CompiledVersion:
    ' We got an error so the Debug statement must
```

```
    ' be working.
    DebugMode = True
End Sub
' Verify that the variant is of the correct type.
Public Sub VerifyVariantType(param As Variant, _
    type_name As String, routine_name As String)

    If Not (TypeName(param) = type_name) Then
        If DebugMode Then
            Stop
        Else
            Err.Raise err_INVALID_PARAMETER, _
                "MyProgram." & routine_name, _
                "Parameter should be of type " & _
                type_name & _
                " but it is of type " & _
                TypeName(param) & _
                " with value " & param
        End If
    End If
End Sub
```

The program calls subroutine SetDebugMode when it starts. After that it can use VerifyVariantType to validate variant parameter types. The following code shows how a subroutine can verify that its parameters are strings.

```
    ' Set the DebugMode variable when we start.
    SetDebugMode
        :
    ' Make sure the parameters are strings.
    VerifyVariantType param1, "String", "MySubroutine"
    VerifyVariantType param1, "String", "MySubroutine"
    VerifyVariantType param1, "String", "MySubroutine"
```

This version automatically determines whether it is running in the development environment or in a compiled executable. The code is more readable and the VerifyVariantType subroutine provides a good place to add error-logging code later.

This method has the disadvantages that it is slightly slower and uses slightly more memory than the previous version. In the previous version, when the conditional compilation symbol DEBUG_MODE is False, the compiler removes the error checking code from the executable version. That reduces the amount of code in the executable. It also means the program does not need to execute an If statement to determine whether or not it is running compiled.

Validate Optional Parameters

In addition to normal parameters, a routine should verify that any optional parameters it receives make sense. For example, if a subroutine takes pairs of numbers as parameters, it should verify that the calling routine has passed in an even number of values. Use the IsMissing function to determine which parameters are present.

Because optional parameters in VB4 are always variants, you should also verify that they have the correct data types and that they have reasonable values.

Program Circles4 draws concentric circles as shown in Figure 5.1. This program uses the DrawCircles subroutine shown in the following code to draw its circles. The routine takes as parameters the center of the circles and the radius of the largest circle. Optional color and aspect parameters let the program specify a color and aspect ratio for the circles. The routine verifies that the color parameter is numeric and that its value is nonnegative.

It also verifies that the aspect parameter is numeric and between 0.25 and 4. Those values allow the program to create a reasonable assortment of ellipses. It is possible that the program might want to create an ellipse with a larger or smaller aspect ratio, but that will be unlikely under most circumstances. If it does turn out to be the case, this routine can be modified to allow more extreme values. In the meantime, the values 0.25 and 4 provide reasonable error checking. If the routine receives the value 0 or 100, there is probably a bug.

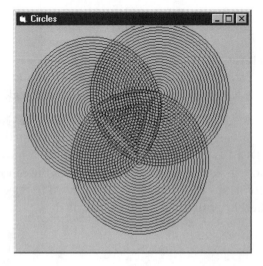

Figure 5.1 Program Circles4 draws concentric circles where you click.

```
' Draw a series of concentric circles.
Private Sub DrawCircles(ByVal X As Single, ByVal Y As Single, _
    ByVal radius As Single, _
    Optional ByVal color As Variant, _
    Optional ByVal aspect As Variant)
Dim clr As Long
Dim asp As Single
Dim r As Integer

    ' If the color is present, verify it is valid.
    If IsMissing(color) Then
        clr = ForeColor
    Else
        If Not IsNumeric(color) Then
            If DebugMode Then
                Stop
            Else
                Err.Raise err_INVALID_PARAMETER, _
                    "Circles.DrawCircles", _
                    "The color parameter must be numeric " & _
                    " but it is of type " & _
                    TypeName(color) & _
                    " with value " & color
            End If
        End If

        clr = CLng(color)
    End If

    ' If the aspect is present, verify it is valid.
    If IsMissing(aspect) Then
        asp = 1#
    Else
        If Not IsNumeric(aspect) Then
            If DebugMode Then
                Stop
            Else
                Err.Raise err_INVALID_PARAMETER, _
                    "Circles.DrawCircles", _
                    "The aspect parameter must be numeric " & _
                    " but it is of type " & _
                    TypeName(aspect) & _
                    " with value " & aspect
            End If
        End If

        asp = CSng(aspect)
    End If

    ' Verify that 0.25 <= aspect <= 4.
    If (asp < 0.25) Or (asp > 4) Then
```

```
            If DebugMode Then
                Stop
            Else
                Err.Raise err_INVALID_PARAMETER, _
                    "Circles.DrawCircles", _
                    "The aspect parameter must be between 0.25 and 4 " & _
                    " but is " & aspect
            End If
        End If

        ' Draw the circles.
        r = radius
        Do While r >= 1
            Circle (X, Y), r, clr, , , asp
            r = r - 4
        Loop
    End Sub
```

Use Default Values

If you use Visual Basic 5 or 6, you can use default values for arguments where a default value makes sense. You can also give more explicit data types to optional variables than variant. Default values and explicit data types let you avoid several kinds of potential errors. For example, the DrawCircles subroutine shown in the previous section no longer needs to check whether optional arguments are present. For those that are present, it no longer needs to verify that they are numeric. It can simply verify that the values it receives fall within a reasonable range.

The following code shows the DrawCircles subroutine used by program Circles5. This program is similar to program Circles4 but it uses default value and explicit typing features for optional parameters. These features are only available in Visual Basic 5 and 6, so do not try to run this program in earlier versions. This code is much more concise than the previous Circles4 code.

```
    ' Draw a series of concentric circles.
    Private Sub DrawCircles(ByVal X As Single, ByVal Y As Single, _
        ByVal radius As Single, _
        Optional ByVal color As Long = vbBlack, _
        Optional ByVal aspect As Single = 1#)
    Dim r As Integer

        ' Verify that 0.25 <= aspect ratio <= 4.
        If (aspect < 0.25) Or (aspect > 4) Then
            If DebugMode Then
```

```
            Stop
        Else
            Err.Raise err_INVALID_PARAMETER, _
                "Circles.DrawCircles", _
                "The aspect parameter must be between " & _
                " 0.25 and 4 but is " & aspect
        End If
    End If

    ' Draw the circles.
    r = radius
    Do While r >= 1
        Circle (X, Y), r, color, , , aspect
        r = r - 4
    Loop
End Sub
```

Note that default values must be hard coded. In Circles4, if the DrawCircles subroutine did not receive a color parameter value, it drew the circles using the form's ForeColor. In Circles5 the default value must be defined in advance by the value vbBlack. If a program needs the kind of increased flexibility demonstrated by program Circles4, it cannot use default values.

Avoid Optional Parameters

An even better way to handle optional parameters than the previous methods is to avoid them completely. If all parameters are required, there are fewer valid ways in which the calling subroutine can invoke the routine. That makes it easier to tell if the program is calling the routine correctly.

It also makes the calling routine easier to understand even when it is correct. Which of the following makes more sense?

```
' With all parameters required:
PrintTextAt 100, 100, "Rod Stephens", ForeColor, BackColor, Font.Size

' With all parameters optional:
PrintTextAt 100, 100, "Rod Stephens", , , Font.Size
```

In the second subroutine call, it is not clear what the missing parameters represent and what values they will receive by default. You can make the calling routine a bit easier to understand if you require all parameters.

Name Optional Parameters

If a routine takes optional parameters, use named arguments in the calling routine. That makes it obvious which arguments are included. It also means you do not need to carefully count all of the commas for omitted arguments to make sure you supply each value in its correct position. You can easily add, remove, and rearrange the arguments without messing up the comma count.

```
' Display text at the indicated spot using the
' specified font properties.
Private Sub PrintTextAt(X As Single, Y As Single, txt As String, _
    Optional font_name As String = "Times New Roman", _
    Optional font_size As Single = 12, _
    Optional is_bold As Boolean = False, _
    Optional is_italic As Boolean = False, _
    Optional is_underlined As Boolean = False, _
    Optional is_struck_through As Boolean = False, _
    Optional fore_color As Long = vbBlack)

    ForeColor = fore_color
    Font.Name = font_name
    Font.Size = font_size
    Font.Bold = is_bold
    Font.Italic = is_italic
    Font.Underline = is_underlined
    Font.Strikethrough = is_struck_through
    CurrentX = X
    CurrentY = Y
    Print txt
End Sub
```

Without named arguments, the program could use the PrintTextAt subroutine as in the following code:

```
Private Sub Form_MouseUp(Button As Integer, Shift As Integer, _
    X As Single, Y As Single)

    PrintTextAt X, Y, "www.vb-helper.com", , , , , , , vbRed
End Sub
```

Now suppose you wanted to make the text appear italicized. It would be relatively difficult to modify this text correctly. You would need to look up the definition of subroutine PrintTextAt and carefully match up the parameters with the arguments already used in the Form_MouseUp event handler. You would then need to insert the new parameter in its correct position.

On the other hand, the following code is easy to modify.

```
Private Sub Form_MouseUp(Button As Integer, Shift As Integer, _
    X As Single, Y As Single)

    PrintTextAt X:=X, Y:=Y, txt:="www.vb-helper.com", _
        fore_color:=vbRed
End Sub
```

To make this code italicize the text, you only need to add the is_italic named argument to the end of the parameter list.

```
Private Sub Form_MouseUp(Button As Integer, Shift As Integer, _
    X As Single, Y As Single)

    PrintTextAt X:=X, Y:=Y, txt:="www.vb-helper.com", _
        fore_color:=vbRed, is_italic:=True
End Sub
```

Use named parameters when you call a subroutine, particularly if you omit some parameters or the parameter list is long.

Validate ParamArray Parameters

The ParamArray keyword lets you create a subroutine that takes any number of parameters. The parameter array is a variant array that must appear as the routine's last parameter. For instance, the ComputeTotal function shown in the following code adds up its arguments and returns the total.

```
' Calculate the total of the routine's arguments.
Public Function ComputeTotal(ParamArray values() As Variant) As Double
Dim i As Integer
Dim total As Double

    For i = LBound(values) To UBound(values)
        total = total + CDbl(values(i))
    Next i
    ComputeTotal = total
End Function
```

ParamArray parameters are always variant arrays containing zero or more elements, each of which is a variant. Variants can contain all sorts of meaningless data, so a subroutine that uses a ParamArray must validate the number, types, and values of the parameters it receives. For instance, the ComputeTotal function should verify that its arguments are numbers.

Although it is possible for a routine to call ComputeTotal with zero or one parameter, this probably indicates a bug in the calling routine. To catch that bug as soon as possible, ComputeTotal should also check that the number of parameters is at least two. If it turns out that the program has a valid reason to pass fewer than two parameters to this function, it can be changed later. Until then, the routine looks for probable bugs by verifying that there are at least two parameters.

```
' Calculate the total of the routine's arguments.
Public Function ComputeTotal(ParamArray values() As Variant) As Double
Dim i As Integer
Dim total As Double

    ' Make sure there are at least 2 items in the
    ' ParamArray.
    If UBound(values) - LBound(values) + 1 < 2 Then Stop

    ' Verify that all ParamArray arguments are numeric.
    For i = LBound(values) To UBound(values)
        If Not IsNumeric(values(i)) Then Stop
    Next i

    ' Proceed with processing.
    For i = LBound(values) To UBound(values)
        total = total + CDbl(values(i))
    Next i
    ComputeTotal = total
End Function
```

Stop or Raise Errors When Appropriate

There are three main actions a routine can take when it receives a bad parameter:

- Stop.
- Raise an error.
- Ignore the parameter and take some reasonable default action.

If the parameter makes no sense whatsoever, the program should stop so you can find the error. For example, if the function takes a variant parameter and it expects a string but receives an integer, it should stop. Then you can figure out why the calling routine is passing it an integer and fix it.

If a function is asked to return the average value of the items in an array and the array contains no items, it should stop. The function cannot take the average of zero items, so it should not pretend to do so. It should stop so you can fix the calling routine.

In each of these cases, the routine could raise an error. Then the calling routine could trap the error and ignore it. That would let the bug remain undetected in the calling routine. Call immediate attention to the error by stopping. It never makes sense to take an average of zero items so the routine should never continue.

There are other times when a value may be valid sometimes but is not currently. For instance, a subroutine may take a filename as an argument. The parameter may contain a valid filename, but the indicated file may not exist. In that case, the argument looks valid, but it is not useful to the program.

This is the sort of error that may occur when the compiled program runs. The user may have deleted a key data file, the file may be mounted remotely on a network that is down, or the file may be on a floppy disk that is not inserted in the floppy drive.

Because the parameter in these cases might sometimes be valid, the routine should not merely stop. Instead, it should raise an error and let the calling routine try to figure out what the problem is. In this example, the calling routine might display a warning and let the user decide whether to retry the file operation or cancel it. If the file is on a missing floppy disk, the user may be able to insert the disk. Then the program could retry the operation and continue successfully.

A routine should never quietly ignore an invalid parameter and take some reasonable default action. Invalid parameters indicate either a problem in the code (the calling routine has a bug) or a problem in the environment (a file is missing). In either case, you should bring the problem to someone's attention so it can be fixed. Highlight the problem instead of hiding it.

Use Tight Restrictions

Restrictions make bugs obvious. When a bug violates the restrictions, it is easy to tell there is a problem.

To catch as many bugs as possible, use the tightest restrictions that are acceptable. Later, if there is a proven need for looser restrictions, you can loosen them.

For instance, suppose the PlotArray subroutine shown in the following code displays a bar graph of data values on a form's background. PlotArray requires that the number of values it is passed be between 10 and 20.

That restriction was chosen somewhat arbitrarily. A program may want to display fewer values, but the result would look a bit empty. A program may also want to display more values, but the form would look crowded. Requiring between 10 and 20 values is reasonable lacking any other information. If it later becomes necessary for the program to display a graph of 50 values, the restriction can be loosened. Until then, the restriction remains tight to guard against obviously invalid values like 2 or 10,000.

```
Private Sub PlotValues(values() As Single)
Dim num_values As Integer
Dim min_value As Single
Dim max_value As Single
Dim i As Integer

    ' Verify that there are between 10 and 20 values.
    num_values = UBound(values) - LBound(values) + 1
    If num_values < 10 Or num_values > 20 Then Stop

    ' Find the biggest and smallest values.
    min_value = values(LBound(values))
    max_value = min_value
    For i = LBound(values) + 1 To UBound(values)
        If min_value > values(i) Then min_value = values(i)
        If max_value < values(i) Then max_value = values(i)
    Next i

    ' Set the form's Scale properties.
    ScaleLeft = LBound(values) - 1
    ScaleWidth = UBound(values) - ScaleLeft
    ScaleTop = max_value
    ScaleHeight = min_value - ScaleTop

    ' Plot the values.
    For i = LBound(values) To UBound(values)
        FillStyle = (i Mod 7) + 1
        Line (i - 1, min_value)-(i, values(i)), , B
    Next i
End Sub
```

To make as many bugs as possible instantly visible, start with tight restrictions and loosen them only when absolutely necessary.

Use LBound and UBound

Chapter 4, "Constants and Enums," recommends that you use constants to define array bounds. For example, the following code uses a constant to declare an array and then initialize its elements to random values between 1 and 99.

```
Option Explicit

Private Const NUM_VALUES = 10
Private Values(1 To NUM_VALUES) As Integer
```

```
' Initialize the random values.
Private Sub Form_Load()
    InitializeValues
End Sub


' Initialize the Values array with random numbers
' between 1 and 99.
Private Sub InitializeValues()
Dim i As Integer

    Randomize
    For i = 1 To NUM_VALUES
        Values(i) = Int(99 * Rnd + 1)
    Next i
End Sub
```

The constant NUM_VALUES makes this code easy to modify. If you change NUM_VALUES to 100, you do not need to modify the InitializeValues subroutine. Because the routine uses the constant to determine the array's upper bound, it will automatically use the new upper bound if you change it.

However, the InitializeValues routine does contain the hard-coded value 1 as the array's lower bound. If you change the array's lower bound to 0 or some other value, the subroutine will not work properly. You could create new FIRST_VALUE and LAST_VALUE constants giving the array's bounds, but that would be needlessly complicated.

A better solution is to make subroutines like InitializeValues use LBound and UBound to determine the array's bounds. Then no matter how you change the array's bounds, the routine will function correctly. In fact, this routine will work even if the array is dynamically resized using the ReDim statement so it has bounds –100 and –75.

```
' Initialize the Values array with random numbers
' between 1 and 99.
Private Sub InitializeValues()
Dim i As Integer

    Randomize
    For i = LBound(Values) To UBound(Values)
        Values(i) = Int(99 * Rnd + 1)
    Next i
End Sub
```

Using this technique, only the code that actually declares the array needs to refer to constants or hard-coded values giving the array's bounds. All other routines can use LBound and UBound to determine the array's current bounds.

When you write routines like this one, carefully consider how the routine will react to typical and unusual upper and lower bounds. For example, how will the routine behave if the lower bound is 0 or 1? What if both bounds are negative? Can it handle the case when the upper and lower bounds are the same?

Notice also that UBound and LBound are undefined for arrays that have not been allocated. For example, the following code generates a subscript out of range error when it tries to determine LBound(Values) and UBound(Values).

```
Option Explicit

Private Const NUM_VALUES = 10
Private Values() As Integer

' Initialize the random values.
Private Sub Form_Load()
    InitializeValues
End Sub

' Initialize the Values array with random numbers
' between 1 and 99.
Private Sub InitializeValues()
Dim i As Integer

    Randomize
    For i = LBound(Values) To UBound(Values)
        Values(i) = Int(99 * Rnd + 1)
    Next i
End Sub
```

If a routine has any special limitations, like requiring the upper and lower bounds to be positive, use Debug.Assert or Stop statements to verify those conditions. The following code uses the Mod operator to map a value into an array. For the Mod operation to work correctly, the array's lower bound must be 0 and its upper bound must be at least 1. This code checks those conditions. It also watches for other potential bugs by verifying that the upper bound is at most 99 and that the value to be mapped is between 0 and 1000.

```
' Map a value into an array.
' Requirements:
'       LBound(arr) = 0
'       UBound(arr) >= 1
' Restrictions:
'       UBound(arr) <= 99
'       0 <= value <= 1000
Private Sub MapValueToArray(arr() As Integer, value As Integer)
Dim u_bound As Integer
Dim l_bound As Integer
Dim num_entries As Integer
```

```
' Get the array's bounds and verify that
' the array has been allocated.
On Error GoTo UnAllocated
u_bound = UBound(arr)
l_bound = LBound(arr)
On Error GoTo 0     ' Resume normal error handling.

' Validate the parameters.
Debug.Assert (value >= 0) And (value <= 1000)
Debug.Assert l_bound = 0
Debug.Assert (u_bound >= 1) And (u_bound <= 99)

' Map the item into the array.
num_entries = u_bound + 1
arr(value Mod num_entries) = value
Exit Sub

UnAllocated:
    If Err.Number = 9 Then
        ' The array has not been allocated.
        Err.Raise err_UNALLOCATED_ARRAY, _
            "MyProgram.MapValueToArray", _
            "Parameter ""arr"" has not been allocated with ReDim"
    Else
        ' Reraise the unknown error.
        Err.Raise Err.Number, _
            Err.Source, Err.Description, _
            Err.HelpFile, Err.HelpContext
    End If
End Sub
```

Use LBound and UBound to make your subroutines robust and easy to modify. Verify requirements and restrictions on bounds to catch potential bugs.

Validate Data Structures

An application should include a series of subroutines that test its supporting data and data structures for errors. These routines can validate data in arrays, check for invalid program options, examine database entries, read and verify the contents of data files, check system registry values, and so forth.

For example, suppose the program displays a corporate organization chart using a TreeView control. The program's data structures include Division, Department, and Employee objects. The data validation routines can verify that:

■ Each Employee has a reference to a valid Department.

■ Each Employee's Department contains a reference to the Employee.

- Each of a Department's Employees holds a reference to the Department.
- Each Department has a reference to a valid Division.
- Each Department's Division contains a reference to the Department.
- Each of a Division's Departments holds a reference to the Division.
- Every Division object is contained in the Divisions global collection.

Validate at Startup

A program should run its data validation routines whenever it starts. That guarantees that the routines are run on a regular basis. If the program's data structures and other components are corrupted, the tests will catch the fact quickly. You can then determine what happened to contaminate the data.

If the data verification routines are fast, you can leave them in the final compiled version of the program. If the data structures are corrupted while end users are using the program, the program should report the fact to you so you can fix it. If you are lucky, you may be able to find the error and fix the data before the users notice the problem.

If the data verification routines are slow, use conditional compilation or a test to see if the program is compiled to run them only in the development environment. You may want to run some of the faster tests in both the development and compiled versions to try to catch some of the more serious errors.

To reduce the impact of the test routines on programmers running the program in the development environment, the tests should occasionally execute the DoEvents statement. That allows the programmer to interact with the user interface while the tests are running. In that case, the programmer must not be able to modify a value or data structure before it has been tested. If the programmer makes a change to the data, it may be inconsistent for a short while and the data validation routines may report an error when none exists.

During design time you can also start the program with a form like the one shown in Figure 5.2. The developer indicates the tests the program should run and clicks the Ok button. The program runs the indicated tests and then continues with its normal functions.

The following code shows one way a program could validate its data before starting normal operation. This is the Load event handler for the program's main form. ValidationForm is the form shown in Figure 5.2. When the user clicks the Ok button, ValidationForm performs the selected data validations before it unloads itself.

Figure 5.2   A startup test form.

```
' Load and validate the data structures.
Private Sub Form_Load()
    ' Load the data structures.
    InitializeData

    ' Validate the data structures.
    ValidationForm.Show vbModal
End Sub
```

Alternatively, you could use the following code to start the program from a Sub Main procedure.

```
' Load and validate the data structures.
Public Sub Main()
    ' Load the data structures.
    InitializeData

    ' Validate the data structures.
    ValidationForm.Show vbModal

    ' Display the program's main form.
    MainForm.Show
End Sub
```

The main drawback to using a validation form is that developers can circumvent the tests by unchecking all the tests. The tests must be run regularly so they can catch errors as soon as possible. The tests do you no good if no one runs them.

Validate at Shutdown

A program should validate its data structures when it is about to exit. These shutdown tests can alert you to problems if the program has corrupted the data structures while it was running.

It is common for a complex program to corrupt its data structures but still continue running for a long time before encountering an error. If one developer corrupts the data but does not realize it, and another developer discovers the error much later, it may be difficult to tell how and when the data structure was contaminated. Shutdown validation routines can at least identify the session during which the data structures were damaged.

You can use the same techniques during shutdown as you can at startup. If the tests are fast, you can perform them all in both the development and final compiled programs. If the tests are slow, you can use conditional compilation or a test to see if the program has been compiled and then skip some or all of the tests in the compiled version. You can even present a form like the one shown in Figure 5.2 to let the developer determine which tests to run.

The following code shows how a program's main form can display a data structure validation form before it unloads.

```
' Validate the data structures and prepare to unload.
Private Sub Form_Unload()
    ValidationForm.Show vbModal
End Sub
```

If the program uses many forms, each can validate the data before it unloads. If the tests are relatively slow, each form can check to see if it is the last form before it performs validation.

```
' Validate the data structures and prepare to unload.
Private Sub Form_Unload()
    ' Validate the data structures if this
    ' is the last form running.
    If Forms.Count < 2 Then ValidationForm.Show vbModal
End Sub
```

Validate While Running

It is often useful to provide a means for developers to run data validation tests on demand. After you determine that a certain combination of commands corrupts the data, you can use the validation tests to help pinpoint the error.

Starting with a consistent data set, run the program. It should pass its startup tests because you are starting with fresh data. Next, perform the first in the series of operations that caused the corruption and run the data validation tests. Perform another step and validate the data again. Continue performing one step and then testing until you find the step that corrupts the data.

If you use a data validation form at startup or shutdown, you can use the same form while the program is running. A simple Test menu containing a Validate Data Structures command can display the form modally.

```
' Present the data structure validation form.
Private Sub mnuTestValidate()
    ValidationForm.Show vbModal
End Sub
```

You can also perform the tests interactively at any time while the program is stopped. Simply enter the command ValidationForm.Show vbModal in the Debug or Immediate window and Visual Basic will present the validation form. When you click the Ok button, the program will perform its validations exactly as if you had displayed the form using a menu command.

Validate Forms and Classes

You can extend the idea of data structure validation to cover forms and classes. When the program creates a new form or class object, that object's Initialize event handler can validate the object's data.

Unfortunately, initialize events do not take any parameters, so often the object cannot fully initialize itself during the Initialize event. For example, an Employee object cannot fill in its Name, EmployeeID, SocialSecurityNumber, and other data values during Initialize. Instead, it can provide the program with a public InitializeData subroutine that takes these values as parameters. After saving the data values, the routine can validate its data.

A form or class can also provide validation during its Terminate event, and it can provide a public method to allow the validation to run at any other times while the program is running. The validation routines can be helpful in tracking down an error that appears after a long series of operations on the objects.

Sometimes it is helpful to have the events of a specific object run a more global data validation routine. For example, when a program destroys an object, it may not have correctly removed that object from its data structures. The object's Terminate event handler can run the program's validation routines to verify that it has been correctly removed from the global data structure.

Clear Unused Variables

When the program is finished using a variable, it should clear it in a way that will expose bugs. Deallocate arrays using the Erase statement. Set object references and variants to Nothing. Give other variables strange values that you can recognize later. For example, set unused integers to –31,425. If you later find a function with a parameter that has value –31,425, you know there is a bug. The calling routine passed the function a variable that should not have been used again.

Setting object references to Nothing also removes the object from memory. As you set different variables to refer to a particular object, Visual Basic keeps track of the number of references to the object. When the reference count reaches zero, Visual Basic knows the program can no longer access the object so it frees the object's memory. The object remains loaded in memory until its last reference goes out of scope or you set the last reference to Nothing.

This can be particularly confusing with forms. The Unload statement unloads a form and clears the form's properties and controls. If the program tries to access any of these values, the program reloads the form and reinitializes all of these values. This can cause a lot of confusion.

For example, the following code creates an EmployeeForm and displays it. It then unloads the form and presents a message box showing the value displayed in the form's txtName TextBox. This makes Visual Basic reload the form with newly initialized values so the text displayed will be whatever is displayed when the form is first loaded.

Later, when the user closes the program's main form, this EmployeeForm is still loaded. Since a Visual Basic program only ends when all forms are unloaded, the program continues running even though no forms are visible.

```
Private EmpFrm As EmployeeForm
    :
Private Sub ShowEmployeeForm()
    ' Create the form.
    Set EmpFrm = New EmployeeForm

    ' Display the form.
    EmpFrm.Show vbModal

    ' Unload the form.
    Unload EmpFrm

    ' Display the txtName value. This reloads the form!
    MsgBox EmpFrm.txtName.Text
End Sub
```

The Unload statement does not execute the form's Terminate event handler because the form is not actually destroyed until its last reference goes out of scope or is set to Nothing.

The following code is similar to the previous code, but it displays the value of the txtName control before it unloads the form. Visual Basic does not reload the form so the TextBox is not reset to its original value. The routine then sets the reference to the form to Nothing. At that point, the form's Terminate event handler executes and the form is removed from memory. When the main form unloads, all forms are unloaded, so the program stops.

```
Private EmpFrm As EmployeeForm
    :
Private Sub ShowEmployeeForm()
    ' Create the form.
    Set EmpFrm = New EmployeeForm

    ' Display the form.
    EmpFrm.Show vbModal

    ' Display the txtName value.
    MsgBox EmpFrm.txtName.Text

    ' Unload the form.
    Unload EmpFrm

    ' Set the only reference to the for to Nothing.
    ' This executes the form's Terminate event handler
    ' and removes the form from memory.
    Set EmpFrm = Nothing
End Sub
```

Always clear unused variables. Set forms and other objects to Nothing to ensure that the objects are actually destroyed.

Use Else Statements

Always use Else clauses in long If Then statements and Select statements. If the program should take specific action when the Else case occurs, put the appropriate code here. If the Else case should never arise, make the program stop so you can determine what caused the unexpected condition.

```
If condition1 Then
    :
ElseIf condition2 Then
    :
```

```
Else
    ' This should never happen.
    Stop
End If
```

This is similar to the technique described earlier for catching errors that can occur when you create a new constant or enumerated value. If the program changes so the If Then or Select statement does something you did not anticipate, the Else clause will let you know so you can find and repair the problem.

Verify Results

An application should automatically verify important results. If the results are incorrect, it should stop so you can fix the problem.

Automatic verification can test a routine extremely thoroughly. For instance, a program might use a network shortest-path calculation to assign employees to jobs. During the development and testing of the program, the shortest-path algorithm may be executed thousands of times. If the algorithm verifies its results each time, it will test itself thoroughly under normal circumstances.

Sometimes you can write a routine to verify the results directly. For instance, to verify that a sorting routine correctly sorted a list, you can simply compare each item to the one before it in the list as in the following code:

```
' Verify the list is sorted.
Private Sub VerifySort(values() As Long)
Dim i As Integer

    ' Verify that each item is at least as large
    ' as the previous item.
    For i = LBound(Values) + 1 To UBound(Values)
        If Values(i - 1) > Values(i) Then Stop
    Next i
End Sub
```

Another method for verifying important results is to use two different routines and then compare their results. If they agree, the result is probably correct. If they disagree, you definitely have a bug in one or both of the routines.

If the two methods are too slow to keep both in the finished program, use conditional compilation directives to remove the slower routine from the final code.

Be certain that the two methods are significantly different. If they use the same techniques, they may both contain the same bugs. For example, because quicksort and heapsort are two very different sorting routines, they are unlikely to contain the same bug.

Even two completely different routines may have shared problems based on invalid assumptions. For example, suppose you write quicksort and heapsort routines to validate each other. You might assume that the list of numbers to be sorted is stored in an array with lower bound 1. The application may actually store values in an array with lower bound of 0. Because you made the same incorrect assumption in both routines, they verify each other even though they are both wrong.

If you remember to make the routines thoroughly verify their assumptions and parameter values, this particular bug is not a problem. When the program first tries to sort a 0-based array, it will see that the array violates its assumptions and it will stop.

You can also reduce the likelihood of making incorrect assumptions by having two different programmers write the two routines. Each may make bad assumptions, but hopefully they will make different bad assumptions and their results will disagree.

Self-Test

Program Bad5, shown in Figure 5.3, violates several of the guidelines described in this chapter. The program randomly generates 50 values in increasing order. Enter a target value and select a search method. Then click the Search button and the program will use the method you selected to find the target. It displays the position of the target in the list and the number of steps it performed during the search. You will find that the binary search uses far fewer steps that the linear search.

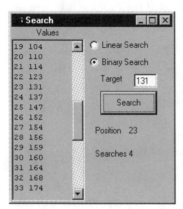

Figure 5.3   Program Bad5 searches for a target value using one of two algorithms.

The following code shows how program Bad5 works. Appendix A, "Self-Test Solutions," contains one possible improved version of this code. Remember that this is not the only possible solution. You can download updated bad and good versions of this program from the Web at www.vb-helper.com/err.htm.

```vb
Option Explicit

' Declare the list of values.
Const NUM_VALUES = 50
Private Values(1 To NUM_VALUES) As Integer

' Randomly initialize some values.
Private Sub Form_Load()
    InitValues
End Sub

' Randomly initialize some values.
Private Sub InitValues()
Dim i As Integer
Dim txt As String

    ' Pick the random values.
    Randomize
    Values(1) = Int(10 * Rnd + 1)
    For i = 2 To NUM_VALUES
        Values(i) = Values(i - 1) + Int(10 * Rnd + 1)
    Next i

    ' Display the values.
    For i = 1 To NUM_VALUES
        txt = txt & Format$(i, "@@") & _
            Format$(Values(i), "@@@@") & vbCrLf
    Next i
    txtValues.Text = txt
End Sub

' Search using the selected method.
Private Sub CmdSearch_Click()
Dim position As Integer
Dim num_searches As Integer

    If optSearchMethod(0).Value Then
        ' Linear search.
        position = LinearSearch(Values, _
            CInt(txtTarget.Text), num_searches)
    ElseIf optSearchMethod(1).Value Then
        ' Binary search.
        position = BinarySearch(Values, _
            CInt(txtTarget.Text), num_searches)
    End If
```

```
    ' Display the results.
    If position = 0 Then
        lblPosition.Caption = "Not found"
    Else
        lblPosition.Caption = Format$(position)
    End If
    lblSearches.Caption = Format$(num_searches)
End Sub


' Use linear binary search to find the target.
Public Function LinearSearch(list() As Integer, _
    target As Integer, num_searches As Integer) As Integer
Dim i As Integer

    For i = 1 To NUM_VALUES
        num_searches = num_searches + 1
        If Values(i) = target Then Exit For
    Next i

    If i <= NUM_VALUES Then
        LinearSearch = i
    Else
        LinearSearch = 0
    End If
End Function


' Use binary search to find the target. For details
' of the algorithm, see Ready-to-Run Visual Basic
' Algorithms, ISBN 0-471-24268-3.
Public Function BinarySearch(list() As Integer, _
    target As Integer, num_searches As Integer) As Integer
Dim min_index As Integer
Dim max_index As Integer
Dim mid_index As Integer

    min_index = 1
    max_index = NUM_VALUES
    Do While min_index <= max_index
        num_searches = num_searches + 1
        mid_index = (min_index + max_index) / 2
        If target = list(mid_index) Then
            BinarySearch = mid_index
            Exit Function
        ElseIf target < list(mid_index) Then
            max_index = mid_index - 1
        Else
            min_index = mid_index + 1
        End If
    Loop
    BinarySearch = 0
End Function
```

Summary

Finding bugs can be easy or hard—the choice is yours. If you write code that quietly ignores data that makes no sense, it will hide bugs so finding them will be difficult. If you write code that jumps up and shouts, "There's a bug here," whenever it sees a suspicious value, the bugs will come to you. This does not excuse you from testing the code, but it can reduce the number of bugs you need to find during testing.

The following Bug Stoppers list the key bug-exposing concepts described in this chapter.

BUG STOPPERS: Exposing Bugs

Verify arguments using Debug.Assert and Stop.

Validate optional parameters.

Use default values for optional parameters.

Use optional parameters only when necessary.

Use named parameters.

Validate ParamArray parameters.

Stop if a condition should never occur. Raise an error for a bad but possible condition.

Use tight restrictions and loosen them later if necessary.

Use LBound and UBound.

Validate data structures at startup, shutdown, and while the program is running.

Validate data structures in forms and classes.

Clear unused variables or set them to strange values that are easy to recognize.

Use Else statements to watch for unexpected conditions.

Verify results.

CHAPTER 6

Being Obvious

C hapter 1, "Programming Philosophy," mentions that programs are written for people, not for computers. Computers do not read comments and do not care if the code is neatly aligned to show scope and structure. For all the computer cares, you could write your program in machine code with no comments or indentation. The computer mindlessly executes one instruction at a time without ever understanding what it is doing.

Code is written primarily so humans can read it. All the work you do to make the code legible is for the benefit of yourself and others who read the code later. With that in mind, it is self-evident that the code should be as obvious as possible. When a human reads the code, its intent should be immediately clear. The code should do what it looks like it does. If the code looks like it does one thing but it actually does another, it will be hard to understand and debug.

This chapter explains techniques you can use to make your code obvious. If you do a good job, a reader should be able to pick up your code and immediately understand what it does and how.

Don't Use Clever Tricks

Clever tricks may be interesting and some are even efficient, but they make it harder for a reader to understand your code. They make what the code is doing less obvious.

For example, here is a straightforward way to swap the values of two variables A and B:

```
Dim A As Integer
Dim B As Integer
Dim tmp As Integer

    ' Do something here. Initialize A and B, etc.
        :
    ' Switch A and B.
    tmp = A
    A = B
    B = tmp
```

I have seen programmers propose the following as a better version because it avoids allocating the temporary variable tmp.

```
Dim A As Integer
Dim B As Integer

    ' Do something here. Initialize A and B, etc.
        :
    ' Switch A and B.
    A = A Xor B
    B = A Xor B
    A = A Xor B
```

This trick is far from obvious. To see how this code works, you need to know these facts about the Xor operator:

- A Xor B = B Xor A
- (A Xor B) Xor C = A Xor (B Xor C)
- A Xor A = 0
- A Xor 0 = A

Knowing these facts, consider the steps in the previous code again. Suppose A and B originally have the values a and b. Then the first statement sets A to A Xor B, which is the same as a Xor b.

```
A = A Xor B
  = a Xor b
```

In the second statement, B is set to A Xor B. The current value of A is a Xor b, so

```
B = A Xor B
  = (a Xor b) Xor b
```

```
= a Xor (b Xor b)
= a Xor 0
= a
```

In the third statement, A is set to A Xor B. The current value of A is a Xor b and the current value of B is a, so

```
A = A Xor B
  = (a Xor b) Xor a
  = a Xor a Xor b
  = 0 Xor b
  = b
```

In the end, A = b and B = a so the values have been switched as desired.

This code is undoubtedly clever, but it is very confusing. Unless the reader has worked through similar examples before or has a lot of experience with the Xor operator, it makes no sense whatsoever.

This code even takes about 50 percent longer than the simpler version. Its only advantage is that it avoids allocating a single 2-byte variable. Two bytes are hardly worth the confusion this trick may cause.

If a clever trick does not make the code much faster, do not use it; use a straightforward implementation instead. If you later discover the routine is a big performance bottleneck and the trick is absolutely necessary, you can change the code later.

Document Tricks

If you must use a clever trick, document it thoroughly. Occasionally, you may find a situation in which a clever trick improves a routine's performance so much that it is worth some risk of confusion. In that case, help future readers by explaining the trick in a comprehensive comment. Make the trick obvious.

Don't Write Routines with Side Effects

When a routine changes the values of its parameters in a way that is not central to the routine's mission, the change is called a *side effect*. For example, suppose the OpenTable subroutine takes the name of a database table as a parameter and it opens the table. When it finishes, the routine changes its parameter to contain a string listing the table's fields separated by commas. This change is unrelated to the main task of opening the table, so it is a side effect.

Side effects can be very confusing. Because they are not central to the routine's mission, the reader often does not expect them to occur. They are not obvious. They are similar to a magician's trick during which the left hand does something while the right hand distracts you. While the user concentrates on the routine's main purpose, the side effect is unnoticed.

To prevent confusion, do not write routines that have side effects. Break confusing behavior into separate routines. For instance, you could break the previous OpenTable subroutine into an OpenTable subroutine that opens the table, and a separate ListFields function that returns a list of the fields in the table.

Note that every function that changes its parameters has side effects. The main purpose of a function is to calculate a return value. Changing a parameter is not central to calculating the return value, so it is a side effect.

Functions that have side effects can be even more confusing than subroutines. For example, the following function SideEffect takes an integer as a parameter, adds 1 to the parameter, and then returns twice the new value.

```
Private Function SideEffect(value As Long) As Long
    value = value + 1
    SideEffect = 2 * value
End Function
```

It is difficult to tell offhand what the values of A, B, and C are after the following code executes. Study the code for a moment and see what you think the new values are.

```
Dim A As Long
Dim B As Long
Dim C As Long

    A = 10
    B = SideEffect(A)
    A = SideEffect(B)
    C = SideEffect(A)
```

This code is not at all obvious. A reader could examine the code for several minutes and still not figure out the correct values. Did you get A = 47, B = 23, and C = 94? How long did it take you to calculate these values? Were you certain of your result?

The following code shows an even more confusing example.

```
A = 7
If (A > 10) And (SideEffect(A) < 100) Then
    A = A * 3
```

```
Else
    A = A * 2
End If
```

This code looks as if it executes the SideEffect function only if the value A is greater than 10. The reasoning is that, if A is less than or equal to 10, the Boolean expression is False no matter what value SideEffect returns, so the program does not invoke SideEffect.

Unfortunately, this is not the way Visual Basic evaluates expressions. The program calls the SideEffect function whether A is greater than 10 or not.

You can reduce confusion by placing functions with side effects on separate lines.

```
A = 7
If (A > 10) Then
    If (SideEffect(A) < 100) Then
        A = A * 3
    Else
        A = A * 2
    End If
Else
    A = A * 2
End If
```

This is still fairly confusing. A better solution is to rewrite the SideEffect function so it does not have any side effects.

Mix Data Types Cautiously

Be careful when you use variables of different data types in a single expression. Visual Basic converts them into compatible data types before it operates on them, but it may not always use the types you expect. The results are sometimes far from obvious.

For example, the following four assignment statements look like they do the same thing, but their results depend on the type of operator and the data types of the operands. In the first statement, Visual Basic sees two integers combined using the & operator. The & operator is a string operator, so the program converts both of the numbers into strings. It then concatenates the strings to give a string result with the value "39."

In the second statement, Visual Basic finds two integers combined with the + operator. Integers are compatible with the + operator, so it simply adds the numbers as integers. The integer result is 12.

In the third statement, Visual Basic must add a string to an integer. Because the operator is +, the system decides that this is a numeric operation so it converts the string 3 into the double 3.0. Now it must add an integer to a double. Since these have different data types, Visual Basic must promote one value so they match. It can change an integer into a double without losing any precision, so that is what it does. It converts the integer 9 into the double 9.0 and adds this to 3.0. The result is a double with value 12.0.

Finally, in the fourth statement, Visual Basic sees two strings. Because they have the same data type, Visual Basic can combine them without any promotion. It adds the strings by concatenating them. The result is the string "39."

```
Dim a As Variant
Dim b As Variant
Dim c As Variant
Dim d As Variant

    a = 3 & 9      ' Result: string "39"
    b = 3 + 9      ' Result: integer 12
    c = "3" + 9    ' Result: double 12.0
    d = "3" + "9"  ' Result: string "39"
```

These four similar statements produce very different results. To be certain of the type of result you get when you mix data types, use the conversion functions CInt, CLng, CStr, and so forth to force Visual Basic to do exactly what you want it to do.

Convert all operands into the data type you want the eventual result to have. Also be sure you use the right kind of operators for that data type. Use + for numeric values and & to concatenate strings. Following these practices makes the code more obvious and will help those who later read the code understand what is happening.

```
Dim a As Variant
Dim b As Variant
Dim c As Variant
Dim d As Variant

    a = CStr(3) & CStr(9)       ' Result: string "39"
    b = CDbl(3) + CDbl(9)       ' Result: double 12.0
    c = CInt("3") + 9           ' Result: integer 12
    d = CDbl("3") + CDbl("9")   ' Result: double 12.0
```

Use & and + Correctly

As the examples in the previous section show, the result of an expression depends in part on the operators the expression uses. If you use the wrong operator, you may get an unexpected result.

To concatenate two strings and produce a new string, use the & operator. To add two numeric values and produce a new numeric value, use the + operator.

The following two lines of code produce completely different results even though they differ only in their operator.

```
a = 8 & 5      ' Result: string "85"
b = 8 + 5      ' Result: integer 13
```

Use the right operators to keep the code obvious.

Mix Booleans and Integers Cautiously

Be extra cautious when you mix Boolean and integer values. The Boolean operators And, Or, Not, and so forth look just like the corresponding bitwise operators you can use to combine and compare numeric values. This can make statements that mix Boolean and integer values very confusing.

For example, if A and B are integers, then the following statement sets the bits in C to 1 where both A and B have bit values 1. Bits where either A or B has value 0 are set to 0.

```
C = A And B
```

On the other hand, if D and E are Boolean values, the following statement sets the variable F to True if D and E are both True.

```
F = D And E
```

Matters are further complicated by the fact that Visual Basic treats an integer as logically False if it has the value 0, and logically True if it has any other value. Now consider the following statement:

```
G = H And I Or J And K
```

The value of G depends on the data types of all of the variables. Even if you know their data types, evaluating this expression would be confusing.

Make this expression understandable by using the CInt and CBool conversion functions. Use parentheses to make the evaluation order obvious. The following code sets G to True if H and I have any common bit set, or if J and K have any common bit set.

```
Dim G As Boolean
Dim H As Integer
Dim I As Integer
Dim J As Integer
Dim K As Integer
    :
    ' Initialize H, I, J, and K.
    :
    G = CBool(H And I) Or CBool(J And K)
```

Using the CBool conversion functions make it obvious that the result is a Boolean value. The CBool function also groups the operands so the evaluation order of the And and Or operators is obvious.

Parenthesize Complex Expressions

Use parentheses to make the evaluation order of complex expressions obvious. This is particularly important when you mix numeric operations with other types of operations.

Intermingled integer and Boolean operations are probably the most confusing. Most people know that multiplication and division take precedence over addition and subtraction. Most programmers can figure out that $10 + 2 * 3$ is the same as $10 + (2 * 3) = 16$ and not $(10 + 2) * 3 = 36$. Even so, adding parentheses makes the statement even more obvious.

Mixing Boolean and bitwise operations makes things much more confusing. Suppose A, B, C, and D are integers. The following lines of code are intended to determine whether A and B share a common bit and C and D share a common bit. Instead, the first line sets the bits in variable E that correspond to bits that are set in all four variables. The second line gives the correct code.

```
E = A And B And C And D
E = CBool(A And B) And CBool(C And D)
```

Use parentheses and conversion functions to make expressions obvious, particularly when you combine values or operations of different data types.

Use Left$

Visual Basic provides string and variant versions of several functions including LCase, Left, LeftB, Mid, Right, Chr, Str, and UCase. The string versions end with a $, as in Left$ and Str$, and return strings. The variant versions including Left and Str return variants containing strings.

If you want to produce a variant, use the variant version of the function. If you want a string, use the string version ending in $. Using the correct functions can prevent confusion later.

The right versions of the functions can also make the code run more quickly. If the data types of the input and result variables do not match the type of the function, Visual Basic may need to perform data type conversions before and after calling the function. In the following code fragment, the variables s1 and s2 are both strings. Left$ returns a string value while Left returns a variant. In one test, the statement using Left took more than 1.5 times as long as the statement that uses Left$.

```
Dim s1 As String
Dim s2 As String

    ' Initialize s1.
        :
    s2 = Left$(s1, 12)
    s2 = Left(s1, 12)
```

Use the proper versions of these functions so the data types of the results are obvious.

Open and Close Files in the Same Routine

If a single routine opens and closes a file, it is easy to verify that the file is being properly closed. With a little reading, it is obvious whether the routine exits without closing the file.

On the other hand, if one routine opens the file and another closes it at some later time, it can be difficult to tell when and if the file is closed. The situation may be even more complicated if the file can be opened and closed in several different routines.

Unless the program needs to keep a file open for a long time, open and close it in the same routine. Keep the routine short and simple so it is easy to understand. Invoke other routines to perform elaborate file processing if necessary.

The following code opens a file, calls the ReadData subroutine to read data from the file, and then closes the file. Putting the complex data reading code in subroutine ReadData allows this routine to be short and simple, even with its error handling code.

```
' Load data from a file.
Private Sub LoadData(file_name As String)
Dim fnum As Integer

    ' Open the file.
    On Error GoTo OpenError
    fnum = FreeFile
    Open file_name For Input As fnum

    ' Read the data.
    On Error GoTo ReadError
    ReadData fnum

    ' Close the file.
CloseFile:
    On Error GoTo 0
    Close fnum

    Exit Sub

OpenError:
    MsgBox "Error" & Str$(Err.Number) & _
        " opening file." & vbCrLf & _
        Err.Description
    Exit Sub

ReadError:
    MsgBox "Error" & Str$(Err.Number) & _
        " reading data." & vbCrLf & _
        Err.Description
    Resume CloseFile
End Sub
```

Put Separate Commands on Separate Lines

Do not use Visual Basic's command separator colon (:) to put more than one command on the same line. This can be confusing and is almost never necessary. It makes the code harder to read and gives no real benefit. It makes no appreciable difference in the speed of the code.

If your code window is too narrow to display the entire line, it may not be obvious that other commands follow to the right of the colon. Someone who reads the code and fails to notice the other commands cannot possibly understand the routine correctly.

One situation in which it may be tempting to put multiple commands on a single line is in a single-line If statement, as shown in the following code.

```
If    NumEmployees    <    10    Then    BuildEmployeeReport    :
ShowEmployeeReport
```

This code is easier to read as a multiline If statement.

```
If NumEmployees < 10 Then
    BuildEmployeeReport
    ShowEmployeeReport
End If
```

One time when you must use a colon is when you execute certain commands interactively in the Debug or Immediate window. The Debug window executes one line at a time and keeps no past history to help with future commands. For example, it cannot remember a For statement and later match it to the corresponding Next statement. To execute a For loop in the Debug window, you must place the entire loop on a single line as in the following code:

```
For i = 1 To 10 : ?my_array(i) : Next i
```

Specify Lower Bounds for Arrays

When you declare an array without specifying its lower bound, it is not obvious what the array's lower bound is. If you have a lot of experience with Visual Basic, you know that arrays usually start with an index of 0. Thus, the following statement allocates six array entries with indexes 0 through 5.

```
' Allocate 6 Person object references numbered 0 through 5.
Dim people(5) As Person
```

This is not obvious. The fact that the statement uses the value 5 to allocate six entries is confusing. Even worse, the file may include an Option Base statement that changes the default lower bound for arrays. While the Dim statement in the following code looks exactly like the previous one, it allocates only five array entries with indexes 1 through 5.

```
Option Explicit
Option Base 1
    :
```

```
' Much later...
' Allocate 5 Person object references numbered 1 through 5.
Dim people(5) As Person
```

To make the code obvious, always explicitly specify a lower bound when you declare an array with bounds. The same principle applies when you resize an array using the ReDim statement.

```
' Allocate 5 Person object references numbered 1 through 5.
Dim people(0 To 5) As Integer

Dim jobs() As Integer
    :
    ' Resize the jobs array.
    ReDim jobs(0 To NumJobs)
```

Don't Use Static Routines

In Visual Basic, if you declare a routine as static, all of the variables declared within the routine are allocated statically. For example, the following two sub-routines are equivalent.

```
Static Private Sub MyStaticRoutine()
Dim i As Integer
Dim j As Integer
    :
End Sub

Private Sub MyStaticRoutine()
Static i As Integer
Static j As Integer
    :
End Sub
```

When you declare a routine as static, it is not obvious within the routine that the variables it contains are static. If the routine declares a lot of variables, a reader who looks at the last few variable declarations may not remember that they are all static.

```
Static Private Sub MyStaticRoutine()
Dim i As Integer
Dim j As Integer
Dim k As Integer
    :
Dim z As Integer
```

```
       :
End Sub
```

This is an even bigger problem if the routine declares other variables far from its beginning, a practice I do not recommend. For example, in the following code the variables i and j are both static.

```
Static Private Sub MyStaticRoutine()
Dim i As Integer
      :
    ' Lots of code.
      :
    Dim j As Integer
      :
End Sub
```

In cases like this, the static keyword may not be visible on the screen so the reader may assume incorrectly that j is not static.

Make static variables obvious by declaring them static individually.

Use Private and Public

Within a subroutine, the Dim statement declares a variable with scope limited to that routine. At the module level, the Dim statement declares a variable with scope limited to that module.

However, scope is somewhat inconsistent if you do not use Private or Public when you declare variables and routines. Variables declared with Dim are private to the module. Subroutines, functions, and property procedures declared with neither Private nor Public are public and available outside the module.

To make the code obvious, always use Private and Public instead of Dim when you declare symbols at the module level. This includes routines, variables, constants, types, and enumerated values. Using Private and Public makes a symbol's scope obvious.

```
    ' This type is defined only within the module.
Private Type PrivateType
      :
End Type

    ' This type is defined within the whole program.
Public Type PublicType
      :
End Type
```

```
' This variable is defined only within the module.
Private PrivateVariable As Integer

' This variable is defined within the whole program.
Public PublicVariable As Integer

' This subroutine is defined only within the module.
Private Sub PrivateSub()
    :
End Sub

' This function is defined within the whole program.
Public Function PublicFunction() As Integer
    :
End Sub
```

Using Private and Public makes a symbol's scope obvious.

Use ByVal and ByRef

When you declare a routine's parameter with the ByVal (by value) keyword, any changes the routine makes will not be returned to the calling routine. The routine works with a separate copy of the parameter so changes are lost when the routine ends.

When you declare a routine's parameter with the ByRef (by reference) keyword, any changes the routine makes are returned to the calling routine. The routine uses the same copy of the variable as the caller so any changes it makes are permanent.

If you declare a parameter with neither ByVal nor ByRef, Visual Basic passes the value by reference. Not only is this not obvious, it is also usually the wrong option. Passing an argument ByVal protects the calling routine from accidental changes to the parameter. To make the caller as safe as possible, every parameter should be passed by value unless part of the routine's purpose is to explicitly change the value of the parameter.

Use ByVal whenever possible. Use ByRef to emphasize the fact that a parameter may be changed by the routine. This makes it obvious that the value may change, and it makes it obvious that you did not simply forget to declare the parameter ByVal.

The following code declares a subroutine that modifies its second parameter but not its first.

```
Private Sub MyRoutine(ByVal num_employees As Integer, _
    ByRef num_jobs As Integer)
        :
```

Note that arrays must always be passed ByRef. Visual Basic does this for efficiency reasons. When you pass a parameter ByVal, Visual Basic makes a separate copy of the value for the routine to manipulate. Copying a large array can take a long time, so Visual Basic passes it by reference instead of by value.

If you do not intend to modify the entries in an array parameter, you can leave the ByRef off to hint that you do not intend to change the values. Visual Basic will not stop the routine from changing them, however.

```
' Print a list of employees without modifying the list.
Private Sub PrintEmployees(employees() As String)
    :
```

One confusing case still occurs when the calling routine passes a value that cannot be modified as a ByRef parameter; for example, if the calling routine uses the value 10 as in the following code. The called routine cannot really modify the value 10 and return the modified result to the calling routine since the value is not stored in a variable.

```
SetTemperature 10, 20
        :
' Change the temperature. Return the previous temperature
' through the temperature parameter.
Private Sub SetTemperature(ByRef temperature As Integer, _
    ByVal duration As Integer)
        :
```

In this situation, Visual Basic creates a temporary variable and places the value 10 in it. Even if the routine modifies the temporary variable, the calling routine will not see the effect.

This is a reasonable course for Visual Basic to take, but it may indicate a bug in the calling routine. The called routine changes its parameter for a reason. Ignoring the change indicates a possible mistake by the caller.

Try not to pass unchangeable values into routines as ByRef parameters. Visual Basic will not warn you if you do, but this may cause a misunderstanding.

Use Line Continuation

If a line gets too long, it may not be obvious that some of it extends beyond the edge of the window. This can be very confusing. Even after the reader realizes there is more to the command, he must scroll the code window back and forth to read the entire statement. The added distraction makes it harder to understand the code. It also prevents the reader from seeing all of the adjacent lines at the same time.

Use line continuation characters to make each line completely visible. Use indentation to show that the subsequent lines are part of the same statement. Unless your project standardizes on a certain size monitor and everyone works with maximized code windows, you should assume the code window is relatively small.

Break lines soon enough that the line continuation characters are visible. If that character is hidden, the statement may look like two separate commands. Proper indentation can warn the reader that something unusual is happening, but the reader may still become confused.

Break long single-line If statements before the Then keyword. This makes it more obvious that the next line is part of the If statement. For example, consider the following statement:

```
If num_processed < num_employees Then _
    ProcessEmployee
```

Now suppose another programmer wants to add a new statement that keeps the user posted about the program's progress. If the programmer does not notice the line continuation character, he might make the change like this:

```
If num_processed < num_employees Then _
    ProcessEmployee
    UpdateStatusBar
```

At a quick glance, this looks correct, but the new UpdateStatusBar command is not contained within the If statement. The scope of the If statement is obvious if the original code is broken before the Then keyword like this:

```
If num_processed < num_employees _
    Then ProcessEmployee
```

Even if the reader does mistakenly add a new line thinking it will lie within the If statement, the result looks suspicious. It is easier to notice that there is a mistake in the following code than it is in the previous incorrect version.

```
If num_processed < num_employees _
    Then ProcessEmployee
    UpdateStatusBar
```

An even better solution is to make long If statements use multiple lines. The difference in performance is tiny and the code is much more obvious.

```
If num_processed < num_employees Then
    ProcessEmployee
    UpdateStatusBar
End If
```

Use Explicit Properties

Controls have default properties. A program can refer to a control's default property by referring to the control. For example, the following two lines of code are equivalent.

```
NumEmployees = CInt(txtNumEmployees.Text)
NumEmployees = CInt(txtNumEmployees)
```

Accessing a control's default property without explicitly mentioning it is not obvious. It forces the reader to remember the control's type and to remember the default property for that kind of control.

Make it obvious which property is being used by explicitly referencing the properties of controls, forms, and other objects.

Eliminate Random Behavior

Random behavior makes bugs hard to find. If you cannot repeat the series of steps that lead to incorrect behavior, you may have a hard time reproducing a bug. You can make things more repeatable by removing random behavior wherever possible.

You cannot remove all randomness from your system because you do not have complete control over the other applications that are running. Still, you can limit the random behavior of your own application by removing randomness wherever you find it.

Certain operations can appear random to a program. Obviously the Rnd statement introduces randomness. Examining the system time, file system, or network connections may also cause unrepeatable behavior. If a subroutine's operation depends on the number of files in a certain directory, it may behave differently when there are different numbers of files. For example, the routine may crash if no files are present. If that occurs very infrequently, it may be hard for you to reproduce the problem.

Pay special attention to code that uses values like system characteristics that are outside the control of the program. While you may be unable to remove these dependencies, you can at least record the values the program uses. Then if an error occurs, you can examine these values to see if they may be related to the problem.

For example, many programs use random numbers generated by the Rnd statement. If you remove this randomness, you may destroy the program. While you cannot eliminate these random numbers, you can control them.

The SeedRnd subroutine shown in the following code initializes the random number generator. It takes a parameter indicating whether it should generate a new random sequence or reuse the previous one.

To generate a new sequence, the routine passes the Randomize statement the number of seconds since midnight. It then saves this seed value in the system registry in case it needs the value again the next time the program runs.

To repeat the previous sequence, the routine uses GetSetting to retrieve the seed value saved in the registry. It passes that value to the Randomize statement so the Rnd function will use the previous sequence of random numbers.

```
' Seed the random number generator. If use_previous
' is true, seed the generator using the previous
' value stored in the system registry. Otherwise
' use the number of second since midnight and save
' that number in the registry.
Public Sub SeedRnd(ByVal use_previous As Boolean)
Dim seed As Long

    If use_previous Then
        ' Get the seed from the registry. Use the
        ' seconds past midnight as a default.
        seed = GetSetting("MyProgram", _
            "Configuration", "RndSeed", Timer)
    Else
        ' Get the seconds after midnight.
        seed = Timer
    End If

    ' Initialize the random number generator.
    Rnd -1
    Randomize seed
```

```
        ' Save the seed for next time.
        SaveSetting "MyProgram", "Configuration", _
            "RndSeed", seed
    End Sub
```

A program should call SeedRnd when it starts. It should not use the Randomize statement anywhere else. Normally the program calls SeedRand with parameter False to make it start a new sequence of random numbers.

If you run across an obscure bug that is hard to reproduce and you think it may be caused by a certain sequence of random numbers, you should pass SeedRnd the value True to make it reuse the same random sequence it used before. If the bug now becomes easily repeatable, you should suspect that it has something to do with the program's use of the Rnd statement. If the bug remains hard to reproduce, you should suspect behavior outside of the program's control.

Perform Short Actions First

Suppose you are reading a subroutine and you come to an Else statement. If it has been a long time since you read the corresponding If clause, you may not remember what condition it tests. This can be even more confusing with a series of nested If statements.

```
If condition1 Then
        :
    ' Many lines of code.
        :
    If condition2 Then
        ' More code.
            :
    Else
        ' More code.
            :
    End If
Else    ' Which condition is this?
    ' Do something brief.
End If
```

You can make the code a bit more obvious if you place short actions first. When the reader reaches the Else clause, the If statement may still be visible on the screen. In that case, it is easy to decipher the meaning of the Else statement.

```
If Not condition1 Then
    ' Do something brief.
Else    ' It is obvious which condition this is.
        :
```

```
    ' Many lines of code.
        :
    If condition2 Then
        ' More code.
            :
    Else
        ' More code.
            :
    End If
End If
```

If all of the actions are long, place a comment next to the Else clause to remind the reader of the condition. In fact, it never hurts to put this kind of comment next to all Else statements even if the amount of code is small.

```
If condition Then
        :
    ' Many lines of code.
        :
Else      ' Not condition.
        :
    ' Many lines of code.
        :
End If
```

The same techniques apply to Select statements.

```
Select Case variable
    Case value1
        ' Do something brief.
    Case value2
        ' More code.
            :
    Case value2
            :
        ' Many lines of code.
            :
End Select
```

Avoid Wizards

Code wizards are designed to simplify programming by automatically generating code to perform common tasks. Unfortunately, they often generate code that is practically unreadable by humans. If there is a problem with the code, it is usually difficult to find and fix. If you later need to use the wizard to regenerate the code, perhaps to specify new parameters, any changes you have made to the code are lost.

Many wizards are all-or-nothing propositions. You should either leave the automatically generated code completely unchanged, or you should use the code only as a starting point for your own code.

If you leave the code unchanged, you can use the wizard to regenerate it later. Since you have made no modifications to the code, you cannot lose any changes you have made. The only change you should consider making is the addition of large comments saying that the code is automatically generated and warning not to edit it.

```
' **********************************************************
' WARNING: This code was automatically generated by the
'          TableReader wizard. Do not modify it manually.
'          If you do, your changes will be lost the next
'          time the wizard runs.
' **********************************************************
```

Alternatively, you can use the wizard to generate a starting point for your own code. After the wizard creates the code, you modify and maintain the code manually and never regenerate it using the wizard. Any changes to the code are your sole responsibility.

While the code initially generated by the wizard may be hard to read, you do not need to rewrite it immediately. If the code works, do not break it by trying to make it easier to read. Instead, wait until you must rewrite the code and then do it properly.

Use Meaningful Names

Give variables and routines meaningful names instead of short abbreviations. There is no advantage to naming a variable EOTW instead of EmployeeOfTheWeek. This only makes the code less obvious and makes the reader focus on memorizing abbreviations instead of learning the program's structure.

You can reasonably use abbreviations that are standard in your industry. For example, in telephone companies the abbreviation POTS stands for "Plain Old Telephone Service" and means basic residential service. A telephone company service system could reasonably include a variable named HasPots because POTS is a well-known telephone company abbreviation.

Most readers will also be able to understand abbreviations that follow a pattern. For example, a group of abbreviations that use the prefix Num to mean Number is reasonably easy to understand.

```
NumEmployees As Integer
NumCompanies As Integer
```

```
NumOrders As Integer
    :
```

Standardize Abbreviations

Standardize any abbreviations you do use. Discuss them with the other developers on the project and develop consistent rules of use. For example, you might decide that Number will be abbreviated Num. If different developers use Num, NumberOf, Number, No, and Count all to mean Number, the code will be confusing.

```
NumEmployees As Integer
NumberOfCompanies As Integer
NoOrders As Integer
NBills As Integer
ItemCount As Integer
    :
```

Use Similar Names for Similar Purposes

Use similar names for similar variables and routines. When a reader learns the meaning of one name, its similarity to other names can help him learn their meanings, too. Suppose the program has routines named PrintEmployeeReport, PrintJobReport, and PrintInventoryReport. The reader will quickly learn that report-printing routines are named PrintXxxReport. He will expect the subroutine that prints tax reports to be named PrintTaxReport. If you name that routine ReportOnTaxes, the reader may become confused.

At the same time, do not use similar variable and routine names for dissimilar purposes. For example, suppose the RemoveCompany subroutine deletes a company record from a database. In that case, the RemoveEmployee subroutine should delete an employee record from the database. It should not merely set the employee's work status to Vacation, leaving the record in the Employees table. Giving these two routines such similar names will mislead the reader into thinking they have similar purposes.

Don't Reuse Variables

If you need a variable for a new purpose, create a new variable instead of reusing an old one. Using the same variable i to loop through two arrays is fine because i is used as a looping variable in both places. Using i as a looping variable in one place and as a file number in another will be very confusing.

```
Dim i As Integer

    ' Search for a specific job number.
    For i = LBound(jobs) To UBound(jobs)
        If jobs(i) = target_job Then Exit For
    Next i
        :
    ' Open a file.
    i = FreeFile
        :
    Open "C:\Data\jobs.dat" For Append As i
```

The problem with this code is that someone modifying the code later may forget what the variable is for and when it is in use for which purpose. If you forget that i is the open file number and you change the code so i is modified while the file is open, you will introduce a bug.

```
        :
    ' Find the smallest job number.
    min_job = jobs(LBound(jobs))
    For i = LBound(jobs) + 1 To UBound(jobs)
        If min_job > jobs(i) Then min_job = jobs(i)
    Next i

    ' Save the smallest job number.
    Print #i, min_number
```

Make the code obvious by creating separate variables for separate purposes.

Use Next i

Use the looping variable's name in Next statements. For example, use the first style shown in the following code.

```
    ' Use this style:
    For i = 1 To 100
        :
    Next i

    ' Do not use this version:
    For i = 1 To 100
        :
    Next
```

This makes the code more obvious. If you are reading the code for a long For loop and you come to the Next statement, using the looping variable's name makes it obvious which loop is ending.

You can make understanding the loop even easier by using a meaningful name for the looping variable. Using the name employee_index instead of i tells the code's reader that the loop manipulates employees in some way. You can make the loop's purpose completely clear with two comments, one before and one after the loop.

```
' Print the employees.
For employee_index = 1 To 100
    :
Next employee_index     ' Print the next employee.
```

Self-Test

Program Bad6 violates several of the guidelines presented in this chapter. This program loads data type information from a data file and displays a summary as shown in Figure 6.1.

The following code shows how program Bad6 works. Appendix A, "Self-Test Solutions," contains an improved version of this code. This is not the only possible solution. You can download updated bad and good versions of this program from the Web at www.vb-helper.com/err.htm.

Note: In the following code, the line

```
If Len(token) > 0 Then output_txt = output_txt & Format(token,
FORMAT_SPECIFIER)
```

```
Data Type Summary                                          _ □ ✕

Data Type          Size              Approx Min         Approx Max
---------          ----              ----------         ----------
Byte               1 byte            0                  255
Boolean            2 bytes           False              True
Integer            2 bytes           -32,768            32,767
Long               4 bytes           -2,147,483,648     2,147,483,647
Single             4 bytes           -3.4e38            3.4e38
Double             8 bytes           -1.8e308           1.8e308
Currency           8 bytes           -9.2e18            9.2e18
Decimal            14 bytes          -7.9e28            7.9e28
Date               8 bytes           January 1, 100     December 31, 9999
Object             4 bytes
String (variable)  10 bytes + length 0 characters       2 billion characters
String (fixed)     length            1 character        ~65,400 characters
```

Figure 6.1   Program Bad6 loads data type information from a data file and displays a summary.

should extend as far as it can and then be truncated at the right edge of the page. It should not be wrapped. Do not extend it beyond the margin or anything fancy like that. Just chop it off, in mid-word if that's where the page ends (that would make the best example). It is demonstrating code that does not wrap.

```
Option Explicit

' Make txtOutput as large as possible.
Private Sub Form_Resize()
    txtOutput.Move 0, 0, ScaleWidth, ScaleHeight
End Sub

' Read the data from the data file.
Private Sub Form_Load()
Dim fnum As Integer

    ' Open the file.
    fnum = FreeFile
    Open App.Path & "\types.dat" For Input As fnum

    ' Read the data.
    LoadData fnum
End Sub

' Read the data file and close it.
Sub LoadData(fnum As Integer)
Const FORMAT_SPECIFIER = "!@@@@@@@@@@@@@@@@@@@@"

Dim output_txt As String
Dim all_data As String
Dim next_line As String
Dim token As String

    ' Read all the data.
    all_data = Input(LOF(fnum), #fnum)

    ' Start with column headers.
    output_txt = _
        Format("Data Type", FORMAT_SPECIFIER) & _
        Format("Size", FORMAT_SPECIFIER) & _
        Format("Approx Min", FORMAT_SPECIFIER) & _
        Format("Approx Max", FORMAT_SPECIFIER)
    output_txt = output_txt & vbCrLf & _
        Format("---------", FORMAT_SPECIFIER) & _
        Format("----", FORMAT_SPECIFIER) & _
        Format("----------", FORMAT_SPECIFIER) & _
        Format("----------", FORMAT_SPECIFIER) & _
        vbCrLf
```

```
    ' Read the lines from the file.
    Do While Len(all_data) > 0
        ' Get the next line.
        next_line = GetToken(all_data, vbCrLf)

        ' Break the line into pieces.
        Do While Len(next_line) > 0
            token = GetToken(next_line, ";")
            If Len(token) > 0 Then output_txt = output_txt &
Format(token, FORMAT_SPECIFIER)
        Loop
        output_txt = output_txt & vbCrLf
    Loop

    ' Display the result.
    txtOutput = output_txt
End Sub

' Get the next delimited token from the string txt.
Function GetToken(txt As String, delimiter As String) As String
Dim p As Integer

    ' Find the delimiter.
    p = InStr(txt, delimiter)

    ' Get the token.
    If p = 0 Then p = Len(txt) + 1
    GetToken = Left(txt, p - 1)

    ' See what's left of the string txt.
    p = Len(txt) - p + 1 - Len(delimiter)
    If p <= 0 Then
        txt = ""
    Else
        txt = Right(txt, p)
    End If
End Function
```

Summary

Maintainable code must be easy to understand. When someone later reads the code, any extra time spent struggling to make sense out of trivial details like variable names and scope is time that could be better spent studying the program's structure. Make your code easy to understand by using the techniques summarized in the following Bug Stoppers.

BUG STOPPERS: Being Obvious

Don't use clever tricks.

Document any clever tricks you do use.

Don't write routines with side effects.

Mix data types cautiously.

Use & and + when appropriate.

Mix Booleans and integers carefully.

Parenthesize complex expressions.

Use the string and variant version of Left$, Mid$, etc.

Open and close files in the same routine.

Put separate commands on separate lines.

Explicitly specify lower bounds for arrays.

Don't use static routines.

Always use Private and Public to specify module-level symbols.

Always use ByVal and ByRef to make calling conventions obvious.

Use line continuation so all the code is visible.

Refer to properties explicitly.

Eliminate or control random behavior.

Perform short actions first in If ... Else and Select statements.

Use wizards cautiously with an all-or-nothing approach.

Use meaningful names, not terse abbreviations.

Standardize any abbreviations you do use.

Use similar names for similar purposes. Use dissimilar names for dissimilar purposes.

Don't reuse variables.

Use the loop variable's name in Next statements.

Comments

Comments help reconcile the two conflicting goals of writing code that can be executed efficiently by a computer and writing code that is understandable to a human. Header-style comments at the beginning of files and routines give readers perspective that helps them better understand the code that follows. Inline comments within the code provide detail the reader needs to easily understand the program.

By increasing the readers' comprehension, comments reduce the chances of bugs being introduced into the code. Better understanding of the code lets developers find bugs faster and fix them more quickly with less chance of error.

This chapter gives general commenting guidelines and standard formats for header-style comments. The exact format does not matter as much as your using some sort of consistent commenting system.

The first three sections that follow describe header-style comments. Use these comments at the beginning of files, routines, and event handlers to give context and background information to the reader. These three sections include example header comments. Appendix B, "Header Comment Templates," contains blank comment templates. You can also download copies of these templates from the book's Web site at www.vb-helper.com/err.htm. You can then paste them into your programs and fill in the blanks.

The remaining sections in this chapter explain guidelines that are applicable to comments in general.

Comment Files

Begin each file with a header comment giving an overview of the file's contents. This comment should include identifying information, description of purpose, entry points, dependencies, known issues, method overview, and declarations.

Identifying Information

Identifying information includes the filename, copyright information, creation date, list of authors, and security level if applicable. It should include any text that you want to appear on printed copies of the file.

Do not underestimate the importance of including the filename here. The name may seem obvious to you when you print the file, but the printout may be copied and sent to others who will need to know where the file is.

If your printer has an option to include the date and the filename in a header or footer on each page, use it. Then you can determine the filename even if you only have a single page from the middle of the file.

Description

The description should explain the file's overall purpose or theme. This should be a short sentence or a paragraph at most. If you cannot explain a module's general purpose in a few sentences, it probably does not represent a clear concept that developers can easily understand. In that case, it would be better to break the file into two or more smaller files, each having a clear purpose.

For .BAS modules, the description should explain the file's theme. For example, "Routines for manipulating three-dimensional matrices."

For .FRM modules, the description should explain what the form is for and what it does. For example, "New job input form where the user enters information to create a new job."

For .CLS modules, the description should explain what the class represents. For instance, "Billing object that represents a single bill to be sent to a customer." It can also include a very brief discussion of the class responsibilities. The method section described shortly contains a more detailed explanation of responsibilities and collaborations.

Entry Points

This section lists the public variables, properties, and routines the module exposes to the rest of the program. It provides a brief description of the purposes of these public items.

This section can be difficult to maintain, particularly early in the development process when programmers change the file's interface frequently. On the other hand, it can also provide a framework for the developers who are building the module. The entry points can be defined and documented during the low-level design process. Then developers can work to make the variables and routines in the module meet these interface goals. Many bugs occur when one routine uses another incorrectly. Defining the public interface for a module early can reduce the chances of misunderstandings between developers and produce more reliable interactions between routines.

Dependencies

This section contains a list of dependencies the file has to other modules. For example, if the code uses functions contained in a certain .BAS module, that module should be listed here.

The dependency list can be helpful in finding bugs. If you trace a problem to this module, the list tells you which other files may be involved. It also lets you know that you may need to update this file if one of the files in the dependency list has changed.

The dependency list is the hardest part of the header comment to maintain. Any developer who changes this module must review the list to make sure the file dependencies are still correct.

Known Issues

Known issues include unsolved bugs, bottlenecks, possible future enhancements, and descriptions of any other issues that should be addressed later. These issues should be described very briefly. If one is particularly complicated, the comment should refer to another source, like a bug tracking system, for further detail.

Method

The method section describes any particularly complex details that make sense on a file level. This may include such things as an explanation of complex algorithms that are not described within the code, an overview of how different routines within the module interact, or a description of a data structure used in the module. Provide references to books or articles if possible to keep this section brief.

For class modules, this section should include a description of the class responsibilities, collaborations, and interactions with other objects in the system.

Declarations

Standard declaration sections follow the main parts of the header information. These sections group type definitions, variable declarations, and constant definitions.

Some of these sections do not apply to all files. For example, forms cannot declare public user-defined types so you do not need a section for them.

Rather than placing API declarations in separate sections, put them all together. For instance, instead of putting API type definitions in one section and API function declarations in another, put them all in a separate API section. This makes updating the code easier when API functions change during different releases of the operating system.

Example File Header

The following example shows a header for a class module. Appendix B, "Header Comment Templates," contains a blank template for a more complete file header comment. You can download the blank template from the book's Web page at www.vb-helper.com/err.htm and paste it into your files.

```
' **************************************************
' File:         RayRect.CLS
' Copyright:    Copyright (c) 1997-1998
'               Yearlong Filibusters, Inc.
' Date Created: 8/20/97
' Authors:      Rod Stephens
'               Michelle Eisgruber
'               Judy Nishimoto
'
' Purpose:
'     A ray traced rectangle in 3-D space.
'
' Entry Points:
'     Sub TraceRay
'         Follow a ray and see if it hits the
'         object. Return the point of intersection.
'
'     NumEmployees As Integer
'
' Dependencies:
'     Matrix.BAS   Matrix manipulation functions.
'
' Issues:
'     Enhancement: Allow transparent surfaces?
'     Enhancement: Define an inside and outside
'
```

```
' Method:
'     See Visual Basic Graphics Programming,
'     Chapter 13, for information on ray tracing.
' ************************************************
Option Explicit


' ************************************************
' Global Definitions
' -------------------------
' Global API Declarations
' -------------------------
Public Type POINTAPI
    X As Long
    Y As Long
End Type

Public Declare Function Polygon Lib "gdi32" _
    Alias "Polygon" ( _
    ByVal hdc As Long, lpPoint As POINTAPI, _
    ByVal nCount As Long) As Long


' -------------------------
' Global Types
' -------------------------
Public Type MyType
    Field1 As Integer
    Field2 As Integer
End Type


' -------------------------
' Global Enums and Constants
' -------------------------
Public Enum PayBands
    PayBand_Engineer
    PayBand_Intern
    PayBand_Manager
End Enum


Public Const SUPPORT_PHONE_NUMBER = "867-5309"


' -------------------------
' Global Variables
' -------------------------
Public NumEmployees As Integer


' ************************************************
' Private Definitions
' -------------------------
' Private API Declarations
' -------------------------
```

```
Private Const SRCCOPY = &HCC0020

Private Declare Function BitBlt Lib "gdi32" _
    Alias "BitBlt" (ByVal hDestDC As Long, _
    ByVal x As Long, ByVal y As Long, _
    ByVal nWidth As Long, ByVal nHeight As Long, _
    ByVal hSrcDC As Long, ByVal xSrc As Long, _
    ByVal ySrc As Long, ByVal dwRop As Long) _
    As Long


' -------------------------
' Private Types
' -------------------------
Private Type MyPrivateType
    Field1 As Integer
End Type


' -------------------------
' Private Constants and Enums
' -------------------------
Private Enum FormColors
    FormColor_Red
    FormColor_Green
    FormColor_Blue
End Enum

Private Const YELLOW_FRUIT = "Banana"


' -------------------------
' Private Variables
' -------------------------
Private NumWorkingEmployees As Byte
```

Comment Routines

Functions, subroutines, and procedures have a lot in common with files. They, too, should begin with header comments giving important information. This should include a brief explanation of the routine's purpose. If you cannot describe the purpose in one sentence, it probably does not perform a single, well-defined task. Because that can make the routine harder to understand and debug, you should probably break it into two or more smaller routines that perform well-defined tasks.

If the routine is so complicated that comments within the code do not give enough detail, add a method section that explains the algorithm. Use references to books and articles to keep the explanation brief.

Next, the header should describe the routine's inputs and outputs. It should explain which variables are modified. These variables should stand out because they are the variables declared ByRef. If the routine is a function or property get procedure, this section should describe the return value. It should also explain any side effects produced by the routine. For example, if the routine modifies a global data structure, it should say so here.

The header comment should then explain any error handling or error generation in the routine. If the code raises an error, the comment should explain when the error is raised and give the error code. The code should be a constant or enumerated value like NETWORK_FILE_NOT_FOUND, not a hard-coded number like 276.

The next section describes any assertions made by the routine. These are verified by the routine and, if an assertion fails, the routine halts. These are different from the errors listed in the previous section. The program can trap errors and continue. When an assertion fails, the routine stops and the program cannot continue.

The header finishes by listing the developers who have worked on the code, the date they made changes, and comments explaining what each developer did.

You may want to leave in sections even if they do not apply to a particular routine. For example, if a function takes no parameters, you may want to use the following comment to make it clear that the input section is blank and not accidentally omitted.

```
' Inputs:
'    None.
```

The following code shows an example function header. Appendix B, "Header Comment Templates," contains a blank template for a routine header comment. You can download the blank template from the book's Web page at www.vb-helper.com/err.htm and paste it into your code.

```
' **************************************************
' Purpose: Sort an array of numbers.
' Method:   See Ready-to-Run Visual Basic
'           Algorithms, p.231-232.
'
' Inputs:
'    numbers    An array of integers to sort.
'
' Outputs:
'    numbers    The numbers are rearranged so they
'               are returned sorted.
'
' Errors:
```

```
'       This routine raises no errors.
'
' Asserts:
'       The number of items in the array is between
'       10 and 100.
'
'       Changed to 10 to 10,000 by Wendy Franklin.
'
' Developer          Date      Comments
' ---------          --------  --------
' Amy Smith            8/20/97 Initial creation.
' Norman Williams     12/21/97 Fixed bug when lower bound < 1.
' Wendy Franklin       4/ 3/98 Changed to allow up to 10k items.
' ************************************************
Public Sub SelectionSort(ByRef numbers() As Integer)
      :
```

Some programmers place a routine's comments after its declaration like this:

```
Public Sub SelectionSort(ByRef numbers() As Integer)

' ************************************************
' Purpose: Sort an array of numbers.
'    :
' More comments
'    :
' ************************************************

     ' The code starts here
        :
```

It doesn't much matter where you put the comments, as long as they are immediately next to the routine and the developers on the project are consistent.

Comment Event Handlers

Event handlers are generally similar to routines, but they have a few key differences. The parameters are specified by the event's definition, so you do not really need to document input and output values in an event handler unless it has unusual side effects. Developers are familiar with the parameters of the more common event handlers. Those who have questions can consult the Visual Basic online help.

Event handlers are invoked by Visual Basic, not other code in the application, so they must never raise errors. The program cannot trap errors generated by code that it does not call directly. If an event handler raises an error, the program crashes. For this reason, event handler comments do not need an errors section. Assertions are still useful in event handlers, though, so the comments should still contain an asserts section.

Finally, the purpose of the event handler is obviously to handle an event. Do not merely repeat that in the purpose section of the comment. Instead, explain what the routine does about the event. State what triggered the event and explain what that means to the program. Do not state, "Handle the user's mouse move event." Instead, say, "If the user is dragging a node, move it to this new position."

The following code shows an example event handler header. Appendix B, "Header Comment Templates," contains a blank template for an event handler header comment. You can download the blank template from the book's Web page at www.vb-helper.com/err.htm and paste it into your code.

```
' **************************************************
' Purpose: The user has clicked the color
'          selection area. Display the selected
'          color.
'
' Method:  Use the Mod operator to determine the
'          row and cloumn clicked. Display the
'          corresponding color in the Colors array.
'
' Outputs: Updates the global value SelectedColor.
'
' Asserts:
'    The number of colors displayed should be
'    either 16 or 256.
'
' Developer           Date     Comments
' ---------           -------- --------
' Mike Johnson        8/20/97 Initial creation.
Private Sub ColorArea_MouseUp(Button As Integer, _
    Shift As Integer, X As Single, Y As Single)
        :
```

Give Context, Not Content

Use comments that provide context to help the reader understand your code. Do not simply repeat what the code does. The comment in the following code is overkill. Any experienced programmer can tell what this statement does.

```
employee = employee + 1    ' Add 1 to employee.
```

Instead, use comments that explain why the code is doing what it does. Make it easier for a programmer of average experience to follow your logic.

```
employee = employee + 1    ' Consider the next employee in the
                           ' array.
```

Comment Portability Issues

Comment code that may break if some other part of the system changes. If something on your computer changes, you can look for these comments to see where bugs may have appeared.

Comment code that may not be portable to other operating systems such as Windows NT, Windows 95, and Windows 3.11. Routines that use API functions, system files, or other system-related objects may stop working when you change or upgrade the operating system.

Comment code that may not work with different software versions such as 16-bit Visual Basic 4 or 32-bit Visual Basic 6. Comment code that may not work with different versions of third-party software such as custom controls or database libraries you may have purchased.

These are all places the code is likely to fail when any of these external components change. Make it easy to find them so you can inspect them quickly.

Comment Plainly

Write your comments in plain, everyday language. The goal is to make comments as easy to read as possible, not to save a few keystrokes.

- Do not write with a stilted corporate style.
- Do not use abbreviations. If a comment is too long, continue it on the next line.
- Do not use acronyms unless they are obvious in your industry.
- Use complete sentences.
- Use proper punctuation.
- Use proper capitalization.

Don't Comment Continued Statements

Visual Basic does not allow you to place comments on a line after a line continuation character. To place a comment on a statement that is continued across more than one line, you must put the comment on the last line. That makes it harder to understand that the comment applies to the whole statement.

```
numbers(i) = _
    numbers(smallest_index) + _
    i ' This is a strange place for a comment.
```

To make this type of comment easier to read, place it before the continued statement.

```
' This is a much better place for the comment.
numbers(i) = _
    numbers(smallest_index) + _
    i
```

Don't Remove Comments

Do not remove comments when you fix bugs or make enhancements, just add to them. Do not remove the old code either, just comment it out. If you later discover that a bug fix was incorrect, you can quickly replace the previous code.

The descriptive comments and commented code give the routine's history. One important use for this history is to determine which routines are buggy. If a lot of bugs have been fixed in a routine, it is likely to contain other bugs.

This is somewhat contrary to intuition. You might think a larger percentage of the bugs have been removed from the routine than from other routines that have had fewer bugs in the past. Actually, a high bug count indicates that the routine probably has some larger design or conceptual flaw. If a routine contains too many bug fixes, it is often better to rewrite it from scratch instead of continuing to patch it.

Format Comments Nicely

Neatness counts. Remember, the intent is to make comments as easy to read as possible. Ugly formatting makes the reader work harder to understand the comments and distracts from the more important task of understanding the code. Which of the following sets of comments is easier to read?

```
' Comments ragged right.
For Each ctl In Controls ' Examine the controls.
    If TypeName(ctl) = "TextBox" Then ' If it is a TextBox:
        If ctl.Text = "" Then ' If the value is missing:
            MsgBox "Enter " & ctl.Name ' Tell the user it's required.
            ctl.SetFocus ' Return to the field.
            Exit Sub ' Let the user enter a value.
        End If
    End If
Next ctl
```

```
' Comments neatly aligned.
For Each ctl In Controls                    ' Examine the controls.
    If TypeName(ctl) = "TextBox" Then       ' If it is a TextBox:
        If ctl.Text = "" Then               ' If the value is missing:
            MsgBox "Enter " & ctl.Name      ' Tell the user it's required.
            ctl.SetFocus                    ' Return to the field.
            Exit Sub                        ' Let the user enter a value.
        End If
    End If
Next ctl
```

Use Lots of Comments

It is hard to use too many comments. Your code may not be as exciting if you explain every little detail, but the idea is to inform, not to entertain. Any comment that increases understanding is a good comment.

In one project I worked on, we followed a rigorous commenting strategy. The program contained a normal number of comments throughout the code. Then far to the right beyond the 80th column, we placed additional comments that explained every single line in excruciating detail. We were all working on 80-column monitors, so you only saw those comments if you wanted to. Most of the time the normal comments were enough, but if you got confused, you could switch to 132-column display to see the extra comments.

When the project was finished, we transferred the program to the company's maintenance organization. Even though you never saw these comments unless you looked for them, the maintenance group decided they were too distracting so they removed them. Their philosophy was, "Use comments only when necessary."

About a month later, they removed a major subsystem from the program and replaced it with a less-functional version they purchased from a third-party vendor. They did this because they could not understand the subsystem we built. The reason they could not understand it was that they had removed all of the comments.

Do not adopt the, "Use comments only when necessary," strategy. Instead, use comments wherever they can help clarify the code.

Self-Test

You might think it makes little sense to include an example of bad comments here. Unfortunately, it is just as easy to write bad comments as it is to write bad code. In fact, because bad comments do not cause syntax errors or faulty behavior, they are easier to write and ignore. Their effects are felt only indirectly through increased bug counts and debugging time.

The comments in the following code violate several of the guidelines described in this chapter. Appendix A, "Self-Test Solutions," contains an improved version of this code.

```
Option Explicit

' True when the user is drawing.
Private Drawing As Boolean

' Save mouse position.
Private LastX As Single
Private LastY As Single

' **************************************************
' Purpose: Start drawing.
'
' Method:  Use the X and Y coordinates to see where
'          the mouse currently is.
' **************************************************
Private Sub picDrawingArea_MouseDown(Button As Integer, _
        Shift As Integer, X As Single, Y As Single)

    ' Set Drawing to true.
    Drawing = True

    ' Record this point's location.
    LastX = X
    LastY = Y
End Sub

' **************************************************
' Purpose: Process the user's mouse move event in
'          the drawing area.
'
' Method:  Use the X and Y coordinates to see where
'          the mouse currently is.
'
' Errors:
'    If the user draws outside the drawing area,
'    raise error OUT_OF_BOUNDS.
```

```
' **************************************************
Private Sub picDrawingArea_MouseMove(Button As Integer, _
        Shift As Integer, X As Single, Y As Single)

    ' If we are not drawing, BAIL OUT.
    If Not Drawing Then Exit Sub

    If X < 0 Or _
       Y < 0 Or _
       X > picDrawingArea.ScaleWidth Or _
       Y > picDrawingArea.ScaleHeight _
    Then        ' Make sure we are in the drawing area
        Err.Raise OUT_OF_BOUNDS, _
            "picDrawingArea", _
            "Cannot draw outside the drawing area."
    End If

    ' Draw a line from (LastX, LastY) to (X, Y).
    picDrawingArea.Line (LastX, LastY)-(X, Y)

    ' Save X and Y.
    LastX = X
    LastY = Y
End Sub


' **************************************************
' Purpose: Finish drawing.
'
' Method:  Set Drawing to False.
' **************************************************
Private Sub picDrawingArea_MouseUp(Button As Integer, _
        Shift As Integer, X As Single, Y As Single)

    Drawing = False
End Sub
```

Summary

Good comments give the reader extra information that makes the code more understandable. By making it easier for readers to understand the code, comments reduce the chances of bugs being introduced into the program. Do not underestimate the power of good comments for preventing bugs.

Table 7.1 summarizes the types of information a header-style comment for a file should contain. Table 7.2 lists information that a routine's header-style comment should include.

Table 7.1 Information in a Header-Style Comment for a File

SECTION	CONTAINS
Idenifying information	Filename, copyright information, author, etc.
Description	The purpose or theme of the file
Entry points	Public routines and variables exposed by the file
Dependencies	Other files on which this one depends
Known issues	Outstanding bugs and possible future enhancements
Method	Information that can help the reader understand the code at the module level
Declarations	Type, constant, Enum, variable, and other declarations

Table 7.2 Information in a Header-Style Comment for a Routine

SECTION	CONTAINS
Purpose	The routine's job
Method	Description of how the routine does its job
Inputs	The meaning of the routine's parameters
Outputs	Explanation of any parameters that are modified
Errors	Errors the routine raises
Asserts	Conditions the routine asserts
History	Author name, date, and description of changes

The following Bug Stoppers summarize more general commenting guidelines.

 BUG STOPPERS: Comments

Begin files with header comments.

Begin routines with header comments.

Begin event handlers with header comments.

Give context, not content.

Comment portability issues so they are easy to find later.

Comment plainly without abbreviations or stilted prose.

Place comments above continued statements, not on their last lines.

Don't remove comments, keep them for history.

Format comments nicely so they do not distract from the task of understanding the code.

Gotchas

This chapter describes several of the most common bugs in Visual Basic programs and ways to avoid them. Most are quite simple once you learn about them. Many are difficult to foresee, however, and they can be very time consuming if you are forced to learn about them by direct experience.

A lot of Visual Basic programmers including myself have wasted a lot of time learning about these gotchas the hard way. After you read this chapter, you should be able to easily avoid the most costly of these mistakes.

Watch Precision in Tests

Checking equality of integers is easy. Two integers are either equal or they are not. Sometimes the equality of floating-point numbers can be a little more confusing. Two floating-point numbers can be very close to the same value and still not be equal.

In the following code, the variable x starts with the value 0. The value 10 / 17 is added to x 17 times. If you multiply 17 by 10 / 17, you get 10, so the final value for x should be 10. Due to round-off errors, however, the value is actually 9.999999. This is not exactly 10, so the test x = 10 in the If statement is false and the message box is not displayed.

```
Private Sub RoundoffProblem()
Dim x As Single
Dim dx As Single
Dim i As Integer

    dx = 10 / 17
    x = 0
    For i = 1 To 17
        ' Do something with x.
            :
        x = x + dx
    Next i

    If x = 10 Then MsgBox "This value is 10."
End Sub
```

This can be even more confusing with double precision floating-point numbers. The following code is similar to the previous routine except it uses double precision numbers. Once again, the test in the If statement is false, so the program does not display the message box.

```
Private Sub RoundoffProblem()
Dim x As Double
Dim dx As Double
Dim i As Integer

    dx = 10 / 17
    x = 0
    For i = 1 To 17
        ' Do something with x.
            :
        x = x + dx
    Next i

    If x = 10 Then MsgBox "This value is 10."
End Sub
```

After the For loop in this routine, x is actually 9.999999999999998. This is not exactly 10, so the program does not display the message box.

To make matters worse, the value of x is so close to 10 that the Format function displays it as 10. The Debug.Print statement and the debugger's quick watch also display x as 10. If you use the format statement, the Debug.Print statement, or Visual Basic's quick watch feature, you will see that x is 10, but the If statement will still not display the message box. This can be extremely confusing. The variable x seems to be 10, but the test x = 10 is false.

To avoid this sort of confusion, never use equality to decide whether two floating-point numbers have the same value. Instead, check whether they are within a certain small distance of each other. For example, the following code fragment shows how to determine whether x is 10 to within 0.00001. This is close enough to equality for most purposes.

```
If Abs(x - 10) < 0.00001 Then MsgBox "This value is
approximately 10."
```

Similarly, never use a simple inequality test (<>) to decide whether two floating-point numbers are different. The following loop runs forever because x is never exactly equal to 10.

```
Private Sub RoundoffProblem()
Dim x As Single
Dim dx As Single

    dx = 10 / 17
    x = 0
    Do While x <> 10
        ' Do something with x.
            :
        x = x + dx
    Loop
End Sub
```

Control Float Loops with While

The previous guideline says you should not test floating-point numbers for equality. If you use a floating-point variable to control a For loop, you are implicitly doing just that. Each time the loop runs, Visual Basic checks to see if the variable has reached the loop's stopping value. This step tests for equality, so it can cause some subtle errors.

The For loop in the following code should execute four times with x equal to 0, 10 / 3, 20 / 3, and 10. It actually executes with x equal to 0, 3.33333333333333, and 6.66666666666667. When the program adds 10 / 3 to x the third time, x becomes roughly 10.0000000000000003. That is greater than 10 so the For loop exits before executing a fourth time. Instead of executing four times, this code runs only three times.

```
Private Sub RoundoffProblem()
Dim x As Double

    For x = 0 To 10 Step 10 / 3
        ' Do something with x.
            :
```

```
        Next x
    End Sub
```

To avoid this kind of problem, eliminate the equality test implicit in the For loop. Use a While loop instead and replace the equality test with the proper inequality. In this case, the code should continue to execute the loop until x is greater than 10 plus a small amount to account for rounding errors.

```
Private Sub RoundoffProblem()
Dim x As Double

    x = 0
    Do
        ' Do something with x.
            :


        x = x + 10 / 3
    Loop While x < 10.00001
End Sub
```

This code executes the For loop statements four times as desired.

Control Float Loops with Integers

If you know how many times you want a loop to execute, use an integer instead of a floating-point number to control the loop. The following code accomplishes the same task as the code from the previous section without the confusing inequality or rounding problems.

```
Private Sub RoundoffProblem()
Dim x As Double
Dim i As Integer

    x = 0
    For i = 0 To 3
        ' Do something with x.
            :


        x = x + 10 / 3
    Next i
End Sub
```

This code executes the For loop statements four times as desired without using the confusing While statement. Despite the fact that this code uses an extra integer variable, the two versions run in almost exactly the same amount of time.

Control Date Loops

Date and time variables are stored internally as floating-point numbers so they are subject to the same rounding errors as other floating-point numbers. The following code should execute a For loop four times with the variable the_time set to 1:00, 1:20, 1:40, and 2:00. Due to rounding, after dx is added to x three times, x has the value 2:00:00.00000000000000001. This is bigger than 2:00, so the loop stops after executing only three times instead of four.

```
Private Sub RoundoffProblem()
Dim the_time As Date
Dim dx As Date

    ' Use 1/3 hour increments.
    dx = 1 / 24 / 3

    For the_time = CDate("1:00 am") To CDate("2:00 am") Step dx
        ' Do something with the_time.
            :
    Next the_time
End Sub
```

This problem has the same solutions as other floating-point looping problems. Use While loops with inequalities instead of For loops controlled by floating-point numbers. If you know how many times you want the loop to execute, use an integer variable to control the loop instead.

The previous example also uses a numeric value to define a time interval. It should use the DateAdd function to be more obvious. Mixing numeric and date functions is confusing and relies on the specific implementation of date variables. The following code shows a better way to handle this problem.

```
Private Sub RoundoffProblem()
Dim i As Integer
Dim the_time As Date

    the_time = CDate("1:00 am")
    For i = 0 To 3
        ' Do something with the_time.
            :

        ' Add 20 minutes to the_time.
        the_time = DateAdd("n", 20, the_time)
    Next i
End Sub
```

This code executes the statements within the For loop four times as desired. Unfortunately, using the DateAdd function is significantly slower than adding floating-point numbers. Even so, this version is much easier to understand so you should use it instead of the previous version. Few programs perform so many date calculations that this kind of loop dominates the program's runtime, so the slightly reduced performance is more than offset by the improved readability.

Don't Resize Inside Loops

Do not change the size of an array or collection while you are iterating over its members. The following code, for example, is meant to remove the odd values from a collection. Unfortunately, Visual Basic calculates the stopping value numbers.Count only when it enters the For loop. As items are removed from the collection, the loop's stopping value does not change even though the number of items in the collection does. If the program removes any items, the index i will eventually run past the collection's ever-decreasing upper bound and the program will crash with a subscript out of range error.

The For loop also increases i even when an item is removed. If the routine removes the first item, the second becomes the new first item. Then i is increased to 2, so the code never examines the new first item, which was the old second item.

```
Dim numbers As New Collection
Dim i As Integer
        :
    ' Initialize the collection.
        :
    ' Remove the odd numbers.
    For i = 1 To numbers.Count
        If numbers(i) Mod 2 = 1 Then numbers.Remove i
    Next i
```

The following code shows one correct method for removing the collection's odd entries. The While loop calculates the continuing condition i <= numbers.Count every time the loop is executed so it can determine when i exceeds the collection's current upper bound. The While loop also allows the program to explicitly determine when to increment i. The code increases i only when it does not remove an item, so it can consider every item in the collection.

```
Dim numbers As New Collection
Dim i As Integer
        :
    ' Initialize the collection.
        :
```

```
' Remove the even numbers.
i = 1
Do While i <= numbers.Count
    If numbers(i) Mod 2 = 1 Then
        ' Remove this item.
        numbers.Remove i
    Else
        ' Consider the next item.
        i = i + 1
    End If
Loop
```

Watch for Circular References

Visual Basic performs automatic reference counting. When you create an object, Visual Basic keeps track of the number of variables referencing that object. If the reference count ever reaches 0, the system knows that the program can no longer access the object, so Visual Basic automatically destroys it. The following code illustrates how the system performs reference counting.

```
Dim obj1 As MyObject        ' Initially these references do not point
Dim obj2 As MyObject        '       to any objects.

    Set obj1 = New MyObject ' Create an object.          Count = 1.
    Set obj2 = obj1         ' obj2 also points to the object. Count = 2.
    Set obj1 = Nothing      ' Only obj2 points to the object. Count = 1.
    Set obj2 = Nothing      ' Nothing points to the object.  Count = 0.
```

Suppose the program creates a Cell object that has a public NextCell variable that is itself a reference to another Cell object. Suppose the program sets the cell's NextCell pointer to reference itself.

```
Dim new_cell As New Cell

    Set new_cell.NextCell = new_cell
    Set new_cell = Nothing
```

Because this object contains a reference to itself, its reference count is not 0, even after the variable new_cell is set to Nothing. The Cell object that new_cell was pointing to still points to itself, so its reference count is 1 and Visual Basic cannot destroy it.

Similarly, a program could build a long chain of cells with the last cell pointing to the first. Both of these situations are *reference loops*. As long as the items in the loop refer to each other, Visual Basic cannot free any of them. The program must explicitly set some of the references to Nothing before the system can free the memory.

Beware of this kind of reference loop. In more complex data structures like trees, networks, and graphs, reference loops can be much harder to detect and remove. Reference loops are one of the few ways a Visual Basic program can permanently lose memory.

Understand Form Lifetime

The lifetime of a form can be confusing. Accessing the values and variables defined by the form can cause behavior you may find strange.

Like other objects in Visual Basic, forms are referenced counted. When you unload a form, you remove it from the screen and destroy the controls it contains. The form object is not completely deleted, however, until the program's last reference to it is set to Nothing. In particular, the variables defined by the form are still available to the program.

For example, the following code creates a form, saves the value 123 in the public ID variable defined in the form's Declarations section, and sets the text displayed by a TextBox control. It then unloads the form. At that point, the controls on the form have been destroyed. However, the public ID variable is still loaded and still contains the value 123 saved by the program. The following code displays this value and sets frm to Nothing so the form is completely destroyed.

```
Dim frm As EmployeeForm

    Set frm = New EmployeeForm        ' Create the form obect.
    frm.Show                          ' Make the form visible.
    frm.ID = 123                      ' Set a public variable's value.
    frm.txtFirstName.Text = "Gomez"   ' Set a control's property.

    Unload frm                        ' Unload the form.

    MsgBox frm.ID                     ' Display the ID.

    Set frm = Nothing                 ' Finish destroying the form.
```

This is confusing enough, but the story gets worse. If you access a control or property on a form that is not loaded, Visual Basic automatically loads it. This is very different from accessing a variable defined by the form.

The following code is similar to the previous example. After loading, initializing, and unloading the form, the code displays the value contained in the txtFirstName text box. Since the form is unloaded, Visual Basic automatically reloads it. That reinitializes txtFirstName to hold whatever value it was assigned at design time. The program then displays that value instead of the name Gomez.

Even worse, Visual Basic reloads the form, so setting the frm variable to Nothing does not destroy it. It removes the program's last reference to the form so it can no longer be used, but the graphical components of the form including its controls are still loaded even though they are not visible. If the user closes all the other forms, this one will still be running so the program will not end.

```
Dim frm As EmployeeForm

    Set frm = New EmployeeForm           ' Create the form obect.
    frm.Show                             ' Make the form visible.
    frm.ID = 123                         ' Set a public variable's value.
    frm.txtFirstName.Text = "Gomez"      ' Set a control's property.

    Unload frm                           ' Unload the form.

    ' The following line reloads the form.
    MsgBox frm.txtFirstName.Text         ' Display the first name text.

    Set frm = Nothing                    ' Remove our reference to the form.
```

This is a common bug. By referencing a form's controls or properties after unloading it, the program reloads the form and keeps it hidden. This is a particularly common mistake in the code a dialog uses to unload itself.

The following code unloads its form. It then sets the form's txtDirectoryName.Text value. That reloads the form. The txtDirectoryName.Text value may look fine to the main program, although other controls on the form will have the values they were assigned at design time. The form will be hidden but running, and that may stop the program from unloading properly.

```
' Close this form.
Private Sub mnuFileSaveAndClose_Click()
    Unload Me

    ' Save the current directory for the
    ' calling program to use.
    txtDirectoryName.Text = CurrentDirectory
End Sub
```

To prevent this particular error, hide the dialog instead of unloading it. That keeps the form loaded so its controls retain their values. The routine that displays the dialog should unload the form.

```
' Close this form.
Private Sub mnuFileSaveAndClose_Click()
    Me.Hide

    ' Save the current directory for the
    ' calling program to use.
    txtDirectoryName.Text = CurrentDirectory
End Sub
```

More generally, you can think of a form as being an object that contains public values defined in its Declarations section. It is connected to another visible object that the user sees as the form containing controls. Loading and unloading apply only to the visible object. To completely destroy the pair, the program must unload the visible object and remove all of its references to the invisible portion.

Initialize All Values

Visual Basic automatically initializes variables to default values. For the most part, those values make sense. For example, numbers are initialized to 0, strings are initialized to empty strings, and object references are initialized to Nothing.

Initialize the variables anyway. Even if you want a variable to start with its default value, initializing it makes that fact obvious. If you really want to save the tiny bit of extra time it takes to initialize the value explicitly, use a comment to emphasize the fact that you want the variable to take its default value. This makes it clear to future programmers that you did not simply forget to initialize the variable.

```
Dim num_employees As Integer      ' Initially 0.
```

Use All Values

If a routine does not use a value after it is set, and the value is not a parameter being returned to the calling routine, you may have a bug. If the value is not needed, it should not be calculated. If you see a situation in which a routine calculates a value but does not use it, figure out why it calculated the value. If the value is truly unnecessary, remove the calculation.

It is common to add code while initially writing a routine, and then to remove it later. A variable that was used in the initial version of the routine may no longer be necessary. This kind of unused variable should be removed from the declarations to prevent later confusion.

Another common example of this problem occurs with API functions. Many programmers assign the return status from an API function to a variable, but then they do not check the status. The following code shows a simple example using the FlashWindow API function. The variable return_status is set but never used.

```
Private Declare Function FlashWindow Lib "user32" _
    Alias "FlashWindow" (ByVal hwnd As Long, _
    ByVal bInvert As Long) As Long
        :
Private Sub FlashTheWindow()
Dim return_status as Long

    return_status = FlashWindow(hwnd, True)
End Sub
```

The program should check the status value to see if the API function succeeded. If the routine does not care whether the API call was successful, it should not assign the return status to a variable. For example, the FlashWindow API function returns a code indicating whether the window was active before the API call. It is not an error code, so, if the program does not care whether the window was active, it can safely ignore the value. In that case, it should treat FlashWindow as if it is a subroutine instead of a function.

```
Private Declare Function FlashWindow Lib "user32" _
    Alias "FlashWindow" (ByVal hwnd As Long, _
    ByVal bInvert As Long) As Long
        :
Private Sub FlashTheWindow()
    FlashWindow hwnd, True
End Sub
```

Do not assign values you never use.

Return a Value

When you write a function, make sure it always returns a value no matter what path the program takes through the code. One technique that makes this easier is to always assign the function's value immediately before any Exit or End statement. To verify that the routine always returns a value, you just need to examine all of the Exit and End statements. If the previous statement does not assign the return value, the value is not explicitly defined.

```
Private Function MyFunction() As Integer
    :
```

```
        If some_condition Then
            MyFunction = 1
            Exit Function
        End If
            :
        If some_other_condition Then
            MyFunction = 2
            Exit Function
        End If
            :
        MyFunction = 3
    End Function
```

Some functions return one value for many paths of execution. You can think of this as the function's default value. If any of several conditions occur, the function returns this value. In cases like this, you can set the function's return value at the very beginning. Then any Exit or End statement that is not immediately preceded by an assignment statement returns the default value.

You can make it easier to verify that the function always returns the correct value by preceding every Exit and End statement with either a value assignment or a comment indicating that the function should return the default value. Then when you inspect the function, you can easily verify that one of these statements is present.

```
    Private Function MyFunction() As Integer
        MyFunction = 0              ' Assume we will return 0.
            :
        If some_condition Then
            MyFunction = 1          ' Return 1.
            Exit Function
        End If
            :
        If some_other_condition Then
            ' Return the default value.
            Exit Function
        End If
            :
        ' Return the default value.
    End Function
```

Some functions modify their return values in complicated ways before returning. Try to restructure the code to match one of the previous simple formats. If you cannot do that, provide extensive comments that help the reader keep track of the function's return value as it changes.

Beware Foreign Syntax

Some statements are valid in Visual Basic and in another programming language, but they have different meanings in the two languages. For example, consider the following code:

```
Dim A As Integer
Dim B As Integer

   A = B = 1
```

The statement A = B = 1 is valid in Visual Basic, C, and C++. In C and C++, this statement assigns the value of 1 to the variables B and A. In Visual Basic, however, this statement is equivalent to A = (B = 1). The variable A is assigned the value of the Boolean expression B = 1. Since B is automatically initialized to 0 when it is created, B does not equal 1 so the expression is False. That means A is assigned the value False and B remains unchanged. In the end, both variables have the value 0.

If you are familiar with another language, beware of that other language's syntax creeping into your Visual Basic code. Visual Basic may execute the code, but you may not get the results you expect.

Never Use GoTo, Except . . .

GoTo statements have a deservedly bad reputation. Improperly used GoTo statements can make a routine totally incomprehensible. They confuse the flow of control through the routine and turn simple loops into confusing tangles.

The following code shows two implementations of the selectionsort algorithm. The first uses GoTo statements instead of the For loops used by the second.

```
Public Sub SelectionSort(ByRef numbers() As Integer)
Dim i As Integer
Dim j As Integer
Dim smallest_value As Integer
Dim smallest_index As Integer

    i = LBound(numbers)
ILoop:
    smallest_value = numbers(i)
    smallest_index = i
    j = i
    GoTo SaveSmallest
JLoop:
```

```
        If numbers(j) >= smallest_value Then GoTo SkipIt
SaveSmallest:
    smallest_value = numbers(j)
    smallest_index = j
SkipIt:
    j = j + 1
    If j <= UBound(numbers) Then GoTo JLoop
    numbers(smallest_index) = numbers(i)
    numbers(i) = smallest_value
    i = i + 1
    If i <= UBound(numbers) Then GoTo ILoop
End Sub

Public Sub SelectionSort(ByRef numbers() As Integer)
Dim i As Integer
Dim j As Integer
Dim smallest_value As Integer
Dim smallest_index As Integer

    For i = LBound(numbers) To UBound(numbers)
        smallest_value = numbers(i)
        smallest_index = i

        For j = i + 1 To UBound(numbers)
            If numbers(j) < smallest_value Then
                smallest_value = numbers(j)
                smallest_index = j
            End If
        Next j

        numbers(smallest_index) = numbers(i)
        numbers(i) = smallest_value
    Next i
End Sub
```

Both of these subroutines work, but the GoTo statements in the first make it much harder to read. They also make it take almost twice as long to run.

Do not use GoTos to control a routine's flow. Use For and While loops instead.

There are only a few reasons you should ever use a GoTo statement in Visual Basic and some of them are discussed in the following sections. Some ways in which you should never use a GoTo include:

- Do not use GoTo to move to an earlier line in the routine. If you want to jump to earlier code, you should probably use a For or While loop instead of a GoTo.

- Do not use GoTo to jump into a loop. Sometimes it is acceptable to use GoTo to exit a loop (see the following sections), but you should never jump into one in this way.

Use GoTo for Error Handling

Visual Basic uses On Error GoTo statements to specify error handlers. When an error occurs, the routine essentially performs a GoTo to jump into the error-handling code. This special use of GoTo is consistent and easy to understand. Programmers who later read a routine that uses On Error GoTo will know that the GoTo leads to an error handler. You can use this form of GoTo because it will not cause confusion.

A routine also executes an implied GoTo when an error handler ends. If the program uses a Resume or Resume Next statement, execution resumes near where the error occurred. These are standard ways for leaving an error handler, so they will not cause confusion either.

The Resume statement also lets a program resume at a specific line. For example, the statement Resume StartHere makes the program jump to the line labeled StartHere. This transfer of control is not standard and is more confusing than simple Resume or Resume Next statements, so you should use it only when absolutely necessary.

One situation in which it may make sense to resume at a specific line is when the routine must perform some cleanup before it exits. For instance, the following code opens a file and reads data from it. If the routine encounters an error, it resumes execution at the beginning of the cleanup code. That ensures that the file is properly closed before the routine ends.

Note that the first thing the cleanup code does is disable error handling with the On Error Resume Next statement. If it did not and the routine encountered an error while inside the cleanup code, it would jump to the error handler. After presenting its message, the error handler would resume execution at the cleanup code again. The program would be stuck in an infinite loop.

```
Private Sub LoadData(ByVal file_name As String)
Dim fnum As Integer

    ' Open a file.
    fnum = FreeFile
    Open file_name For Input As #fnum

    ' Read from the file, process data, etc.
    On Error GoTo ReadError
        :
    ' Continue into the clean up code.

CloseFile:
    ' Close the file.
```

```
        On Error Resume Next
        Close #fnum


        Exit Sub

ReadError:
        MsgBox "Error" & Str$(Err.Number) & _
            vbCrLf & Err.Description

        ' Go to the file cleanup code.
        Resume CloseFile
    End Sub
```

This code can be restructured to remove the confusing Resume statement with a simpler Resume Next statement. The following routine moves the complex file reading code into the ReadData subroutine. If an error occurs inside Read-Data, this routine uses the Resume Next statement to continue execution after ReadData. This code is easier to understand than the previous version.

```
Private Sub LoadData(ByVal file_name As String)
Dim fnum As Integer

        ' Open a file.
        fnum = FreeFile
        Open file_name For Input As #fnum

        ' Read from the file, process data, etc.
        On Error GoTo ReadError
        ReadData fnum

        ' Close the file.
        Close #fnum
        Exit Sub

ReadError:
        MsgBox "Error" & Str$(Err.Number) & _
            vbCrLf & Err.Description
        Resume Next
    End Sub
```

Use GoTo to Simplify

GoTo is sometimes also used when the alternative would be more awkward and confusing. For example, a single GoTo statement can allow a program to break out of a deeply nested series of loops. The following code executes a series of loops. If it finds the condition value(i, j, k) = 0, it uses a GoTo statement to break out of all of the loops in one step.

```
        Do While Timer < stop_time
            For i = 1 To 100
                For j = i + 1 To 1000
                    ' Do something here.
                        :
                    If value(i, j) = 0 Then GoTo ExitLoops
                Next j
            Next i
        Loop

ExitLoops:
```

Compare this to the following code that breaks out of the loops without using a GoTo statement. This code is reasonable, but the previous version is simpler.

```
    Dim found_entry As Boolean

        found_entry = False
        Do While Timer < stop_time
            For i = 1 To 100
                For j = i + 1 To 1000
                    ' Do something here.
                        :
                    If value(i, j) = 0 Then
                        found_entry = True
                        Exit For
                    End If
                    if found_entry Then Exit For
                Next j
                if found_entry Then Exit For
            Next i
            if found_entry Then Exit Do
        Loop
```

Exit in One Place

Some developers believe that every routine should always exit from a single point. That makes it easy to verify that any special cleanup code is properly executed.

The following subroutine opens two data files and reads from them. It uses error handlers with appropriate Resume statements to ensure that it closes the files properly and always exits at the same Exit Sub statement.

```
    Private Sub LoadData( _
        ByVal file_name1 As String, _
        ByVal file_name2 As String)

    Dim fnum1 As Integer
```

```
Dim fnum2 As Integer

    ' Open the files.
    On Error GoTo OpenError1
    fnum1 = FreeFile
    Open file_name1 For Input As #fnum1

    On Error GoTo OpenError2
    fnum2 = FreeFile
    Open file_name1 For Input As #fnum2

    ' Read from the file, process data, etc.
    On Error GoTo ReadError
        :

    ' Close the files.
CloseFile1:
    On Error GoTo CloseError2
    Close #fnum2

CloseFile2:
    On Error GoTo CloseError1
    Close #fnum1

LoadDataDone:
    On Error Resume Next

    ' Always exit here.
    Exit Sub

    ' ******************************
    ' Error handlers (code omitted).
OpenError1:
        :
    Resume LoadDataDone

OpenError2:
        :
    Resume CloseFile1      ' Close file 1 only.

ReadError:
        :
    Resume CloseFile2      ' Close both files.

CloseError2:
        :
    Resume CloseFile1      ' Close file 1 only.

CloseError1:
        :
    Resume LoadDataDone    ' We've cleaned up all we can.
End Sub
```

Making a routine exit at a single point generally requires lots of error handlers, GoTos, and labeled lines. This example required six On Error statements, five error handlers, and eight labeled lines. This makes the routine look somewhat cluttered, but most of this code is required anyway, no matter how the routine is organized. The subroutine in this example must handle errors in quite a few situations. It must be prepared to close zero, one, or both of the files depending on which files are open. Handling all those situations makes the routine fairly complex in any case.

Exit before Error Handlers

Always place an Exit Sub statement before error-handling code so the routine does not continue past the end of the normal code and fall into the error handlers.

```
        :
    ' Done with normal processing.
    Exit Sub

    ' ***************
    ' Error handlers.
    ' ***************
OpenFileError:
        :
```

Place error handlers together at the end of the routine. Don't mix error-handling code with normal code.

Don't Use IIF

The IIF statement has the syntax

```
variable = IIF(expression, true_value, false_value)
```

Here, expression is a logical expression. This statement gives the variable the value true_value if the expression is True and false_value if it is False.

IIF is confusing so you should not use it. Use an If Then Else statement instead. The following code compares the times required by IIF and If Then Else. The If Then Else statement is not only easier to understand, it also takes only 25 percent as long as IIF.

```
Private Sub TimeIIF()
Const NUM_TESTS = 100000
Dim start_time As Single
```

```
Dim stop_time As Single
Dim i As Long
Dim txt As String

    ' Try IFF.
    start_time = Timer
    For i = 1 To NUM_TESTS
        txt = IIf(i < 5000, _
            "It's a smaller value", _
            "It's a larger value")
    Next i
    stop_time = Timer
    MsgBox Format$(stop_time - start_time, "0.00")

    ' Try If Then Else.
    start_time = Timer
    For i = 1 To NUM_TESTS
        If i < 5000 Then
            txt = "It's a smaller value"
        Else
            txt = "It's a larger value"
        End If
    Next i
    stop_time = Timer
    MsgBox Format$(stop_time - start_time, "0.00")
End Sub
```

IIF also has interacts strangely with routines that have side effects because it always evaluates both assignment values whether the condition is True or not. In the following code, IFF executes both TrueFunction and FalseFunction even though it does not really need the value of FalseFunction.

```
variable = IIF(True, TrueFunction, FalseFunction)
```

Prevent confusion by using If Then Else instead of IIF.

Watch for Overflow and Underflow

Watch out for expressions that can produce overflow or underflow. For example, the following function produces an overflow error if its input parameter is greater than 16383. It produces an underflow if the parameter is less than −16384.

```
Function DoubleIt(ByVal x As Integer) As Integer
    DoubleIt = 2 * x
End Function
```

Underflow errors are easy to overlook. You must be sure you consider variables with both large positive and negative values.

If it is easy to determine what parameter values will produce errors, use Debug.Assert or Stop statements to verify that the values are acceptable. Use an On Error statement to catch the error in more complicated situations and in the compiled version of the program.

```
Function DoubleIt(ByVal x As Integer) As Integer
    Debug.Assert (x >= -16384) And (x <= 16383)

    DoubleIt = 2 * x
End Function
```

Watch for Divide by 0

Watch for expressions that could cause a divide-by-0 error. If an expression includes division, check the denominator to see if can ever be 0. Use Debug.Assert, Stop, and On Error statements to prevent the routine from crashing.

```
Function Invert(ByVal x As Integer) As Integer
    Debug.Assert x <> 0

    Invert = 1 \ x
End Function
```

Be Aware of Argument Promotion

Be certain you understand how the types of variables change when they are passed to routines or used in expressions. Use parentheses and data type conversion functions to force Visual Basic to handle the values as you intend.

Think about how variable promotion can interact with the other guidelines discussed in this chapter. For example, after the following code runs, it looks as if x and y should have the same value. However, when the program reaches the statement y = 0#, Visual Basic promotes y to the double data type. During the For loop, y retains more precision than x, which is only a single. At the end of the loop, x has the value 9.999999 while y has the value 10.0000004172325. These values are not exactly equal, so the message box never appears.

```
Private Sub PromotionProblem()
Dim x As Single
```

```
Dim y As Variant
Dim dx As Single
Dim i As Integer

    dx = 10 / 17
    y = 0#
    x = y
    For i = 1 To 17
        ' Do something with x and y.

        x = x + dx
        y = y + dx
    Next i

    If x = y Then MsgBox "The values are equal."
End Sub
```

Do not rely on Visual Basic to behave as you expect. Make the results of expressions obvious to developers who read the code later.

Avoid Error Codes

The problem with functions that return error codes is that you must remember to check them. If a routine returns an error code and the program ignores it, you will not be aware that a problem may be occurring. On the other hand, if a routine raises an error, you cannot fail to notice it. You must trap the error with an On Error statement or the program will crash.

Try to use routines that always work. You do not need to handle errors that cannot arise. If you cannot use an error-proof routine, use one that raises errors when it fails instead of returning a status code.

If neither of those options is available, be certain you check the function's status code. Visual Basic allows a program to treat a function as if it were a procedure if the program does not want the function's return value. For example, the LineTo API function draws a line to a specified point and returns a nonzero value if it is successful. The following code shows how a program can invoke LineTo with and without the return code.

```
Private Declare Function LineTo Lib "gdi32" Alias "LineTo" _
    (ByVal hdc As Long, ByVal x As Long, ByVal y As Long) As Long
        :
Private Sub DrawLines()
Dim status As Long

    ' Treat as a subroutine, ignoring the return code.
    LineTo hdc, 100, 200
```

```
        ' Check the return code.
        status = LineTo(hdc, 200, 300)
        Debug.Assert (status <> 0)
    End Sub
```

If you use a function that returns a status code, do not ignore the code. See if the routine succeeded and take appropriate action if it did not.

Don't Assume Variable Sizes

Do not assume variable sizes will remain the same forever. For example, do not assume integers take 4 bytes and that doubles take 8. Those values probably will not change in the near future, but stranger things have happened. At some point in the future, when most computers use 128-bit addressing, doubles could change to 16 or 32 bytes. Use the Len and LenB functions to see how large variables are if you need to know.

Don't Assume Constant Values

Do not assume constant values defined by Visual Basic will never change. In particular, do not assume that True will always have the value −1. False is likely to remain 0, but the value of True has been redefined by other languages like Pascal in the past. It could happen in Visual Basic.

If you need to assign the value 0 or −1 to a variable depending on the results of a Boolean expression, use an If statement, not a simple assignment.

```
    Dim X As Integer

    X = (A = B)         ' Don't use this method.

    If (A = B) Then     ' Use this method instead.
        X = -1
    Else
        X = 0
    End If
```

Self-Test

Program Bad8 violates several of the guidelines presented in this chapter. The program, shown in Figure 8.1, presents a sorted list of numbers. Enter a number and click the Search button to make the program try to find the number in the list.

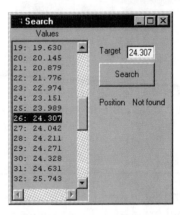

Figure 8.1   Program Bad8 failing to locate the number 24.307.

Unfortunately, program Bad8 practically never finds the correct number. In fact, it does not even correctly generate a sorted list. Some of the numbers are not in sorted order. If the program obeyed all of the guidelines described in this chapter, it would not have these problems.

```
Option Explicit

' The list of values.
Private Const NUM_VALUES = 50
Private Values(1 To NUM_VALUES) As Variant

' Initialize the data.
Private Sub Form_Load()
    InitializeData
End Sub

' Create some random data.
Private Sub InitializeData()
Dim i As Integer
Dim last_value As Integer ' The last value assigned.
Dim txt As String

    Randomize

    ' Initialize the random numbers with each
    ' value slightly bigger than the previous one.
    last_value = 10
    For i = 1 To NUM_VALUES
        Values(i) = last_value + Rnd + 0.01
        last_value = Values(i)
    Next i
```

```vb
    ' Display the values.
    For i = 1 To NUM_VALUES
        txt = txt & Format$(i, "@@") & ": " & _
            Format$(Values(i), "0.000") & vbCrLf
    Next i
    txtValues.Text = txt
End Sub

' Search for the target.
Private Sub CmdSearch_Click()
Dim position As Integer

    position = LinearSearch(Values, txtTarget.Text)
    If position < 1 Then
        lblPosition.Caption = "Not found"
    Else
        lblPosition.Caption = Format$(position)
    End If
End Sub

' Locate a target item using linear search. If the
' target is not found, return 1 less than the
' smallest array index.
Public Function LinearSearch(list() As Variant, _
    target As Variant) As Integer
Dim i As Integer

    For i = LBound(list) To UBound(list)
        ' See if we found the target.
        If list(i) = target Then
            LinearSearch = i
            Exit Function
        End If

        ' If the values are too big, we passed
        ' where it should be so it's not here.
        If list(i) > target Then Exit For
    Next i
End Function
```

Summary

Visual Basic is safer than many programming languages, but it still has its share of traps for the unwary. The Bug Stoppers that follow summarize the guidelines for avoiding the traps that are discussed in this chapter.

BUG STOPPERS: Gotchas

Watch precision in tests.

Control float loops with while.

Control float loops with integers.

Control date loops with while loops or integers.

Don't resize arrays or collections inside loops that access them.

Watch for circular object references.

Understand when forms load and unload.

Initialize all values.

Use every value you calculate or remove the calculation.

Make sure functions always define their return values.

Beware of using the syntax from other programming languages.

Never use GoTo except for error handling or to simplify code.

Never use GoTo to jump backwards in the code.

Never use GoTo to jump into a loop.

Exit in one place.

Place all error-handler code together at the end of the routine.

Use an Exit Sub statement before error handlers.

Do not use IIF, use If Then Else instead.

Watch for overflow and underflow.

Watch for divide-by-0 errors.

Use parentheses and data type conversion functions to control variable promotion.

Avoid functions that return status codes, but check them when you use such a function.

Use Len and LenB to determine variable sizes.

Do not assume constant values will never change.

PART THREE

Development

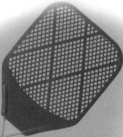

The chapters in Part 3 deal with development at a higher level than those in Part 2. Chapters 3 through 8 discuss specific coding guidelines that reduce the number of bugs in a program, and that make bugs easier to find when they do occur.

The following chapters cover higher-level design and optimization issues. A poor design can set the stage for bugs before developers even write the first line of code. These chapters expose some of the design pitfalls that can doom a project to disaster before it starts. They also emphasize some important high-level concepts you can use to make your code more manageable.

CHAPTER 9

Design

This book does not explain the design process itself. Data flow diagrams, functional decomposition, entity-relationship diagrams, and other design techniques are beyond the scope of this book. For information on design and life cycle processes in general, you should read a book on those subjects.

This chapter explains some of the design hazards that can snare unwary developers and make a good project turn bad. The first several sections deal with high-level design issues. The rest cover more detailed guidelines for subroutine design.

Design for Uniformity, Simplicity, Elegance

At all levels of design, you should treat matters as uniformly as possible. Maximize the common attributes of the different parts of the system. The more similar they are, the easier they will be to understand. You will need less time to generate low-level designs for pieces of the system that are similar to other pieces you have worked on before. By basing one part of the system on techniques that worked successfully in another, you can code more quickly and with fewer mistakes.

Later, when you discover bugs, you can apply the things you learn fixing one bug to look for others. For instance, if all reporting routines are similar, a bug in one indicates there may be a similar bug in the others.

A single elegant design is also usually apparent to users. They need to learn fewer new concepts to master the different parts of the system. The user interface will also probably reflect the uniform design.

On the other hand, I have seen several mainframe systems that contained literally hundreds of data entry and reporting screens. Most were designed and built completely separately with very little common design. The screens were inconsistent and awkward. A user had to be an expert in each of the many screens to use them. Consequently, most of the users never made use of the vast majority of the screens. They were hard to maintain and hard to use, making them relatively expensive for the small return they gave.

Make the design uniform to reduce bugs, promote maintainability, and increase user productivity.

Avoid Creeping Featuritis

As a project progresses, developers are often tempted to add new features. An enhancement might be easy because of other code that has already been written for something else. A customer might see a prototype and decide, "Gee, if they can do this, they should also be able to . . ." Adding features like this is called "creeping featuritis" or "bells and whistles disease."

Do not add these extra features. Write them down and think about adding them to a future release, but do not include them in the release in which they are proposed. If the users cannot prove a feature is absolutely necessary, leave it for later. If a feature is not in the original product specification, it is probably unnecessary and the users can probably wait for it.

The original system was not designed to support these enhancements. Adding extra features during the coding phases of the project may cause subtle changes in the project and may force other parts of the system to change to accommodate. That causes bugs. In the best case, large parts of the system may need to be redesigned. In the worst case, the development team will try to force the new features into the old design. The result is more bugs and decreased maintainability.

Last-minute features can also add confusion to the user interface. What was once an elegant program becomes cluttered with confusing menus and options that most of the users never wanted in the first place. The fact that the original design did not include the new features is apparent to the users.

Besides, you probably have enough to do already. If you are so far ahead of schedule that you think you can add extra features, think again. Wait until the project is completed and tested. Then, if you still have extra time, you can consider adding new features. Or better still, you can get a head start on the next release.

Start with Minimal Functionality

Whenever you have the choice between doing just barely what is required and doing something extra, start simple. Do not provide features you do not need. Extra features are extra places to add bugs. If you later discover that you really do need a new capability, you can add it then. If you find that you do not need the extra feature, you will have saved a lot of time that you would have wasted writing, debugging, and testing the feature.

A closely related principle is to avoid unnecessary flexibility. Extra functionality creates additional work for you. Unnecessary flexibility makes it more difficult to detect bugs, even if it creates no extra work.

For example, suppose you are considering two designs for a subroutine that displays a list of five integers in a PictureBox. The first design takes five integer parameters and simply displays them. The second design takes a ParamArray as a parameter so you can pass it any number of arguments. This version would not take much extra work to implement, and in some ways might even be simpler. It creates a much larger number of test cases, however.

The first design requires that the routine take exactly five integer arguments. The second allows the routine to take fewer or more arguments. Because ParamArrays are variant arrays, the arguments can be strings, singles, or objects. They can even be other variant arrays containing more objects. Instead of testing simple variations using five integers, you need to consider all these strange cases.

If you just need the subroutine to display five integers, make it do just that. If you later find that you also need to display seven doubles, you can enhance it then or write a new routine for that purpose.

Avoid "Not Invented Here" Syndrome

Most programmers like to write code, particularly fast, clever, interesting code. This gives them a bias toward building instead of purchasing a product off the shelf. Building is almost always a mistake. Programming, debugging, and later maintaining even the simplest tools is very expensive. You will save time and money in the long run if you purchase tools already built by someone else.

Often a prepackaged tool does not provide the exact functionality you want. For example, a graphing control may not provide exactly the kind of three-dimensional plot you have in mind. Before you decide to build your own ActiveX graphing control, ask yourself if you really need that one kind of plot. Is it worth spending months of time programming, testing, and debugging the control? Is it worth adding another potential source of bugs to the project and increasing the project's chance of failure? Probably not.

The same principle applies to code you can obtain from another part of your company. If another group has already done the work for you, use what they have. Do not modify it unless absolutely necessary. Once you make changes, you take on the burden of writing, testing, and debugging your changes.

Avoid the Bleeding Edge

Most programmers like to work with cutting-edge tools and techniques. Unfortunately the "cutting edge" is very close to the "bleeding edge." New tools contain bugs. That may be fine if you are producing an experimental proof-of-concept application that aims to test available technology. It can be disastrous in a project that must produce a usable product in a reasonable amount of time.

If you use a brand new product that has not been thoroughly tested by other users, you may end up performing extended beta testing for the product. If you can, wait for the second or third release.

Use a less-functional but more-mature product instead. Isolate the product so you can replace it with a more advanced model later, but let someone else do the tool company's debugging for them. You probably have more than enough work to do building and debugging your own software without paying someone else so you can help debug theirs.

Avoid Third-Party Products

Keep your use of third-party products to a minimum. Suppose your project uses several different custom controls, a third-party database, a couple extra libraries, and special-purpose scanning hardware and software. The next time you upgrade your operating system, something is likely to break. Often it will take a lot of time just to figure out which product is at fault. Many vendors will waste a lot of your time pointing fingers at each other instead of fixing their products.

When you do know which product is to blame, you may need to install an upgrade. This will cost you extra money and may make some other product fail. That may cause you to upgrade the second product and that may cause something else to go wrong. It may take a long time and a lot of money before you again find a stable combination of upgraded products.

Another problem with third-party products is that they often do not provide support for old versions. Suppose you find a bug in a product two years after you buy it. The vendor refuses to repair the bug because that code is three revisions old, so you are forced to upgrade. The new version makes another product fail and you are stuck testing a bewildering combination of upgrades trying to find compatible versions of all of your third-party tools. Even worse, one of the products may no longer exist. Then your only choice may be an extensive rewrite of your program.

Avoid these hassles by minimizing the number of third-party products you use. Generic Visual Basic code is more likely to work with later versions of Visual Basic than any third-party product.

Also use the most generic tools possible. If a product is relatively simple, it is more likely to work when you must upgrade other products.

Note that the goal of avoiding third-party products contradicts the earlier goal of avoiding the "not invented here" syndrome. You need to carefully study the alternatives. Consider not only the risks of possible version conflict in the future, but also how hard it will be to build, debug, and maintain the code yourself.

Optimize Design, Not Code

Perform optimizations during high- and low-level design, not during coding. Changes to design can have a large impact. Changes during coding usually produce little improvement and make the code more complicated.

If you know part of the system will be slow, pick efficient algorithms for that part of the system. If a subroutine needs to manage a huge amount of data, design efficient data structures for it. These sorts of optimizations can make a meaningful difference in the system's performance.

On the other hand, adjusting a few lines of code while leaving the underlying design unchanged is unlikely to give a vast improvement in performance. It will probably make the design less clear so it will increase the chances of bugs appearing. Tweaking one or two lines of code may speed up part of the program by a few percent. Changing the underlying algorithm can make a difference of several orders of magnitude.

After the routine is written, if you find it has an unexpected performance problem, redesign it and rewrite it from scratch. Do not try to modify the code one line at a time. You will achieve a better result if you start over and do the job properly instead of trying to patch the existing routine.

This does not mean you need to be intentionally stupid. If there is an easy way to improve performance in a subroutine, do it. However, if the change makes the code less readable, more likely to contain or hide a bug, or harder to maintain in the future, stick with a straightforward implementation until you prove it is not fast enough.

Defer Optimization

Most programs spend more than 95 percent of their time running in less than 5 percent of the code. Effort spent optimizing the remaining 95 percent of the code is wasted. It would be much more productive to spend the same amount of energy optimizing the critical 5 percent.

During the design phase, if you are fairly certain you know where the critical 5 percent of the code lies, spend some extra time designing efficient algorithms for that code. Unfortunately, it is often hard to know in advance which code will be the most critical. In that case, defer optimization until you have the program running correctly. Then some simple tests will tell you where you should spend extra time optimizing. Chapter 15, "Profiling," discusses some ways to identify performance bottlenecks.

Deferring optimization saves the time you might have wasted improving the performance of routines that do not need it. It also avoids making those routines more complicated than necessary so they are easier to code, debug, and maintain. Finally, it is usually easier to optimize a program that runs correctly than it is to find the bugs in code that is fast but unnecessarily complex.

Indent Consistently

Consistent indentation makes code more readable. The following subroutine uses no indentation or blank space so it is relatively hard to read.

```
Private Sub DrawBall()
' Fix the part of the image that was covered.
BitBlt picCanvas.hDC, _
OldX - BallR, OldY - BallR, BallD, BallD, _
picHidden.hDC, OldX - BallR, OldY - BallR, SRCCOPY
OldX = CurX
OldY = CurY
```

```
' Redraw the ball.
picCanvas.Circle (CurX, CurY), BallR
' Update the display.
picCanvas.Refresh
End Sub
```

The following version is much easier to read because it uses indentation and blank lines.

```
Private Sub DrawBall()
    ' Fix the part of the image that was covered.
    BitBlt picCanvas.hDC, _
        OldX - BallR, OldY - BallR, BallD, BallD, _
        picHidden.hDC, OldX - BallR, OldY - BallR, SRCCOPY
    OldX = CurX
    OldY = CurY

    ' Redraw the ball.
    picCanvas.Circle (CurX, CurY), BallR

    ' Update the display.
    picCanvas.Refresh
End Sub
```

Indent code within If statements and loops to show the program's structure. Indent continued lines to show that they are part of the previous line. The third, fourth, and fifth lines in the previous code examples show the right and wrong way to continue long lines of code. In the first example, it takes some serious study to determine that these three lines are actually a single statement. In the second example, the line continuation is obvious.

Indent the code inside a subroutine because it executes at a different level of scope than code outside the routine. Some programmers indent variable declarations within a routine because they are at the same level of scope as the code within the routine.

```
Private Sub MySub()
    Dim name_counter As Integer
    Dim student_number As Integer

    For student_number = 1 To NumStudents
        :
    Next student_number
End Sub
```

I am accustomed to keeping variable declarations at the same level as the routine's declaration. This separates the variable declarations more firmly from the code.

```
Private Sub MySub()
Dim name_counter As Integer
Dim student_number As Integer

    For student_number = 1 To NumStudents
        :
    Next student_number
End Sub
```

Either method is fine as long as you are consistent.

Remove or Assert Assumptions

Either remove or assert every assumption. For example, a subroutine that sorts the items in an array can use LBound and UBound to determine the array's bounds. In that case, the routine may not need to make any assumptions about the array's bounds.

However, if the routine does make assumptions about the array's bounds, it should use Debug.Assert or Stop statements to verify that the bounds meet those assumptions. The most straightforward implementation of the heapsort algorithm, for example, assumes the lower array's lower bound is 1. A heapsort routine should use Debug.Assert or Stop to verify that assumption.

Note that in either case, the routine assumes that the array has been allocated. LBound and UBound generate errors if the array has not yet been allocated. The following code shows how a program can protect itself if in this situation.

```
Private Sub SortArray(arr() As Integer)
Dim l_bound As Integer
' (Other declarations omitted)
    :

    ' Verify that the array has been allocated.
    On Error GoTo UnAllocated
    l_bound = LBound(arr)
    On Error GoTo 0    ' Resume normal error handling.
    ' Verify assumptions.
        :

    ' Sort the array.
        :
    Exit Sub

UnAllocated:
    If Err.Number = 9 Then
        ' The array has not been allocated.
```

```
        Err.Raise err_UNALLOCATED_ARRAY, _
            "MyProgram.MapValueToArray", _
            "Parameter ""arr"" has not been allocated with ReDim"
    Else
        ' Reraise the unknown error.
        Err.Raise Err.Number, _
            Err.Source, Err.Description, _
            Err.HelpFile, Err.HelpContext
    End If
End Sub
```

Catch Invalid Situations

When a routine encounters a situation that should never arise, it should let someone know about it. For example, a subroutine that expects a variant parameter to contain a filename should never receive a parameter that contains an array of integers. That situation never makes sense and there is no reasonable way the routine can figure out what to do.

During the design phase, the routine can use Debug.Assert or Stop to make the program stop when it encounters an invalid situation. In a final program in which the debugging code has been removed, the routine should raise an error using the Err.Raise statement. While the calling routine probably cannot handle the error, it can try to continue running.

In any case, the routine should always tell someone about the error. It should not quietly ignore the error and continue.

Raise Errors for Exceptions

If a routine encounters an exceptional condition, it should raise an error. This forces the calling routine to take exceptional action using an error handler. If a routine that saves data into a file cannot open the file, that is an important and exceptional condition. It should force the calling routine to take action by raising an error.

During normal situations, if a routine must return information to the calling routine, it should return the information through a parameter passed ByRef or through its return value if it is a function. A routine should not raise an error under normal circumstances.

Consider a routine that searches a phone directory for a specific name. Depending on the user's input, this routine may fail to find the specified person. Failing to find a person is a normal situation so the routine should not raise an error. It should return a status code indicating whether it succeeded or failed. The calling routine must check the status code to see whether it found the person it wanted.

Note that Microsoft's Common Dialog Control violates this guideline. If a program sets the control's CancelError property to True, the control raises an error when the user cancels a file selection operation. It would be better if the control provided a Canceled property that indicated whether the user canceled the operation.

Use Enums for Status Codes

Use enumerated types or constants to define status codes. Do not use True, False, or magic numbers. The following statement uses a function named Open-DataFile. It is not clear from the code whether OpenDataFile returns True when it is successful or when it fails.

```
If OpenDataFile(file_name) Then ...
```

In the following version it is obvious that the If statement executes its code when the function fails.

```
Enum ofStatus
    ofOpenFailed
    ofOpenOk
End Enum
        :
    If OpenDataFile(file_name) = ofOpenFailed Then ...
```

Using Enums for status values not only makes the code more obvious, it also makes creating new status codes easier. Suppose a function returns True to indicate success and False to indicate failure. Now suppose you later discover that the function can fail in more than one way and the calling routine needs to know how it failed. Making the function accommodate this change is difficult. If the function returns enumerated status codes instead of True and False, adding a new status code is easy.

Return the Worst Data Possible for Errors

When a routine encounters an error and returns an error status code, it should return the worst possible value. This encourages the calling routine to check the status code before it uses the return values.

For example, suppose a routine searches an array for a book's title and returns the book's index in the array. If it cannot find a book, the routine should return an error status code. For instance, it could set its return value to –32,767. If the programmer who wrote the calling function does not check the status code and tries to use this return value, the program will probably crash and the error will be obvious. On the other hand, if the search routine returns the value 0, the calling routine might be able to continue, depending on the lower bound of the array. This bug would be much harder to find.

Note that Visual Basic default values look quite sensible. For example, the default value for an uninitialized integer is 0. If a routine does not take specific action to return unreasonable values like –32,767, the result may look useable to the calling routine.

Don't Use One Input for Multiple Purposes

Do not use the same input variable for multiple purposes. For example, you could write a routine that draws lines, circles, and ellipses. The first parameter indicates the type of shape. For circles, the next four parameters are the coordinates of the line's end points. For circles, the next three parameters give the coordinates of the circle's center and its radius. For ellipses, the next four parameters give the ellipse's minimum and maximum X and Y values.

These parameters mean different things under different circumstances and that makes them confusing. Parameters should not have different meanings in different parts of the routine.

One solution is to redefine the parameters so they have consistent meanings. In this case, the four parameters after the first could specify the minimum and maximum X and Y values for the shape no matter which shape is being drawn.

Another solution is to create separate parameters for each shape. To draw a line, for example, the calling routine would omit the other parameters.

Perhaps the best solution is to break this routine into three separate routines, one for each shape. The combined routine really performs three very different functions and there is little profit in making it one subroutine anyway.

Visual Basic's Line statement is a good example of a routine asked to do too much. The Line statement can draw either a line or a rectangle depending on whether the third parameter contains a B. Conceptually, drawing a line and drawing a rectangle are not similar tasks. The only thing they have in common is that they can be specified using the coordinates of two points. Because they are conceptually different, these tasks should be performed by separate routines.

Don't Use One Output for Multiple Purposes

Do not use the same output variable for multiple purposes. You could write a ControlValue function that returns a variant containing a ScrollBar's numeric value if the parameter is a ScrollBar, a TextBox's string value if the parameter is a TextBox, a RadioButton's Boolean state if the parameter is a RadioButton, and so forth.

Resist the temptation. This function would be very confusing to use because it returns values that are conceptually very different.

Keep Separate Tasks Separate

Make each routine perform just one conceptual task. If it performs more than one task, using it can be confusing. Visual Basic's Circle method is a good example. It allows you to draw both circles and ellipses.

To draw a circle, the program passes the Circle method the coordinates of the circle's center and its radius. That is a reasonable way to specify a circle and makes perfect sense.

To draw an ellipse, you add another parameter containing the ellipse's aspect ratio. That is remarkably counterintuitive. Probably very few programmers think of drawing ellipses using the center of the ellipse, a radius, and an aspect ratio.

The radius and aspect ratio parameters do not even always specify the same values. If the aspect ratio is greater than 1.0, the radius gives the ellipse's height and the width is the radius divided by the aspect ratio. If the aspect ratio is less than 1.0, the radius gives the ellipse's width and the height is the radius times the aspect ratio.

This ridiculous situation arises because the developers of Visual Basic were thinking of circles and ellipses as two different kinds of objects. The center and radius parameters make drawing circles intuitive. The aspect ratio parameter is tacked on to make the routine draw ellipses as well.

The developers could have redefined the routine's functionality so it performed one conceptual task. For example, they could have built a single Ellipse routine to draw ellipses. It could take as parameters the ellipse's minimum and maximum X and Y coordinates. In fact, this is the way the API Ellipse function works. Because a circle is just a special kind of ellipse, this routine draws circles without any extra confusion. If the difference in the X coordinates is the same as the difference in the Y coordinates, the result is a circle.

Alternatively, the Ellipse routine could take as parameters the coordinates of the ellipse's center and its width and height. In this case, if the width and height are the same, the result is a circle.

Finally, this confusion could have been completely avoided by using separate Circle and Ellipse routines.

Do not cause similar confusion in your programs. Make each routine perform a single conceptual task. If a routine performs several functions, break it into two or more separate routines that each performs a single task.

Examine Decisions Closely

Whenever a program makes a choice, it can make the wrong choice. Decisions are more prone to errors than simple calculations, so you should study decisions carefully.

An If statement clearly makes a decision. Select statements are structurally very similar to long If Then Else statements, so they also make decisions.

Loops make decisions in less obvious ways. Every time a For or Do loop executes, Visual Basic checks the loop's ending condition to see if the loop should stop. The logic behind these decisions can be confusing in a Do While loop where the exit condition is complicated.

Exit statements represent the decision to break out of a loop or routine, so you should consider them carefully. Finally, On Error statements set the stage for a later decision to go to a particular error handler when an error occurs.

Carefully examine all of these decision points so you are sure they make sense.

Use FreeFile

Use FreeFile to obtain an unused file number before you open a file. It is remarkable how many Visual Basic programmers simply use the number 1 for all of their file operations. If you use a constant instead of FreeFile and you ever integrate your code with another routine that uses the same file number, you may encounter strange bugs.

Assigning the file number to a variable also lets you use a meaningful name to represent the file. The following code opens a data file and reads the number of items stored in the file. It then uses the ReadItem subroutine to read the items from the file. If ReadItem also uses FreeFile to find unused file numbers, it can open other files if it needs to without interfering with this routine.

```
Dim input_file As Integer
Dim num_items As Integer
Dim item As Integer

    ' Open the data file.
    input_file = FreeFile
    Open input_file_name For Input As input_file

    ' Read the number of items.
    Input #input_file, num_items

    ' Read the items.
    For i = 1 To num_items
        ' Use the ReadItem routine to read the next
        ' item from the file.
        ReadItem input_file
    Next i

    ' Close the data file.
    Close input_file
```

Use ByVal

Use ByVal whenever possible. If a routine's parameter is declared ByVal, any changes made by the routine do not return to the calling routine. This reduces the chances that the routine will make accidental changes that will effect the caller.

If changes to a parameter must be visible to the calling routine, the routine should declare the parameter ByRef. This emphasizes the fact that the parameter will be modified so the programmer writing the calling routine can easily see that changes will return to the calling routine.

```
Private Sub CallBoth()
Dim X As Integer

    X = 0
    ' X is now 0.

    PassedByVal X
    ' X is still 0.

    PassedByRef X
    ' X is now 2.
End Sub

' ByVal so changes do not return to the caller.
```

```
Private Sub PassedByVal(ByVal X as Integer)
    X = 1
End Sub


' ByRef so changes return to the caller.
Private Sub PassedByRef(ByRef X as Integer)
    X = 2
End Sub
```

If you change a parameter from ByVal to ByRef, carefully examine the code to see if the value is changed during the routine. If so, making the parameter ByRef will probably create bugs. You can avoid this by using a temporary variable in place of the original variable during calculations.

If you change a parameter from ByRef to ByVal, carefully examine all calling routines. If they expect the parameter's value to change and it does not, the result is probably a bug.

Separate Debug and Nondebug Code

Nondebug code should not use debug variables, and vice versa. If these types of code share variables, the program may behave differently during runtime and design time. Variables that exist in the debugging environment may have different values or may not even exist in the final compiled program.

In the following code, the variable X is defined only when the DEBUG_MODE compiler constant is True. If the final version of the program sets DEBUG_MODE to False, Visual Basic will refuse to compile the program because X is undefined.

```
Private Sub MySub()
#If DEBUG_MODE Then
    Dim X As Integer
#End If

Dim i As Integer

    X = 1
    For i = 1 To 10
        X = X * i
    Next i
End Sub
```

The following code is even trickier. When DEBUG_MODE is False, the subroutine does not create a local variable named X. Because there is another variable named X at the module global scope, the routine uses that variable instead. The program will compile and run, but it will behave differently than it would if DEBUG_MODE was True.

```
Private X As Integer

Private Sub MySub()
#If DEBUG_MODE Then
    Dim X As Integer
#End If

Dim i As Integer

    X = 1
    For i = 1 To 10
        X = X * i
    Next i
End Sub
```

Debug code can also cause problems if it modifies nondebug variables. The following code compiles and runs but produces different results in debug and nondebug versions.

```
Private Sub MySub()
Dim i As Integer
Dim X As Integer

    X = 1
    For i = 1 To 10
        X = X * i

        #If DEBUG_MODE Then
            X = X + 1
        #End If
    Next i
End Sub
```

This example is somewhat contrived, but this problem can be subtle. For example, if the debugging code calls a subroutine, it may not be immediately apparent whether the routine modifies its parameters. If it does, the program's debug and nondebug versions may be quite different.

Avoid all these issues by keep debug and nondebug code as separate as possible.

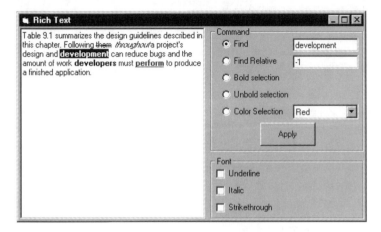

Figure 9.1   Program Bad9 is a crude text editor.

Self-Test

Program Bad9 violates some of the guidelines presented in this chapter. The program, shown in Figure 9.1, is a rather crude text editor. Select text in the text box. Then select a command in the command area and click the Apply button to perform the command. Click on checkboxes to change the selected text's font styles.

Program Bad9 is awkward to use and its code is difficult to understand. Both of these problems are caused mainly by the fact that the program violates several of the guidelines presented in this chapter. The program's bad code follows. Appendix A, "Self-Test Solutions," contains a greatly improved version of the program.

```
Option Explicit

Private Const cmd_FIND = 0
Private Const cmd_FIND_RELATIVE = 1
Private Const cmd_BOLD = 2
Private Const cmd_UNBOLD = 3
Private Const cmd_COLOR = 4

Private Const chk_UNDERLINE = 0
Private Const chk_ITALIC = 1
Private Const chk_STRIKETHROUGH = 2

' True when the program is changing display values.
Private SettingValues As Boolean
```

```vb
' Apply the selected command.
Private Sub cmdApply_Click()
    If optCommand(cmd_FIND) Then
        ' Find and select the indicated text.
        FindText
    ElseIf optCommand(cmd_FIND_RELATIVE) Then
        ' Find and select the indicated text.
        FindTextRelative
    ElseIf optCommand(cmd_BOLD) Then
        ' Color the selection bold.
        ColorSelection "Bold"
    ElseIf optCommand(cmd_UNBOLD) Then
        ' Unbold the selection.
        rchMainText.SelBold = False
    ElseIf optCommand(cmd_COLOR) Then
        ' Color the selection.
        ColorSelection cboSelColor.Text
    End If

    rchMainText.SetFocus
End Sub

' Find and select the indicated text.
Private Sub FindText()
Dim txt As String
Dim pos As Integer

    txt = rchMainText.Text
    pos = InStr(txt, txtFindText.Text)
    If pos = 0 Then
        Beep
    Else
        rchMainText.SelStart = pos - 1
        rchMainText.SelLength = Len(txtFindText.Text)
    End If
End Sub

' Find and select the indicated text skipping the
' indicated number of copies.
Private Sub FindTextRelative()
Dim txt As String
Dim target As String
Dim targetlen As Integer
Dim pos As Integer
Dim skip As Integer
Dim trials As Integer

    txt = rchMainText.Text
    target = txtFindText.Text
    skip = CInt(txtSkip.Text)
```

```
    ' If skip >= 0, search forward from here.
    If skip >= 0 Then
        pos = rchMainText.SelStart + 1
        For trials = 0 To skip
            pos = InStr(pos + 1, txt, target)
            If pos = 0 Then Exit For
        Next trials
        If pos = 0 Then
            Beep
        Else
            rchMainText.SelStart = pos - 1
            rchMainText.SelLength = Len(txtFindText.Text)
        End If
    Else
        ' Skip < 0. Search backwards.
        targetlen = Len(target)
        trials = 0
        skip = -skip
        For pos = rchMainText.SelStart To 1 Step -1
            If Mid$(txt, pos, targetlen) = target Then
                trials = trials + 1
                If trials >= skip Then Exit For
            End If
        Next pos

        If pos <= 0 Then
            ' We didn't find it.
            Beep
        Else
            rchMainText.SelStart = pos - 1
            rchMainText.SelLength = targetlen
        End If
    End If
End Sub


' Color the selected text.
Private Sub ColorSelection(color As String)
    Select Case color
        Case "Red"
            rchMainText.SelColor = vbRed
        Case "Green"
            rchMainText.SelColor = vbGreen
        Case "Blue"
            rchMainText.SelColor = vbBlue
        Case "Black"
            rchMainText.SelColor = vbBlack
        Case "Bold"
            rchMainText.SelBold = True
    End Select
End Sub
```

```
' Switch the value of the font's property.
Private Sub chkFontOption_Click(Index As Integer)
Dim value As Integer

    ' Ignore the event if the program is making the change.
    If SettingValues Then Exit Sub

    value = (chkFontOption(Index).value = vbChecked)
    Select Case Index
        Case chk_UNDERLINE
            rchMainText.SelUnderline = value
        Case chk_ITALIC
            rchMainText.SelItalic = value
        Case chk_STRIKETHROUGH
            rchMainText.SelStrikeThru = value
    End Select


    rchMainText.SetFocus
End Sub


' Update the check boxes.
Private Sub rchMainText_SelChange()
    ' Do not trigger a click event.
    SettingValues = True

    ' Check the SelUnderline property.
    Select Case rchMainText.SelUnderline
        Case True
            chkFontOption(chk_UNDERLINE).value = vbChecked
        Case False
            chkFontOption(chk_UNDERLINE).value = vbUnchecked
        Case Else ' More than one value.
            chkFontOption(chk_UNDERLINE).value = vbGrayed
    End Select

    ' Check the SelItalic property.
    Select Case rchMainText.SelItalic
        Case True
            chkFontOption(chk_ITALIC).value = vbChecked
        Case False
            chkFontOption(chk_ITALIC).value = vbUnchecked
        Case Else ' More than one value.
            chkFontOption(chk_ITALIC).value = vbGrayed
    End Select

    ' Check the SelStrikeThru property.
    Select Case rchMainText.SelStrikeThru
        Case True
            chkFontOption(chk_STRIKETHROUGH).value = vbChecked
        Case False
            chkFontOption(chk_STRIKETHROUGH).value = vbUnchecked
```

```
        Case Else ' More than one value.
            chkFontOption(chk_STRIKETHROUGH).value = vbGrayed
    End Select

    SettingValues = False
End Sub
```

Summary

The following Bug Stoppers summarize the design guidelines described in this chapter. Following them throughout a project's design and development can reduce bugs and the amount of work you must perform to produce a finished application.

BUG STOPPERS: Development

Design for uniformity, simplicity, and elegance.

Avoid creeping featuritis and bells and whistles disease.

Start with minimal functionality.

Avoid the not invented here syndrome.

Avoid the bleeding edge.

Avoid third-party products.

Optimize design, not small pieces of code.

Defer optimization.

Indent consistently.

Remove or assert assumptions.

Assert or Stop for invalid situations.

Raise errors for valid but exceptional situations.

Use Enums for status codes.

Return the worst data possible for errors.

Don't use one input variable for multiple purposes.

Don't use one output variable for multiple purposes.

Keep separate tasks separate.

Examine decision points closely.

Use FreeFile to obtain unused file numbers.

Use ByVal whenever possible to prevent confusing side effects.

Separate debug and nondebug code.

CHAPTER 10

Encapsulation

Encapsulation is the process of wrapping up a set of features or behavior in a neat package to hide complexity from other parts of a program. For example, an Employee class might represent employee objects. The class might contain elaborate data structures and complicated subroutines. The rest of the program, however, can treat employee objects in a fairly simple way.

Many object-oriented programmers think of encapsulation as a new idea that applies only to classes and objects. Actually, many other programming constructs have provided encapsulation for decades.

This chapter explains some of the ways you can encapsulate data and behavior in a program to reduce the program's complexity. Reduced complexity makes the program easier to implement, debug, and maintain over time.

Hide Internals

Never write a routine that relies on the internals of another routine or class. If a routine relies on the way another routine works, modifying the second may break the first. If you need to fix a bug in one, you may introduce a new bug in the other.

Keeping track of the way different classes and routines interact with each other can be difficult. Minimize the interactions by keeping the classes and routines as tightly encapsulated as possible. They should not expose anything outside their own code unless absolutely necessary.

Encapsulate with Classes

Use classes to encapsulate functionality, and hide implementation details inside the class. Public routines and property procedures let the rest of the program access the features of the class without knowing the details of how the class works internally. All of the details of how the class stores and manipulates its data should be kept private within the class.

For instance, suppose an EmployeeList class stores a list of employees in an array. It provides a FindEmployee routine that takes an employee's name as a parameter and returns the employee's index in the array. The main program can then access the array to learn more about the employee.

This class provides weak encapsulation. The main program knows that the employee information is stored in an array and it can directly access the array. As the program grows, you may decide it would be more efficient to store the employee information in a tree-data structure. Making this change would require you to rewrite all the parts of the program that previously accessed the data using the array.

Now consider a different version of the class. It provides a routine that locates an employee and returns a user-defined data type holding all of the information about that employee. This class provides better encapsulation for the employee list. The main program does not know how the list is stored or accessed, and it does not access any of the class data structures directly. If you change the way this class stores its information, you will not need to change the rest of the program.

Count Object Creation and Destruction

Count the objects created and destroyed by a program by placing code in Class_Initialize and Class_Terminate event handlers. Before the program ends, check the object counts. If a count is not 0, some object was created that was not destroyed. This could indicate a bug or a memory leak.

The following code shows a Cell class. Each Cell object includes a reference to another Cell. The variable NumCells is declared publicly in a .BAS module and is used to count Cell object creation and destruction.

```
' The next cell in the cell's linked list.
Public NextCell As Cell

Private Sub Class_Initialize()
    NumCells = NumCells + 1
End Sub

Private Sub Class_Terminate()
    NumCells = NumCells - 1
End Sub
```

Visual Basic performs automatic reference counting. When you create an object, Visual Basic automatically keeps track of the number of variables referencing that object. If the reference count ever reaches 0, the system knows that the program can no longer access the object, so Visual Basic automatically destroys it.

Suppose the program creates a Cell object and sets its NextCell pointer to itself.

```
Dim new_cell As New Cell

    Set new_cell.NextCell = new_cell
    Set new_cell = Nothing
```

Because this object contains a reference to itself, its reference count is not 0, even after the variable new_cell is set to Nothing. The Cell object that new_cell used to point to still points to itself, so its reference count is 1 and Visual Basic cannot destroy it. This is one of the few ways you can create a memory leak using Visual Basic code. If the program executes this code many times, it may use up a lot of memory. Eventually, the program may use up all of the available memory and crash.

However, if you check the value of NumCells before the program ends, you will find there are cells that were created but never destroyed. Once you know the problem exists, you can start hunting for the cells. Instead of having an enigmatic crash, you have a simple bug.

This is a trivial example and is unlikely to happen in a real program. More complex data structures such as balanced trees, sparse arrays, and networks are much more likely to cause this sort of problem.

I often use this object-counting technique to verify that complex data structures have been properly destroyed. Occasionally, I have been surprised to find that a data structure that I thought was properly cleaned up had not been completely destroyed. That let me find the bug quickly and painlessly.

Initialize Objects

Classes provide an Initialize event that fires when an object is created. Initialize the object's state in the Initialize event handler if possible. That way, you can never forget to perform the initialization.

Unfortunately, the Initialize event handler does not take parameters so it can only perform initialization that is the same for every object in the class. If you need to perform object-specific initialization, create a public InitializeObject routine to do so. Name the initialization routine for every class InitializeObject so it is obvious what routine to call. The program should use InitializeObject to initialize each object immediately after creating it.

If you need this kind of initialization, give the class a private Boolean variable Initialized. The InitializeObject routine should set this value to True. All other public routines and property procedures should assert that the control has been initialized before they provide access to the object as shown in the following code.

```
Private Initialized As Boolean
Private TreeRoot As Boolean
    :
' Save the tree's root for later use.
Public Sub InitializeObject(tree_root As TreeNode)
    Set TreeRoot = tree_root

    Initialized = True
End Sub

' Draw this node and those under it.
Public Sub DrawSubTree()
    ' Make sure we're initialized.
    Debug.Assert Initialized
        :
End Sub
```

If the program tries to use an object before it is properly initialized, the program's Assert statement makes the bug immediately obvious.

Use Property Procedures

Use property procedures instead of public variables to expose values outside a form, class, or module. Property procedures give you more control over the value. If you later need to change the way the value is stored, you can do so without modifying the outside program. Property procedures also allow you to create read-only values.

For example, suppose a dispatch program uses a Map class to store map information. The Distance property get procedure shown in the following code returns the shortest distance between two points. Because there is no corresponding property let procedure, the application can read this value but cannot change it.

```
' The number of locations.
Private mNumLocations As Integer

' Private distance array. Dimensioned
'     (1 To mNumLocations, 1 To mNumLocations)
Private mDistance() As Single

' Other declarations.
   :
' Return the distance between two locations.
Property Get Distance(ByVal from_point As Integer, _
    ByVal to_point As Integer)

    Distance = mDistance(from_point, to_point)
End Property
```

Now suppose the program grows until the map is too large to store all the distance information in an array. The map of a moderately large city might contain 10,000 locations. Storing all the distances between pairs of locations in an array would require 10,000 * 10,000 = 100 million entries taking up 400MB of memory.

In that case, you might rewrite the Distance property get procedure so it calculates the distance between two points whenever it is needed instead of storing the distances in an array. As long as the procedure's parameters and return value remain unchanged, the rest of the program will continue to work without changes.

Property procedures also provide an important debugging opportunity. Suppose you know the value ProgramCount is being set to an invalid value somewhere in a complicated piece of code. If ProgramCount is a public variable, you must search out every place it is set and look for the invalid change. If ProgramCount is a property procedure, you can simply set a break point inside the procedure. Then when you run the program in the debugger, you can see exactly where the value is changed. You can use the debugger's call stack command to see which routine is modifying the value and where.

Many programmers overlook the fact that you can create property procedures in a .BAS module. Property procedures in .BAS modules give you all the advantages of property procedures in classes and forms, including better encapsulation and the equivalent of read-only public variables.

Use Implements

Visual Basic 5 introduced the Implements keyword. You can use Implements to make the code more manageable and to improve performance in Visual Basic 5 and 6.

Suppose your program needs to use more than one class that provides the same features. For example, the Car and Truck classes might both provide Location, Speed, Mileage, and FuelCapacity property procedures. In addition, they would also provide features that are specific to their different kinds of objects. In cases such as this, you can define an interface class to define the features shared by the Car and Truck classes.

Create a new Vehicle class. In this class, define the features that Car and Truck should share. For this example, create public variables named Location, Speed, Mileage, and FuelCapacity.

Next, create a new Car class. After the class module's Option Explicit statement, add the statement Implements Vehicle. This statement makes Visual Basic create a new Vehicle symbol in the Car class. It also makes Visual Basic build property procedure stubs for the public variables defined in the Vehicle class. If you open the class in the Visual Basic editor, you will find the name Vehicle in the object box in the upper left of the edit window. The procedures box lists the public symbols defined by the Vehicle class. Figure 10.1 shows the Visual Basic editor displaying an empty Vehicle object's Mileage property get procedure.

You still need to create the procedures defined by the Vehicle class yourself, but using Implements has several advantages. First, it standardizes the interface defined by the Vehicle class. You do not need to worry about the Car providing

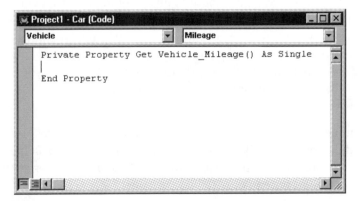

Figure 10.1 The Vehicle_Mileage property procedure defined by the Vehicle class.

Speed as an integer and the Truck class providing it as a single. Speed is defined for both classes by the Vehicle class so they must be the same.

Implements also allows the program to treat Car and Truck objects polymorphically. This means that they can be used interchangeably under some circumstances.

Suppose the MakeTrip subroutine takes as a parameter either a Car or Truck object and then simulates a trip by that object. The program can pass this routine either a Car or a Truck object. As long as the routine uses only properties and methods that are actually implemented by the object, it does not need to know what kind of object it is. The following code shows how this routine might be defined.

```
Public Sub MakeTrip(veh As Object)
    ' Do whatever is needed for the trip.
        :
End Sub
```

Unfortunately, the program could also pass this routine any other kind of object including a Form or a control. If the program uses the Implements keyword to make Car and Truck implement the Vehicle interface, you can declare the parameter to be of type Vehicle instead of type Object. That lets Visual Basic verify that the object passed to the routine actually implements the Vehicle interface. It can provide better error checking and it allows Visual Basic to manage the object more efficiently.

```
Public Sub MakeTrip(veh As Vehicle)
    ' Do whatever is needed for the trip.
        :
End Sub
```

Use the Implements keyword to standardize the features implemented by similar classes. Implements keeps the classes synchronized, allows Visual Basic to perform better error checking, and gives better performance.

Encapsulate with Types

In some ways, user-defined types (UDTs) are similar to classes without routines. A UDT is a simple data structure that groups related pieces of data together in a convenient package. For example, the following code shows part of the definition of an Employee data structure.

```
Type Employee
    empLastName As String
    empFirstName As String
```

```
        empSalary As Single
        empId As Integer
        empSSN As String * 11
        empHomePhone As String * 12
        empOfficePhone As String * 12
           :
    End Type
```

User-defined types encapsulate the data needed to represent a complex object. They allow the program to manipulate data entities easily while ignoring any unnecessary details. For example, a payroll application might use the previously defined Employee type. Different payroll routines could pass an employee's data around without worrying about the details of what was inside. When a routine needed some data, it would be readily available. For instance, the subroutine that actually generates checks could examine the data structure's name, address, Social Security number, and other fields as necessary.

Use UDTs to hide complexity from the program while keeping all of the data readily available for those routines that need it.

Encapsulate with Controls

ActiveX controls are a lot like classes. Both provide public methods, events, and property procedures to interact with the outside program. In many ways, a class is simply a control with no visible interface.

Even the simplest Visual Basic program uses controls, so every Visual Basic programmer is familiar with them. While some programmers may not have mastered classes and object-oriented programming, they all know how to use controls. Take advantage of that preexisting experience by building ActiveX controls to encapsulate behavior.

Controls have the advantage that you can distribute them in binary form. That means you can sometimes upgrade a control without recompiling an application. As long as you do not change the control's public interface, you can upgrade it quickly and easily without rebuilding the rest of the application.

You can also allow other developers to use only the compiled OCX version of the control. That hides more detail from them so they are less likely to write code that relies on the control's internals. If they cannot see the source code, they cannot easily tie their code to the control's internal idiosyncrasies.

Encapsulate with Modules

Many programmers overlook the fact that they can use modules to encapsulate data and functionality. A module can contain private variables, data structures, and routines that it needs but that are not needed by other parts of the program. To maximize encapsulation, as many of the module's details as possible should be private.

For example, a work assignment program might keep a list of items sorted in priority order. The CreateJob subroutine creates a new job and adds it to the list. Subroutine GetNextJob fills in a user-defined data structure to describe the next job that must be worked.

These subroutines could be placed inside a module. The list of jobs is stored using variables private to that module. All the rest of the program sees are the CreateJob and GetNextJob subroutines. The complexity of the job list is hidden from the main program. The jobs could be stored in an array, linked list, priority queue, tree, or some other data structure.

Encapsulating the details of the job list within the module makes it easier to think about the rest of the program. While you concentrate on other parts of the code, you can ignore the job list internals.

Encapsulating the job list also prevents the rest of the program from relying on the particular implementation of the list's internals. If you later find a bug in the way the list is stored, you can fix it without breaking the rest of the program.

Group related routines in the same module so they are easy to find. Do not include unrelated routines in a module. This decreases the encapsulation provided by the module because the unrelated routine can access the module's private data. One module should contain all of the routines related to one topic and nothing more.

Encapsulate with Subroutines

If you use the same code more than once, place it in a subroutine. By calling the routine, you can reuse the code without having to write several copies. A less-obvious benefit of subroutines is that you only need to debug, test, and maintain one copy of the code. If duplicate code is replaced with a subroutine, you do not need to worry about keeping the separate copies synchronized when you make changes.

One opportunity for reducing code duplication that is often overlooked is in form management code. If you perform the same task for many forms, write a subroutine in a .BAS module to do it. Make the routine take the form it should manipulate as a parameter. For example, the following routines save and restore a form's size and position in the system registry.

```
' Save the form's size and position.
Public Sub SaveFormPosition(frm As Form)
    SaveSetting "MyProgram", "Layout", frm.Name & " Left", frm.Left
    SaveSetting "MyProgram", "Layout", frm.Name & " Top", frm.Top
    SaveSetting "MyProgram", "Layout", frm.Name & " Width", frm.Width
    SaveSetting "MyProgram", "Layout", frm.Name & " Height", frm.Height
End Sub


' Reload the form's size and position.
Public Sub LoadFormPosition(frm As Form)
Dim l As Single
Dim t As Single
Dim w As Single
Dim h As Single

    ' Get the settings.
    l = GetSetting("MyProgram", "Layout", frm.Name & " Left", _
        Format$(frm.Left))
    t = GetSetting("MyProgram", "Layout", frm.Name & " Top", _
        Format$(frm.Top))
    w = GetSetting("MyProgram", "Layout", frm.Name & " Width", _
        Format$(frm.Width))
    h = GetSetting("MyProgram", "Layout", frm.Name & " Height", _
        Format$(frm.Height))

    ' Size and position the form.
    frm.Move l, t, w, h
End Sub
```

Instead of placing code to save and load these values in each form, you can make the forms invoke these subroutines. A form could use these routines to set and save its size and position when it is loaded and unloaded, as shown in the following code:

```
Private Sub Form_Load()
    LoadFormPosition Me
End Sub


Private Sub Form_Unload(Cancel As Integer)
    SaveFormPosition Me
End Sub
```

Encapsulate Errors

When a routine fails during design, it should stop to alert developers to the problem so they can fix it. In the final compiled version, the program must continue running even if an unexpected error occurs. This can be very difficult for some programs. If an operation completes only partially, it may leave data in an ambiguous state from which it is hard to continue.

To minimize this kind of problem, routines should encapsulate their errors. They should hide the effects of their errors from calling routines. When a routine fails, it should undo any changes it has made to global data structures. Then the calling routine can continue operating without needing to know how much the routine accomplished before it failed.

One common example occurs during file input. If the input routine fails, it must be sure to properly close the file. The following code shows how a routine can guard against errors and ensure that the input file is closed no matter when the error is encountered.

```
Private Sub LoadData(ByVal filename As String)
Dim fnum As Integer

    ' If we fail now, the file is closed.
    On Error GoTo FileOpenError
    fnum = FreeFile
    Open filename For Input As fnum

    ' If we fail now, the file is open.
    On Error GoTo FileReadError

    ' Read the data from the file.
        :

    ' Close the file.
    Close fnum

    ' If we fail now, the file is closed.
    On Error GoTo FileClosedError

    ' Do any other processing that is necessary.
        :
    Exit Sub

FileOpenError:
    ' Error opening the file. It is closed.
    MsgBox "Error" & Str$(Err.Number) & _
        " opening file " & filename & "." & _
```

```
            vbCrLf & Err.Description
        Exit Sub

    FileReadError:
        ' Error reading from the file. It is open.
        MsgBox "Error" & Str$(Err.Number) & _
            " reading file " & filename & "." & _
            vbCrLf & Err.Description

        ' Close the file.
        Close fnum
        Exit Sub

    FileClosedError:
        ' Error after the file is closed.
        MsgBox "Error" & Str$(Err.Number) & _
            " processing data from file " & filename & "." & _
            vbCrLf & Err.Description
        Exit Sub
    End Sub
```

Chapter 12, "Error Handling," and Chapter 13, "Standard Error Handlers," explain error handling and subroutine cleanup in greater detail.

Encapsulate with Variables

A program can use variables to simplify its code. For example, if you need to use the results of a complex expression several times, calculate the expression once and save the result in a variable. Then examine the variable several times instead of reevaluating the expression each time.

The following code uses the same complex expression in two places.

```
If ((PlayerNumber Mod 2) = 1) And (PlayerTeam = MovingTeam) Then
    ' Do something.
        :
End If
    :
If ((PlayerNumber Mod 2) = 1) And (PlayerTeam = MovingTeam) Then
    ' Do something else.
        :
End If
    :
```

The following code does the same thing without repeating the complex expression.

```
Dim correct_player As Boolean

correct_player = _
    ((PlayerNumber Mod 2) = 1) And (PlayerTeam = MovingTeam)

If correct_player Then
    ' Do something.
        :
End If
    :
If correct_player Then
    ' Do something else.
        :
End If
    :
```

This code has several advantages. It is easier to read. Assigning the expression to a well-named variable clarifies the expression's purpose. It makes the If statements easier to read and understand. It also keeps the expression in one place. If the way the program calculates the expression changes, you do not need to worry about keeping multiple copies of the expression synchronized. In many cases, evaluating the expression once also makes the code run faster.

The only reason you should repeat an expression is if some value in the expression may have changed. In the previous example, if PlayerNumber changes between the If statements, the routine must reevaluate the expression.

Save Property Values

A common trick for optimizing code is to save property values in temporary variables. Accessing a variable is much faster than accessing a property. If a routine uses the property value many times, it can use a temporary variable to save time. The following example shows how a subroutine can work with a string variable instead of repeatedly accessing a text property value.

```
Dim car_name As String

car_name = txtCarName.Text
' Work with car_name instead of txtCarName.Text.
    :
```

Not only does this technique save time, it also makes the code easier to read. Long sequences of object references can be particularly cumbersome. The following code uses a variable to refer to an inconveniently long object expression.

```
Dim font_size As Single

    font_size = frmPreview.picPrintPreview.Font.Size
    ' Work with font_size instead of the long expression.
        :
```

Use variables to simplify complex expressions and long sequences of object references.

Use With

Use With statements to simplify code that uses long sequences of object references. The following code uses a With statement so it does not need to use the expression TheGame.Player(1).txtPlayerName several times.

```
With TheGame.Player(1).txtPlayerName
    If .Text = "" Then
        .Text = "REQUIRED"
        .Font.Bold = True
    Else
        .Font.Bold = False
    End If
End With
```

Alternatively, you could use a variable to simplify the expression as explained in the previous section.

Don't Use Nested Withs

Nested With statements can be confusing. As the nested statements begin and end, the reader must remember which statement is in effect. The following code is legal but confusing.

```
    ' Name or number but not both should be non-blank.
With TheGame.Player(1).txtPlayerName
    If .Text = "" Then
        With TheGame.Player(1).txtPlayerNumber
            If .Text = "" Then
                .Text = "REQUIRED"
                .Font.Bold = True
            Else
                .Font.Bold = False
            End If
        End With
    Else
```

```
        ' Blank the number.
        With TheGame.Player(1).txtPlayerNumber
            .Text = ""
            .Font.Bold = False
        End With
    End If
End With
```

Use temporary variables to avoid the long object expressions without using extra With statements.

```
Dim txt_name As TextBox
Dim txt_number As TextBox

    ' Name or number but not both should be non-blank.
    Set txt_name = TheGame.Player(1).txtPlayerName
    Set txt_number = TheGame.Player(1).txtPlayerNumber

    If txt_name.Text = "" Then
        If txt_number.Text = "" Then
            txt_number.Text = "REQUIRED"
            txt_number.Font.Bold = True
        Else
            txt_number.Font.Bold = False
        End If
    Else
        ' Blank txtPlayerNumber.
        txt_number.Text = ""
        txt_number.Font.Bold = False
    End If
```

Don't Repeat Code

If you repeat a piece of code, you need to test and debug each piece separately. You also must keep the different occurrences of the code synchronized. If you change one but forget to change another, you will introduce a bug.

Rewrite the code so you use the code in only one place. This code repeats the scaling, rotating, and projection code twice.

```
If move_to_origin Then
    ' Translate the object to the origin.
    MoveToOrigin Polytope

    ' Scale, rotate, and project the object.
    ScaleObject Polytope, object_scale
    RotateObject Polytope, object_rotation
```

```
        PerspectiveProject Polytope, CenterOfProjection

        ' Translate the back to its original position.
        MoveBack Polytope
    Else
        ' Scale, rotate, and project the object.
        ScaleObject Polytope, object_scale
        RotateObject Polytope, object_rotation
        PerspectiveProject Polytope, CenterOfProjection
    End If
```

This version performs each task only once.

```
    If move_to_origin Then
        ' Translate the object to the origin.
        MoveToOrigin Polytope
    End If

    ' Scale, rotate, and project the object.
    ScaleObject Polytope, object_scale
    RotateObject Polytope, object_rotation
    PerspectiveProject Polytope, CenterOfProjection

    If move_to_origin Then
        ' Translate the back to its original position.
        MoveBack Polytope
    End If
```

Notice that the second version uses the same If statement twice. If this statement involves a complex expression, use a variable to simplify it as in this example.

Encapsulate Library Calls

Place library declarations and calls in separate modules. Place API declarations and function calls in one module, declarations for an expression parsing library in another, and so forth. Write Visual Basic routines to encapsulate the library calls so the main program does not depend on the details of how they work.

Library calls sometimes change when a new version of a library is released. If the calls are encapsulated in a module, you can easily review them to see if you need to make changes whenever you install a new version of the library. If a call has changed, you can change the wrapper routine you built in a single place instead of looking for calls scattered throughout the application.

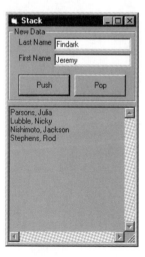

Figure 10.2 Program Bad10 manipulates a stack.

Self-Test

Program Bad10, shown in Figure 10.2, violates some of the guidelines described in this chapter. This program implements a *stack*, a kind of list where items are added and removed from the same end of the list. Because items are removed in last-in-first-out order, stacks are sometimes called *LIFO lists* or *LIFOs*.

For historical reasons, adding an item to a stack is called *pushing* the item onto the stack. Removing the top item from the stack is called *popping* the item off of the stack.

Enter values in the program's Last Name and First Name fields and click the Push button to add an item to the stack. Click the Pop button to remove the most recently added item.

Program Bad10 is fairly simple, but it disobeys several of the rules described in this chapter. Such a simple program can get away with some of these violations. In a more complex program, however, they could cause a lot of trouble. The source code for program Bad10 follows. Appendix A, "Self-Test Solutions," contains an improved version of the program.

```
Option Explicit

' The data for a person.
Private NumPeople As Integer
Private LastNames() As String
Private FirstNames() As String
```

```vb
' Add an item to the stack.
Private Sub cmdPush_Click()
    ' Create space for the new person.
    ReDim Preserve LastNames(1 To NumPeople + 1)
    ReDim Preserve FirstNames(1 To NumPeople + 1)

    ' Save the new person's data.
    LastNames(NumPeople + 1) = txtLastName.Text
    FirstNames(NumPeople + 1) = txtFirstName.Text
    txtLastName.Text = ""
    txtFirstName.Text = ""

    ' Enable the Pop button.
    cmdPop.Enabled = True

    ' Update the number of people.
    NumPeople = NumPeople + 1

    ' Display the list.
    DisplayList
End Sub

' Remove the top item from the stack.
Private Sub cmdPop_Click()
    ' Display the person's values.
    txtLastName.Text = LastNames(NumPeople)
    txtFirstName.Text = FirstNames(NumPeople)

    ' Remove the last person.
    If NumPeople - 1 > 0 Then
        ReDim Preserve LastNames(1 To NumPeople - 1)
        ReDim Preserve FirstNames(1 To NumPeople - 1)
    Else
        Erase LastNames
        Erase FirstNames
    End If

    ' Enable this button only if there are
    ' people left.
    cmdPop.Enabled = (NumPeople - 1 > 0)

    ' Save the new number of people.
    NumPeople = NumPeople - 1

    ' Display the list.
    DisplayList
End Sub

' Display the people in the stack.
Private Sub DisplayList()
```

```
Dim i As Integer
Dim txt As String

    For i = 1 To NumPeople
        txt = LastNames(i) & ", " & _
            FirstNames(i) & _
            vbCrLf & txt
    Next i
    txtList.Text = txt

    ' The last name field is where the user will
    ' start editing the new data.
    txtLastName.SetFocus
End Sub
```

Summary

Encapsulation hides detail from code that does not need to know about it. Encapsulation lets you concentrate on one piece of code while ignoring irrelevant complexity.

There are many ways you can take advantage of encapsulation in your programs. The key is to represent complex things with simpler things. Use variables to represent complex expressions or object references. Use UDTs to represent complicated data structures. Use subroutines, classes, and modules to represent even more complex entities and behaviors. Take advantage of encapsulation in all its forms.

The following Bug Stoppers summarize the encapsulation concepts explained in this chapter.

 BUG STOPPERS: Encapsulation

Hide the internals of a routine from other routines.

Encapsulate with classes.

Look for memory leaks by counting object creation and destruction.

Initialize objects.

Use property procedures instead of public variables.

Use the Implements keyword to define interfaces and improve performance.

Encapsulate with user-defined types.

Encapsulate with controls.

Encapsulate with subroutines.

Encapsulate with modules.   **(Continues)**

BUG STOPPERS (CONTINUED)

Use variables to avoid recalculating expressions.

Use variables to avoid recalculating property values.

Keep as much private as possible in classes and modules.

Use With to simplify using objects.

Use variables instead of nested With statements.

Do not repeat code.

Encapsulate library calls so you can easily change them later.

CHAPTER 11

Optimization

Optimization and bug proofing are often conflicting goals. Code designed for speed and efficiency is often harder to test and debug than code written for readability. Many programmers are more than happy to make a program illegible and impossible to debug in the name of efficiency.

This chapter does not explain specific techniques for optimizing a program's performance. It does describe some techniques you can use to make optimization safer. Following these guidelines, you can optimize your Visual Basic program and still keep it readable and relatively bug free.

Note that these optimizations apply to compiled executables in Visual Basic 5 and 6. If you are running an earlier version, you can skip this chapter.

Optimize Algorithms

Optimize algorithms on a large scale instead of individual lines of code. Small changes to a routine will probably not produce large improvements. After spending a lot of effort rewriting and debugging a few key lines of code in a subroutine, you might realize a few percent improvement in speed. On the other hand, changing the fundamental algorithm might make the routine orders of magnitude faster.

Modifying a few lines here and there is also likely to introduce bugs. When you rewrite an entire routine, you need to understand the routine's purpose and underlying approach. You cannot even begin until you have a reasonable understanding of the routine. On the other hand, it is easy to rewrite a single line of code without understanding the larger context. In that case, you are much more likely to make a seemingly innocuous change that interacts badly with some other code that you do not fully understand.

None of this means that you need to code stupidly and skip obvious chances to improve the code. If there is a more efficient way to write a particular routine, by all means, use it. Do not spend a huge amount of time perfecting every line of code, however. Initially concentrate on making the code easy to understand and modify. You can always change it later if necessary.

Defer Optimization

Near the beginning of a project, focus on getting the program running correctly. Concentrate on writing clear, straightforward code that will be easy to test, debug, and maintain over time. Do not spend time optimizing the code until later.

Usually, more than 95 percent of a program's time is spent in less than 5 percent of the code. Once you have the program running correctly, you can identify the 5 percent that is most time consuming and concentrate your optimization efforts there. That will probably produce a much bigger improvement in performance than scattering your optimization efforts throughout the 95 percent of the code that is already fast enough.

Concentrating on writing code that is easy to debug also gives you a solid foundation to build on during optimization. If the code is robust and bug resistant, you can concentrate on optimization without wasting huge amounts of time chasing bugs.

Optimize as late as possible. Get the program running bug free first.

Profile First

Before you start optimizing, profile the program's execution. See how long the program spends in each routine and determine where it spends most of its time. You can use a profiling tool like the Visual Basic Code Profiler described in Chapter 15, "Profiling." You can also perform tests using the Timer function. For example, the following code prints the time spent in each of three subroutines into the Debug window.

```
Private Sub LoadData()
Dim start_time As Single
Dim stop_time As Single
Dim fnum As Integer

    ' Open the file.
    fnum = FreeFile
    Open "C:\City.dat" For Input As Fnum

    ' Read the header information.
    start_time = Timer
    LoadHeader fnum
    stop_time = Timer
    Debug.Print "LoadHeader: " & _
        Format$(stop_time - start_time, "0.00")

    ' Read the node information.
    start_time = Timer
    LoadNodes fnum
    stop_time = Timer
    Debug.Print "LoadNodes: " & _
        Format$(stop_time - start_time, "0.00")

    ' Read the link information.
    start_time = Timer
    LoadLinks fnum
    stop_time = Timer
    Debug.Print "LoadLinks: " & _
        Format$(stop_time - start_time, "0.00")
End Sub
```

Once you have profiled the code, identify the routines that take up most of the program's time. Some you will be unable to improve significantly. For example, a routine that downloads data over a slow modem line will be slow no matter how efficiently you rewrite the code. Focus on code where you can make a meaningful difference.

Comment Optimizations

Many programmers do not add comments when they modify code to improve its performance. They think, particularly near the end of the project, that optimization is more important than clarity.

By adding comments to the code as you optimize it, you can have both speed and clarity. When you change the code, document the change. If the new code is complex, explain how it works. If the old code is easier to understand, comment it out instead of removing it. Then, later developers can compare the two versions of the code.

Whether you modify the code to fix a bug, add a new feature, or to optimize, modifying code is more likely to produce bugs than writing original code is. Treat optimization as bug fixing and use comments to document the changes.

Use Slow Debugging Code

It does not matter how slow debugging code is as long as it is tolerable to the developers. If the code will be removed by compiler constants in the final version, it need only be fast enough to be usable during design and debugging. Do not waste time optimizing code that will be eliminated from the final program anyway. Spend extra time optimizing the debugging code only if it is so inefficient that it is slowing down development.

Be sure you disable the debugging code before you profile the program to find the 5 percent of the code that uses 95 percent of the program's time. If you generate timing statistics with the debug code running, you will not be able to tell which code really needs optimization.

Understand Visual Basic's Optimizations

The Visual Basic compiler provides several optimization features that you should understand. These optimizations apply when you create a compiled executable. Using some of the optimizations, you may be able to improve your program's performance without making any changes to the code.

Be very careful when you use these options. They disable checks that allow Visual Basic to detect certain conditions and raise errors. They seriously weaken Visual Basic's ability to recover from errors.

For example, if you disable array bounds checking, Visual Basic cannot tell when the program tries to access an array element that lies outside of the array. In that case, the program cannot catch the error using an On Error statement. If you are lucky, the program will crash without warning. If you are unlucky, it will modify some other piece of memory that lies where the missing array entry would be if it existed. That can create a bug that is extremely hard to find.

Because these optimizations apply only to the compiled version of the program, they can make the program's compiled and noncompiled versions behave differently. That can lead to some bugs that are very hard to detect and fix.

To access the advanced optimizations in Visual Basic 5 and 6, select the Project Properties command from the bottom of the Project menu. Select the Compile tab and then click the Advanced Optimizations button to see the dialog shown in Figure 11.1.

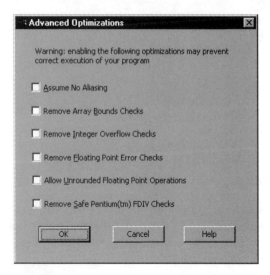

Figure 11.1 Visual Basic's Advanced Optimizations dialog.

The advanced optimizations are described in the following sections.

Assume No Aliasing

This option tells Visual Basic that no variable is referenced by more than one name at the same time. For example, suppose you pass a parameter declared by reference using the ByRef keyword to a routine. The routine knows the variable by the parameter's name. The calling routine knows the variable by its original name. Within the MySub routine shown in the following code, the variable A is referred to by the name A and X at the same time.

```
Private A As Integer

Private Sub Caller()
    MySub A
End Sub

Private Sub MySub(ByRef X As Integer)
    ' Here the variable is known as A and X.
        :
End Sub
```

This optimization allows Visual Basic to make the code run faster. It will not necessarily work, however, unless the code never uses aliased names.

You should not use this optimization unless you never pass parameters ByRef. Keep in mind that ByRef is the default, so the following definition of MySub is just as dangerous as the previous one.

```
Private Sub MySub(X As Integer)
    ' Here the variable is known as A and X.
        :
End Sub
```

Remove Array Bounds Checks

This option disables Visual Basic's array bounds checks. Normally, Visual Basic checks array accesses to ensure that the access is within the array's bounds. If the program tries to access an index outside the array's bounds, Visual Basic generates a subscript out of range error.

If you disable array bounds checking, Visual Basic does not make this check. If the program tries to access an entry outside the array's bounds, the program may crash. Even worse, it may write over the piece of memory that lies where the missing array entry should be.

Error handlers cannot catch this error. If this check is disabled, the following code may crash the program. If array bounds checks are enabled as usual, the error handler catches the error and presents a message box.

```
Private Sub UnsafeSub()
Dim arr(1 To 5) As Integer
Dim i As Integer

    On Error GoTo OutOfBounds

    ' Access items outside the array's bounds.
    For i = 1 To 10
        arr(i) = i
    Next i
    Exit Sub

OutOfBounds:
    MsgBox "Error" & Str$(Err.Number) & _
        vbCrLf & Err.Description
End Sub
```

Disable array bounds checks only if you have thoroughly tested your program and you are certain it never tries to access elements outside of any array. Of course, if the program uses no arrays, it cannot violate array bounds so you can disable array bounds checks.

Remove Integer Overflow Checks

Normally, Visual Basic checks every integer calculation to see if the result is too big to fit in an integer. If it finds that the result will overflow the integer data type, Visual Basic raises an overflow error.

If you disable this option, the program will not notice the error and it will perform the calculation anyway. When the system performs an operation that overflows, the result can be quite strange. For example, 20,000 + 20,000 = 40,000. The largest value that can fit in an integer is 32,767, so calculating 20,000 + 20,000 normally causes an integer overflow. If you disable integer overflow checks, the result is –25,536.

If you run the following code with integer overflow checks enabled, the program catches the overflow and presents an error message. If you disable integer overflow checks, the code displays the value –25,536.

```
Private Sub UnsafeSub()
Dim A As Integer

    On Error GoTo OverflowError
    A = 20000 + 20000
    MsgBox Format$(A)
    Exit Sub

OverflowError:
    MsgBox "Error" & Str$(Err.Number) & _
        vbCrLf & Err.Description
End Sub
```

Disable integer overflow checks only if you have thoroughly tested your program and you are certain it never performs integer operations that may result in an overflow. If the program never uses integer calculations, you can disable integer overflow checks.

Remove Floating-Point Error Checks

Just as it checks for integer overflow errors, Visual Basic examines floating-point calculations looking for errors. It checks for values out of range and divide by zero errors. If you disable floating-point error checks, the program will not notice these errors and the program may generate some strange results.

For example, if you execute the following code with floating-point checks disabled, the code sets the value of A to a special infinite value. Then the message box displays the string "1.#INF." If you run the code with floating-point checks enabled, Visual Basic catches the error and presents a division by zero error message.

```
Private Sub UnsafeSub()
Dim A As Single

    On Error GoTo FloatError
    A = 10 / 0
    MsgBox Format$(A)
    Exit Sub

FloatError:
    MsgBox "Error" & Str$(Err.Number) & _
        vbCrLf & Err.Description
End Sub
```

Disable floating-point checks only if you have thoroughly tested your program and you are certain it never performs floating-point operations that may result in an error. If the program does not use any floating-point operations, you can disable floating-point checks. However, keep in mind that Visual Basic may automatically promote integer values to floating-point values. For example, the following code does not directly use any floating-point values. When it reaches the statement A = 10 / 0, Visual Basic decides that the result of the division should be a floating-point number. The result is a divide by zero error that Visual Basic cannot catch if floating-point checks are disabled.

```
Private Sub UnsafeSub()
Dim A As Variant

    On Error GoTo FloatError
    A = 10 / 0
    MsgBox Format$(A)
    Exit Sub

FloatError:
    MsgBox "Error" & Str$(Err.Number) & _
        vbCrLf & Err.Description
End Sub
```

Allow Unrounded Floating-Point Operations

This option allows Visual Basic to optimize certain floating-point operations. As a side effect, the program may store variables with greater precision than you expect. The program may consider two extremely close values to be different when you think they are the same.

Situations like these, where the program uses too much precision, can be a problem even when this optimization is not enabled. For example, in the following code the variable x starts with the value 0. The value 10 / 17 is added to x 17 times. If you multiply 17 by 10 / 17, you get 10, so the final value for x should be 10. Due to round-off errors, however, the value differs from 10 by roughly 2E-15. This is not exactly 10, so the test x = 10 in the If statement is false. Unfortunately, the Str$ command does not represent x with enough precision for you to see that x is not 10. The message box displays the rather confusing string, "The value is not 10, it is 10."

```
Private Sub RoundoffProblem()
Dim x As Double
Dim dx As Double
Dim i As Integer

    dx = 10 / 17
    x = 0
    For i = 1 To 17
        ' Do something with x.
            :
        x = x + dx
    Next i

    If x = 10 Then
        MsgBox "The value is 10."
    Else
        MsgBox "The value is not 10, it is" & _
            Str$(x) & "."
    End If
End Sub
```

If you examine the value of x using the Format$ function, or if you display it in the Immediate window using the Debug.Print command, you receive a similarly confusing result. As far as you can tell, x is 10; yet x = 10 is false.

The way to solve this problem is to not use equality to determine whether floating-point numbers are equal. Instead, see if they differ by some very small amount as in this code:

```
If Abs(x - 10) < 0.00001 Then
```

If you use this technique to avoid problems with floating-point numbers stored at very high precision, you can allow unrounded floating-point operations.

Remove Safe Pentium FDIV Checks

If you select this option, the program may produce incorrect results on computers with the infamous Pentium FDIV bug. Use this option only if you are certain you will not perform any floating-point calculations that will cause the bug or if you are sure you will never run the program on a Pentium that has this bug.

Figure 11.2 Program Bad11 is not safe for all optimizations.

Self-Test

Program Bad11, shown in Figure 11.2, performs operations that make some of Visual Basic's optimizations unsafe. The program is a crude array manager. Enter an array index in the Index box. Enter a floating-point value in the Value box and click the Set button to save the value in the indicated array position. Click the Get button to see what value is currently in that array position.

Examine the code that follows and try to determine why it makes the optimizations unsafe. Appendix A, "Self-Test Solutions," contains an improved version of the code.

```
Option Explicit

Private Values(1 To 100) As Single

Private Sub cmdGet_Click()
Dim index As Integer

    On Error GoTo GetError
    index = CLng(txtIndex.Text)
    txtValue.Text = Format$(CellValue(index))
    Exit Sub

GetError:
    MsgBox "Error" & Str$(Err.Number) & _
        " getting value." & vbCrLf & _
        Err.Description
End Sub

Private Sub cmdSet_Click()
    On Error GoTo SetError
    CellValue(txtIndex.Text) = txtValue.Text
    Exit Sub
```

```
SetError:
    MsgBox "Error" & Str$(Err.Number) & _
        " setting value.· & vbCrLf & _
        Err.Description
End Sub


' Return the indicated array cell value.
Public Property Get CellValue(ByVal index As Integer) As Single
    CellValue = Values(index)
End Property


' Set the indicated array cell value.
Public Property Let CellValue(ByVal index As Integer, _
    new_value As Single)

    Values(index) = new_value
End Property
```

Summary

Probably the biggest optimization mistake developers make is optimizing too soon. Wait until most of the program's features have been correctly implemented before you begin optimization. Then profile the code and work with a plan instead of trying to improve randomly selected sections of code. The following Bug Stoppers summarize these and the other optimization guidelines discussed in this chapter.

 BUG STOPPERS: Optimization

Optimize algorithms, not lines of code.

Defer optimization until the program runs correctly.

Profile the program before you optimize.

Use comments to explain optimizations.

Do not worry about slow debugging code.

Understand Visual Basic's optimizations.

PART FOUR

Error Handling

In a complicated program, it is extremely difficult to remove absolutely every bug. You may test a program for a long time without finding any new bugs, but you can never be completely sure you have found them all. That means the program's final compiled version must be prepared to handle bugs that arise unexpectedly.

In addition, even a perfectly debugged program remains subject to random occurrences in the Windows environment. Other programs may exhaust the system's memory so your program cannot run properly. The user may accidentally delete an important file or part of the system registry. These situations create errors the program must handle, but they are not bugs.

The chapters in Part 4 explain runtime error handling topics. They show how to detect and manage bugs and unexpected conditions that might otherwise crash the program. Using proper error handling techniques, a program can continue to operate even when it runs into unanticipated errors.

CHAPTER 12

Error Handling Fundamentals

This chapter explains the family of On Error statements Visual Basic uses to handle errors. It tells how a program installs and removes error handlers, and it explains some of the idiosyncrasies of error handling code. After reading this chapter you will be able to write basic error handlers to protect your programs from the unexpected.

Use On Error

A Visual Basic program uses the On Error statement to register error handling code. This statement can take one of three forms:

- On Error GoTo 0
- On Error Resume Next
- On Error GoTo line

These forms tell Visual Basic what it should do when the program encounters an error. The three forms are described in the following sections.

On Error GoTo 0

On Error GoTo 0 is relatively straightforward. It simply cancels any currently installed error handler assigned by a previous On Error GoTo line or On Error Resume Next. If the program encounters an error after this statement executes, it crashes.

On Error Resume Next

On Error Resume Next makes the program ignore errors. When it encounters an error, the program continues execution after the statement that caused the error.

When a program uses On Error Resume Next, it should check the Err object after every operation that might cause an error. If the value Err.Number is nonzero, the operation caused an error and the program can take special action.

The program should check Err.Number immediately after the statement in question. Certain other actions reset the Err object and remove the previous error information.

Many programs use On Error GoTo Next when they present a common dialog to the user. The CommonDialog control's CancelError property indicates whether the control should raise an error if the user cancels the dialog. The following code fragment shows how a program can use CancelError to decide whether to continue an action such as loading a file.

```
' Generate an error if the user cancels.
dlgOpenFile.CancelError = True

' Ignore errors for now.
On Error Resume Next

' Present the dialog.
dlgOpenFile.ShowOpen

' See if there was an error.
If Err.Number = cdlCancel Then
    ' The user canceled. Do nothing.
    Exit Sub
ElseIf Err.Number <> 0 Then
    ' Unknown error. Take more action.
        :
End If

' Resume normal error handling.
On Error GoTo 0
```

On Error GoTo Line

The On Error GoTo line statement registers a new error handler. If the program encounters an error, it passes control to the error handler beginning at the indicated line number or label. The error handler can then take appropriate action.

The following code shows a simple error handler that catches unexpected errors and describes them to the user.

```
Private Sub DoSomething()
    ' Install the error handler.
    On Error GoTo UnexpectedError

    ' Do stuff.
        :

    ' Do not pass through into the error handler code.
    Exit Sub

UnexpectedError:
    ' Describe the error to the user.
    MsgBox "Unexpected error" & _
        Str$(Err.Number) & _
        " in subroutine DoSomething." & _
        vbCrLf & _
        Err.Description
    Exit Sub
End Sub
```

Leave Error Handlers

There are several ways a program can leave error handling code and return to normal execution.

- Resume
- Resume Next
- Exit Sub/Function/Property
- End Sub/Function/Property
- Err.Raise

These different methods are described in the following sections.

Resume

The Resume statement continues execution by repeating the statement that caused the error. If the statement is still incorrect, the program will raise the error again. This may put the program in an infinite loop. To avoid an infinite loop, do not use the Resume statement unless something in the error handler should have fixed the problem.

For example, the following code tries to load a file that might be stored on a floppy disk. If it fails, the code reports the error and asks the user if it should try again. If the disk is not in the floppy drive, the user can insert it and click the Retry button. The program then uses the Resume statement to try to open the file again. If the program fails again, it returns to the error handler to give the user another chance to fix the problem. The program continues looping from the Open statement to the error handler and back until the user fixes the problem or clicks the Cancel button. If the user clicks Cancel, the error handler exits the subroutine without opening the file.

```
Private Sub LoadData(ByVal filename As String)
Dim fnum As Integer

    ' Open the file.
    fnum = FreeFile
    On Error GoTo OpenError
    Open filename For Input As fnum

    ' Read the data.
    On Error GoTo ReadError
        :

    ' Close the file.
    On Error GoTo CloseError
    Close fnum
    Exit Sub

OpenError:
    ' We could not open the file. Ask the user
    ' if we should retry.
    If MsgBox("Error" & _
            Str$(Err.Number) & _
            " opening file " & filename & "." & _
            vbCrLf & Err.Description & vbCrLf & _
            "Check that the disk is properly " & _
            "inserted and click the Retry button.", _
            vbRetryCancel, _
            "Error opening file") = vbRetry _
    Then
        ' Try again at the same statement.
```

```
        Resume
    End If

    ' Otherwise cancel the file loading.
    Exit Sub

ReadError:
    MsgBox "Error" & _
        Str$(Err.Number) & _
        " reading file " & filename & "." & _
        vbCrLf & Err.Description

    ' Close the file.
    Close fnum
    Exit Sub

CloseError:
    ' Error closing the file.
    MsgBox "Error" & _
        Str$(Err.Number) & _
        " closing file " & filename & "." & _
        vbCrLf & Err.Description
    Exit Sub
End Sub
```

Resume Next

Resume Next makes the program continue execution at the statement after the one that caused the error. This is a useful action if the program and user cannot reasonably correct the error, but the program can continue running without the statement completing.

For example, the following code tries to convert a string value into a date using the CDate function. If it fails, the error handler assigns the current date to the start_date variable and uses that as a default value.

```
Private Sub ValidateStartDate(ByVal date_string As String)
Dim start_date As Date

    ' Install the error handler.
    On Error GoTo InvalidDate

    ' Convert the string into a date.
    start_date = CDate(date_string)

    ' Do something with the date.
        :
```

```
    ' Do not pass through into the error handler code.
    Exit Sub

InvalidDate:
    ' It's an invalid date string. Use today.
    start_date = Date
    Resume Next
End Sub
```

Note that this is probably not the best way to handle this situation because it silently handles the error instead of making it obvious. If the user entered the invalid value, the program should politely tell the user there is a problem and ask for a new value. If the string was passed to this routine from another part of the program, the program may contain a bug. It should stop during design mode or raise an error in the final compiled version so someone can fix the problem.

Exit Sub/Function/Property

If the routine cannot continue with its task, it can use Exit Sub, Exit Function, or Exit Property to exit immediately. The following code shows a new version of the previous routine. If the date string is invalid, this version tells the user and then exits.

```
Private Sub ValidateStartDate(ByVal date_string As String)
Dim start_date As Date

    ' Install the error handler.
    On Error GoTo InvalidDate

    ' Convert the string into a date.
    start_date = CDate(date_string)

    ' Do something with the date.
        :

    ' Do not pass through into the error handler code.
    Exit Sub

InvalidDate:
    ' It's an invalid date string. Tell the user and leave.
    MsgBox "The start date """ & _
        date_string & _
        """ is invalid. Please enter a new one."
    Exit Sub
End Sub
```

When a routine exits in this way, the calling routine cannot tell that an error occurred. That means you should use this technique only when the calling routine can properly continue whether this routine succeeded or not. If the caller must know that this routine failed, the code should use the Err.Raise statement described shortly.

End Sub/Function/Property

If the error handler code continues to the routine's End Sub, End Function, or End Property statement, the routine exits just as if it had executed the Exit statement described in the previous section. For example, the end of the previous subroutine could be written:

```
InvalidDate:
    ' It's an invalid date string. Tell the user and leave.
    MsgBox "The start date """ & _
        date_string & _
        """ is invalid. Please enter a new one."
End Sub
```

Sometimes it can be a little confusing for the error handler to just drop off the end of the routine like this. This version also creates the opportunity for a new bug. A developer who later adds a new error handler to the end of the routine may not notice that the code drops through the end of the routine. If the new error handler is added without a preceding Exit statement, the old error handler will continue into the new one. If the following code encounters an invalid date, it presents the user with two error messages instead of one.

```
InvalidDate:
    ' It's an invalid date string. Tell the user and leave.
    MsgBox "The start date """ & _
        date_string & _
        """ is invalid. Please enter a new one."

ReadFileError:
    ' Error reading the data file.
    MsgBox "Error reading the data."
        :
End Sub
```

To prevent this kind of mistake, do not allow an error handler to continue to the routine's End statement. Use an Exit statement to leave the routine instead.

Err.Raise

The Err object provides a Raise method that allows a program to generate errors. It can create new errors or reraise old ones. The syntax for the Raise method is

```
Err.Raise Number, [Source], [Description], [Helpfile], [Help-
context]
```

Number. The error number. To create a new error code in a class module, add vbObjectError to your number. For example, vbObjectError + 1001.

Source. The name of the object or application generating the error. For objects, use the format Project.Class. For routines, use the format Project.Routine. For example, MyProgram.LoadData.

Description. A string describing the error. If you set Number to a standard Visual Basic error code like 9 for subscript out of range, you can omit Description to make Visual Basic use a standard description string.

Helpfile. The full name of a help file that gives more information on the error.

Helpcontext. The context ID for this error's topic in the help file.

If a routine cannot handle an error itself, it should raise a new error that makes sense within its context. For example, the following routine attempts to read a data file. If the file is not found, the FileOpenError error handler raises the myappErrNoInputFile error. This gives the calling subroutine more information than Visual Basic's initial file not found error. The error Visual Basic generates indicates that some file was not found. The new error explains that an input data file was not found. The Err.Description field even includes the name of the file that was not found.

```
' Define application error constants.
Private Const myappErrNoInputFile = vbObjectError + 1000
    :
' Define Visual Basic error constants.
Private Const vbErrFileNotFound = 53
    :
Private Sub ReadInputData(ByVal file_name As String)
Dim file_number As Integer

    ' Open the file.
    file_number = FreeFile
    On Error GoTo FileOpenError
    Open file_name For Input As file_number

    ' Process the file.
    On Error GoTo FileReadError
        :
    ' Process the file here.
        :
    ' Close the file.
    Close file_number
    Exit Sub
```

```
FileOpenError:
    ' There was an error opening the file.
    If Err.Number = vbErrFileNotFound Then
        ' It's a file not found error. Convert it
        ' to myappErrNoInputFile.
        Err.Raise myappErrNoInputFile, _
            "MyApp.ReadInputData", _
            "Could not open input file """ & _
                file_name & """."
    Else
        ' It's some other error. Reraise it so some
        ' other routine can catch it.
        Err.Raise Err.Number, _
            Err.Source, _
            Err.Description, _
            Err.HelpFile, _
            Err.HelpContext
    End If
    Exit Sub

FileReadError:
    ' There was an error reading the file.
        :
    Exit Sub
End Sub
```

A program could invoke this subroutine using code similar to the following. The error handler uses the information stored in the Err object by the Raise method to present a message to the user.

```
On Error GoTo DataInputError
ReadInputData "c:\mydata.dat"
Exit Sub

DataInputError:
    ' There was an error loading the data.
    MsgBox "Error" & Str$(Err.Number) & _
        " loading the input data." & vbCrLf & _
        Err.Description
```

Routines that present messages to users normally format the error information as shown in the previous code. To make that formatting as simple as possible, routines should not format the error description in the Raise statement. For example, the following code formats an error's description.

```
Err.Raise myappErrNoInputFile, _
    "MyApp.ReadInputData", _
    "Error" & Str$(myappErrNoInputFile) & _
    " opening the input file."
```

When this error occurs, the error handler that catches the error will probably display a message like this one:

```
Error -2147220504 loading the input data.
Error -2147220504 opening the input file.
```

Leave the formatting to the routine that actually records the error or presents the message to the user.

Define Error Constants

Microsoft says normal error messages lie in the range of 1 to 65,535. They reserve the range 1 to 1000 for use by Visual Basic, and some of the values between 31,000 and 31,037 are already used by Visual Basic. You can use other values to define your own error codes.

Microsoft also recommends that you define new error constants for classes by adding a value to the constant vbObjectError as in the following code:

```
Private Const myclassErrNoInputFile = vbObjectError + 1000
```

If you follow these rules, your error codes will not overlap Microsoft's. Unfortunately, this does not guarantee that your error code will not collide with other error constants defined by other developers or libraries you use.

One method for preventing confusion is to define a base value similar to vbObjectError for your constants. Then define error codes in terms of that constant. For example, a ray-tracing package might define error codes as in the following code:

```
Public Const rayErrorBase = 45300
Public Const rayParametersNotSet = rayErrorBase + 1
Public Const rayInvalidSphereFormat = rayErrorBase + 2
Public Const rayLightAtEye = rayErrorBase + 3
    :
```

If you later discover that your error codes collide with those of another developer or library, you can quickly redefine all of the error codes by changing the error base value.

Keep Error Handlers Separate

End every error handler with Resume, Resume Next, Exit Sub/Function/Property, End Sub/Function/Property, or Err.Raise. Never allow the code to fall through from one error handler into another. This can produce some clever code, but it can produce confusion as well.

For example, the following code falls through its error handlers to close the file it has opened.

```
Private Sub LoadData(ByVal filename As String)
Dim fnum As Integer

    ' The file is not yet open.
    On Error GoTo FileIsClosed

    ' Open the file.
    fnum = FreeFile
    Open filename For Input As fnum

    ' The file is now open.
    On Error GoTo FileIsOpen

    ' Read the data.
        :

    ' Fall into the error handlers to close the file.
    On Error Resume Next

FileIsOpen:
    ' Close the file.
    Close fnum

FileIsClosed:
    ' Perform any final tasks.
        :

    ' Fall through to the End Sub.
End Sub
```

This code has a number of problems. First, it is confusing. Another developer who tries to add a new error handler would be likely to make a mistake and cause a bug. This code also does not signal its errors. Instead, it quietly continues as if nothing has gone wrong. It hides bugs that might otherwise be easy to fix.

Prevent confusion and possible bugs by keeping error handlers separate.

Understand Error Handler Scope

When a program encounters an error, Visual Basic checks to see if an error handler is presently installed in the current routine. If so, control passes to that error handler.

If no error handler is in effect, Visual Basic moves up the call stack to the calling routine to see if an error handler is currently installed there. If so, the system resumes execution at that error handler.

If no error handler is installed in the calling routine either, Visual Basic continues moving up the call stack until it finds a routine with an error handler installed. If it runs off the top of the stack before it finds an active error handler, the program crashes.

Execution of all Visual Basic code begins with either an event handler or the Main subroutine. That means you can guard against almost all errors if you place error handlers in every event handler and the Main subroutine (if the program uses one). Then, no matter where the program encounters an error, control eventually passes up through the call stack to the event handler or Main subroutine that started the code. The error handler installed at that point can handle the error.

Don't Nest Error Handlers

Error handler code runs a little differently from other code. No other error handler can be active within another error handler's code. In other words, an error handler cannot use On Error GoTo to define an error handler to catch its mistakes. If an error handler uses On Error GoTo, the new error handler only takes effect when the error handler finishes and returns control to the main code sequence.

This sort of thing can be very confusing. If Subroutine2 raises an error in the following code, it is not clear whether control passes to the Error1 or Error2 error handler. Control passes to Error1 if Subroutine1 ran correctly, but it passes to Error2 if Subroutine1 also generated an error.

```
        On Error GoTo Error1
        Subroutine1
        Subroutine2
        Exit Sub

    Error1:
        On Error GoTo Error2
```

```
    MsgBox "Error1:" & Str$(Err.Number) & "." & vbCrLf & _
        Err.Description
    Resume Next

Error2:
    MsgBox "Error2:" & Str$(Err.Number) & "." & vbCrLf & _
        Err.Description
    Resume Next
```

Avoid this confusion by not using On Error statements within error handler code. Keep all On Error statements in the main code sequence.

Write Bugproof Error Handlers

If an error occurs while an error handler is running, Visual Basic raises the new error up the call stack to any calling routine that has an error handler defined. In that case, the original error handler loses control and cannot finish whatever it was doing. It cannot finish closing files and performing other cleanup chores. For this reason, error handler code must be as bugproof as possible.

Unfortunately, error handlers are bug prone. They are often complicated and they execute when something else has already gone wrong and the state of the system may be uncertain. Many error handlers are not adequately tested. In part that is because error handlers are usually difficult and tedious to test. Programmers also spend most of their time working under more normal conditions so they have less experience working under the strange circumstances that sometimes arise when errors occur.

To make error handlers a little safer, move risky operations into a subroutine. The subroutine can protect the error handler using its own On Error statement. Note that the subroutine must handle its errors completely. It cannot raise an error of its own. If it does, control passes out of the original error handler and moves up the call stack.

In the following code, subroutine RiskySub may generate an error. If it does, it calls subroutine LogError to write error information into a log file. LogError might fail, so it protects itself with an On Error Resume Next statement. If it does fail, LogError continues instead of raising a new error so the error handler in RiskySub does not lose control.

Note that when subroutine LogError exits, Visual Basic clears the Err object. If RiskySub needs to use the Err.Number and Err.Description values later, it must save those values before it calls LogError.

```
Private Sub RiskySub()
Dim err_number As Long
Dim err_description As String

    On Error GoTo Error1
    ' Do something that might cause an error.
        :
    Exit Sub

Error1:
    ' Save the error values because they will be
    ' cleared when we successfully call LogError.
    err_number = Err.Number
    err_description = Err.Description

    ' LogError logs the error safely, protecting
    ' us with its own On Error statement.
    LogError err_number, "MyApp.RiskySub", err_description

    ' Reraise the error.
    Err.Raise err_number, _
        "MyApp.RiskySub", _
        err_description
End Sub

Private Sub LogError(ByVal err_number As Long, _
    ByVal err_source As String, ByVal err_description As String)

    ' Make sure we do not fail.
    On Error Resume Next

    ' Log the error.
        :
End Sub
```

Always Be Prepared

Errors can happen at practically any time. Even if the program is completely
bug free, there are parts of the environment that are outside of the program's
control. The user might have several memory-intensive programs running and
they may prevent your program from allocating the memory it needs. The user
might open a floppy drive door while your program is trying to read from that
drive. A word processor might have locked a file the program needs.

The program must always be prepared to handle unexpected errors. During the
design phase, the program can stop so you can identify the problem. In its final
compiled version, the program should record the error and continue as gracefully as possible.

Being always prepared for failure means the program must always have an error handler registered and ready to run. At a minimum, all event handlers and the Main subroutine must use error handling. Most programs should also handle errors in other subroutines at a more local scope instead of letting them propagate all the way up the call stack to the event handlers.

Event handlers must be prepared to handle every kind of error. A routine may generate an error directly, or a subroutine it calls may generate the error. The event handler should record and handle the error smoothly if possible. It should at least catch the error and ignore it so the program can continue running.

Clean Up

When a routine fails during the project's design phase, it should stop and alert you to the problem. In the final compiled version, the program should continue running as normally as possible. Continuing could be extremely difficult if the routine that fails leaves the program in some uncertain state.

To allow the program to keep running, a routine that fails should clean up any mess it has made. It should restore global variables and data structures to the state they were in before the routine began. The calling routine can then assume the routine is either successful or that it cleans up its mess.

If a routine's failure means the calling routine cannot continue properly, it should also undo any changes it has made. It can then fail and return control to the routine that called it.

In the worst case, when none of the routines can continue executing, control passes all the way back to the event handler that started the action. If the event handler fails, the program must ignore the event. The behavior the user wanted to trigger will not occur, but otherwise the program should continue normally.

For instance, suppose the user clicks on a button that starts a complex process. Somewhere deep within the series of subroutine calls, an unrecoverable error occurs. As each subroutine fails, it cleans up after itself. Control eventually returns to the button's Click event handler. The error handling code in that routine displays a message telling the user that the program cannot perform the desired task, and then it exits. Control returns to Visual Basic's event handling loop and the program is ready to run as if the user had never clicked the button. The rest of the program's code can run safely because each of the routines that failed cleaned up their messes.

For a more complex example, suppose a program uses an object of the DispatchScenario class named TheScenario to store information about a dispatching system. The LoadScenario subroutine that follows loads data about a particular dispatch problem from a file into a new DispatchScenario object. If the routine fails, it destroys the new DispatchScenario object it has created. It calls the DestroyScenario subroutine to destroy the pieces of the data structure. This leaves the program as it was before the routine was called so the program can continue running.

Only if the routine successfully creates the new scenario object does it destroy the old object and replace it with the new one.

```
' Global DispatchScenario object.
Private TheScenario As DispatchScenario

' Define error constants.
Private Const myappErrScenarioFileNotFound = 1
    :

' Load a dispatch scenario from a file.
Private Sub LoadDispatchScenario(ByVal file_name As String)
Dim new_scenario As DispatchScenario
Dim file_number As Integer
        :
Dim err_number As Long
Dim err_description As String

    ' Open the file.
    On Error GoTo FileOpenError
    file_number = FreeFile
    Open file_name For Input As file_number
        :
    ' Create the new scenario object.
    Set new_scenario = New DispatchScenario

    ' Read the data from the file.
    On Error GoTo FileReadError
        :
    ' Close the file.
    Close file_number

    ' We have successfully created the new
    ' scenario object. Destroy the old one and
    ' replace it with the new object.
    DestroyScenario TheScenario
    Set TheScenario = new_scenario
    Exit Sub

FileOpenError:
    ' Raise a new error.
    Err.Raise myappErrScenarioFileNotFound, _
        "MyApp.LoadDispatchScenario", _
        "Could not open scenario file """ & _
```

```
            file_name & """." & vbCrLf & Err.Description
        Exit Sub

    FileReadError:
        err_number = Err.Number
        err_description = _
            "Could not read scenario file """ & _
            file_name & """." & vbCrLf & Err.Description

        ' Close the file.
        Close file_number

        ' Destroy the objects created so far.
        DestroyScenario new_scenario
        Set new_scenario = Nothing

        ' Raise a new error.
        Err.Raise err_number, _
            "MyApp.LoadDispatchScenario", _
            err_description
        Exit Sub
    End Sub
```

Handle Errors in Objects

A program's code is executed directly or indirectly from its event handlers and from the Main subroutine if one is installed. The program can use normal error handlers to catch and handle errors that occur within this code.

However, there are times when code is not under the direct control of the program. For example, suppose you have built an ActiveX control using Visual Basic 5 or 6. That control might contain a Timer control with a Timer event handler that generates an error under certain circumstances. That event is independent of the main program, so the program cannot trap any errors it generates. If the Timer event raises an error, the program crashes.

Similarly, an ActiveX control might contain a Click event or any other event that generates an error. Once again, the error occurs while the program's code is not running. The program cannot trap the error, so it crashes.

To prevent this from happening, you must ensure that ActiveX controls handle any errors generated by their event handlers. As usual, the code should stop to point out errors at design time. In the final compiled version, the control should properly recover from its error if it can.

If it cannot recover, the control still must not raise an error because that will crash the program. Instead, it should raise an Error event. The main program can use the control's Error event handler to watch for errors.

For instance, the WebStocks control graphs the value of one or more stocks. It periodically updates itself using the Web. The following code shows how the WebStocks control protects the main program when its timer event handler tries to update the control.

```
' Define error codes for programs to use.
Private Const wstkErrorBase = vbObjectError + 1000
Public Enum sbtnErrors
    wstkWebUpdateError = wstkErrorBase + 1
    wstkInitializeError = wstkErrorBase + 2
        :
End Enum


' Declare the Error event that we raise
' when there's a problem.
Event Error(number As Long, source As String, description As String)

' When the timer control fires its event,
' update the graph data from the Web.
Private Sub tmrUpdateFromWeb_Timer()
    ' Catch any errors.
    On Error GoTo UpdateFromWebError

    ' Do whatever's necessary to update the control.
        :
    Exit Sub

UpdateFromWebError:
    ' Raise an Error event (not an Err.Raise error).
    RaiseEvent Error(wstkWebUpdateError, _
        "WebStocks.WebUpdate", _
        "Periodic Web update failed with error:" & _
        vbCrLf & Space$(8) & Format$(Err.number) & _
        "-" & Err.description)
End Sub
```

The main program can watch for errors using code like the following:

```
' Watch for errors generated by the wstkUtilities
' WebStocks control.
Private Sub wstkUtilities_Error(number As Long, _
    source As String, description As String)

    Select Case number
        Case wstkWebInitializeError
            ' Take special action for this error.
                :
        Case ...
```

```
            ' Handle other cases.
                :
        Case Else
            ' Handle unknown cases.
            MsgBox "Error " & Format$(number) & _
                " in " & source & "." & _
                vbCrLf & vbCrLf & description
    End Select
End Sub
```

If the WebStocks control performed an operation that caused a divide by 0 error, the program would display a message like this one:

```
Error -2147220503 in WebStocks.WebUpdate.

Periodic Web update failed with error:
        11-Division by zero
```

Handle Other Object Errors

ActiveX controls you build are not the only objects that can generate errors outside of the main program's control. Any other control or server object that generates errors when it has not been directly called by the program can raise a potentially fatal error.

The Data control handles this problem much as is described in the previous section. When it encounters an error that cannot be trapped, it normally attempts to handle the error itself by presenting a message to the user. You can use the control's Error event handler to override this default behavior.

For example, suppose a program contains a Data control connected to a database. It also contains a TextBox that is bound to an integer data field selected by the Data control. Now suppose the user enters the letter X into the TextBox and tries to use the Data control to move to the next record. The Data control tries to update the current record and store the value X in the integer data field. That is an invalid data conversion, so the control fails.

Instead of raising a fatal error, the Data control raises its Error event. The main program can use the control's Error event handler to catch the error and take action. When it has finished, the program can set the Error event handler's response parameter to tell the Data control what to do next. If the program leaves response with its default value vbDataErrDisplay, the Data control presents the generic message "Data type conversion error." If the program sets response to vbDataErrContinue, the Data control remains silent. This gives the program a chance to fix the problem or present a message of its own.

Break on Errors

Visual Basic's development environment provides several different options for handling errors. To set these options, select the Tools menu's Options command. In Visual Basic 4, click on the Advanced tab. In Visual Basic 5 and 6, click the General tab. The result is a dialog similar to the one shown in Figure 12.1.

The three break options are in the upper right. If you select Break on All Errors, the program enters break mode whenever an error occurs, whether an error handler is in effect or not. This option can help you locate the source of an error before the error handler takes control.

When you select the Break in Class Module option, the program enters break mode if an error occurs inside a class object and that object has not defined an error handler. Normally in this situation, control would return to the main program's error handlers. When this option is set, the program stops even if the main program has an active error handler defined. This option is useful for locating errors in class modules and ActiveX controls.

When you select the Break on Unhandled Errors option, the program only enters break mode if it encounters an error when no error handler is defined. This option is useful for testing code to make sure you cannot generate any uncaught errors.

Use these three options to catch errors at different stages during project development. When you are working on a class, break on errors in the class. If you cannot figure out where an error handler is being invoked, break on all errors. Once you have a class working well, break only on unhandled errors.

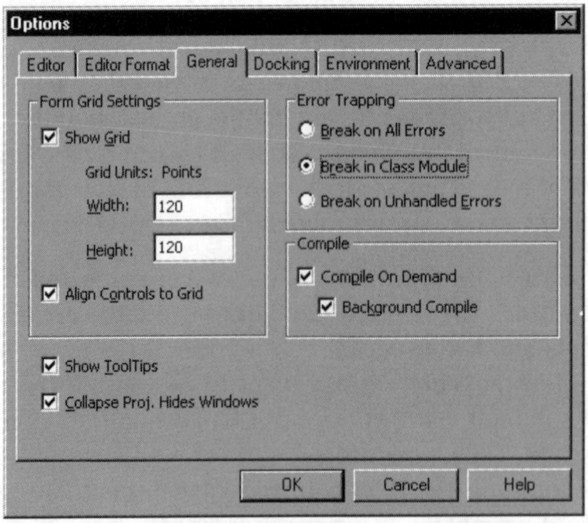

Figure 12.1 Selecting break options in Visual Basic 5.

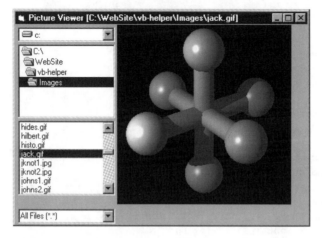

Figure 12.2 Program Bad12 displaying a bitmap file.

Self-Test

Program Bad12, shown in Figure 12.2, uses no error handling. It also contains a few bugs that cause it to crash under certain circumstances. The program lets you view graphics files quickly and easily. Use the ComboBox at the bottom to specify the kinds of files you want to examine. Use the drive, directory, and file list boxes to select a graphic file. When you select a file, the program displays the image stored in the file.

Review the code and decide how to add error handlers to it. Appendix A, "Self-Test Solutions," contains an improved version of the program that uses proper error handling to protect the program.

```
Option Explicit

' Load cboPatterns with file selection patterns.
Private Sub Form_Load()
    cboPatterns.AddItem "Bitmaps (*.bmp)"
    cboPatterns.AddItem "GIF (*.gif)"
    cboPatterns.AddItem "JPEG (*.jpg)"
    cboPatterns.AddItem "Graphic (*.bmp;*.gif;*.jpg)"
    cboPatterns.AddItem "All Files (*.*)"

    ' Start with the first choice (bitmaps) selected.
    cboPatterns.ListIndex = 0
End Sub

' Make the controls as big as possible.
Private Sub Form_Resize()
Const GAP = 60
```

```
Dim wid As Integer
Dim hgt As Integer

    ' Put drvDrives at the top.
    wid = drvDrives.Width
    drvDrives.Move GAP, GAP, wid

    ' Put cboPatterns at the bottom.
    cboPatterns.Move GAP, ScaleHeight - cboPatterns.Height, wid

    ' Make dirDirectories and filFiles split the
    ' rest of the available height.
    hgt = (cboPatterns.Top - drvDrives.Top - _
        drvDrives.Height - 3 * GAP) / 2
    dirDirectories.Move GAP, drvDrives.Top + _
        drvDrives.Height + GAP, wid, hgt
    filFiles.Move GAP, dirDirectories.Top + _
        dirDirectories.Height + GAP, wid, hgt
End Sub

' The user selected a new pattern.
' Make filFiles use the selected pattern to list files.
Private Sub cboPatterns_Click()
Dim choice As String
Dim file_pattern As String
Dim start_pos As Integer
Dim end_pos As Integer

    ' Find the pattern between parentheses.
    choice = cboPatterns.List(cboPatterns.ListIndex)
    start_pos = InStr(choice, "(")
    end_pos = InStr(choice, ")")
    file_pattern = Mid$(choice, start_pos + 1, _
        end_pos - start_pos - 1)

    filFiles.Pattern = file_pattern
End Sub

' The user has picked a new drive.
' Update the directory list.
Private Sub drvDrives_Change()
    dirDirectories.Path = drvDrives.Drive
End Sub

' The user has picked a new directory.
' Update the file list.
Private Sub dirDirectories_Change()
    filFiles.Path = dirDirectories.Path
End Sub
```

```
' The user has picked a file.
' Display it.
Private Sub filFiles_Click()
Dim fname As String

    ' Display the selected file's full name
    ' in the form's caption.
    fname = filFiles.Path + "\" + filFiles.filename
    Caption = "Picture Viewer [" & fname & "]"

    ' Display the picture.
    MousePointer = vbHourglass
    DoEvents
    imgView.Picture = LoadPicture(fname)
    MousePointer = vbDefault
End Sub
```

Summary

The Bug Stoppers that follow summarize the fundamental error handling concepts explained in this chapter. Probably the most important is to always be prepared to handle any kind of error. Even the most thoroughly debugged application can experience all sorts of strange errors through no fault of its own. Be ready to handle these unforeseen errors with robust, carefully tested error handlers.

 BUG STOPPERS: Fundamentals

Use On Error statements.

Leave error handlers using Resume, Resume Next, Exit, or Err.Raise, not End.

Define error constants using an error base.

Keep error handlers separate.

Understand error handler scope.

Do not install an error handler within another error handler.

Write bugproof error handlers.

Always be prepared for errors.

Make routines clean up their messes.

Handle errors in your objects.

Handle errors in objects you don't create.

Use the project options to break on errors.

CHAPTER 13

Standard Error Handlers

C hapter 12, "Error Handling Fundamentals," explains in general how error handlers work. This chapter describes several specific error handlers you can use to cope with unexpected errors in your final compiled application.

When an unexpected error occurs, the program has two goals: to continue running safely and to notify you of the error so you can fix the problem. Chapter 12 described several techniques you can use to help a program continue running safely. For example, if every routine cleans up any data global structures it has modified, it is easier for calling routines to survive the failure.

There are several ways a program can report an error to developers. Some possibilities include:

- Presenting a message to the user who then reports the message to developers
- Writing a message into a file
- Creating a new record in a database
- Sending email to developers

The following section explains a systematic approach to error treatment that allows a program to trap and handle as many errors as possible. The rest of this chapter describes specific error handlers that use the previously listed methods to notify you and other developers when an error occurs.

Use a Systematic Approach

Use a systematic approach to ensure that the program catches every error. Agree with other developers on the strategy to take. If you all use the same methods, your error handlers will be easier to understand.

Most of a program's code is executed by an event handler or by the Main subroutine if one is selected. To trap every error possible, event handlers and Main should always have error handlers that are prepared to handle any kind of error. Then even if the routines called by this code do not have error handlers of their own, these error handlers will catch the error.

When an event handler traps an error caused by a routine it calls, it cannot give very detailed information. It can check the Err object to learn the error's code and description, but it cannot determine where the error occurred. You can get a more precise location for the error if you place an error handler in every routine in the program.

One strategy for systematically handling every error begins by placing an error handler in every routine in the application. The following code shows the error handler's initial structure. All this code does is present a message box describing the error.

```
Private Sub MySub()
    On Error GoTo MySub_Error

    ' Do whatever the routine needs to do.
        :

    Exit Sub

MySub_Error:
    ' Handle unexpected errors.
    MsgBox "Unexpected error " & _
    Format$(Err.Number) & _
        " in MyModule.MySub." & vbCrLf & _
        Err.Description

    ' Clean up any modified data structures.
        :

    ' Reraise the error.
    Err.Raise myappGradeRatioError, _
        "MyApplication.MySub", _
        "Divide by zero calculating grade ratio."
End Sub
```

As you develop and test the program, you will discover errors you had not antic-ipated. When you learn about new errors that may occur, analyze them to decide how they should be handled. If an error can be prevented, modify the code to prevent it.

If the error handler can take action to fix a problem, add the proper code to the error handler. For example, if the error indicates that a floppy disk is not present, the error handler might tell the user and ask if it should cancel its oper-ation or try to read the file again. It can then exit the routine or use a Resume statement to try to read the file once more. See Chapter 12, "Error Handling Fundamentals," for more information on this kind of behavior.

If you find an error that seems likely to occur and that you know the program cannot handle, add code to the Select statement to exit the routine appropri-ately. The following code shows how a routine might exit when it encounters a divide by zero error.

```
MySub_Error:
    Select Case Err.Number
        Case 11
            ' Divide by zero. We cannot handle this.
            ' Clean up any modified data structures.
                :

            ' Reraise the error.
            Err.Raise myappGradeRatioError, _
                "MyApplication.MySub", _
                "Divide by zero calculating grade ratio."

        ' Handle other errors
            :

        Case Else
            ' Handle unexpected errors.
                :
    End Select
End Sub
```

Even after you have thoroughly tested and debugged the application, the Else clause in the error handler's Select statement handles errors you did not encounter while testing.

Catch Error Events

Ideally, a control handles its own errors and the program never needs to know something is amiss. For critical errors, a control should raise an Error event. To be certain your program catches this kind of error, check all nonstandard controls for Error events. If a control has an Error event, write an event handler to determine what has happened. Handle the situation as you would in a normal Visual Basic error handler.

A poorly designed control may raise an exception or allow an error to pass untrapped. In that case, the program may be unable to trap the error and it will crash. For example, suppose the user's clicking on the control makes it enter a calculation that generates a divide by zero error. Because the main program's code is not running, it cannot trap the error. If the control does not handle the error, the program crashes.

There is little you can do about this kind of error unless you have access to the control's source code.

Present Error Messages

The simplest strategy for handling errors is to describe the error to the user. The user can then tell you and other developers about the error. The following code shows a minimal error handler. It simply invokes subroutine ShowErrorMessage to display the error message.

```
Private Sub MySub()
    On Error GoTo MySubError

    ' Do whatever this routine needs to do.
      :

    Exit Sub

MySubError:
    ' Display a non-speecific error message.
    ShowErrorMessage "ShowError.cmdRaiseError_Click"
    Exit Sub
End Sub
```

Subroutine ShowErrorMessage uses the MakeErrorMessage function to build an appropriate error message. If the program's DEBUG_MODE constant is set to True and the Err.HelpFile value is not blank, the message box displays a Help button. During design, you can click on the Help button to get information that may help you understand the error. This information will be meaningless to a user who is not a programmer, so the Help button is not displayed when DEBUG_MODE is False. Note that the MsgBox function does not provide these help features in Visual Basic 4 and earlier versions.

ShowErrorMessage takes the name of the routine that has caught the error as a parameter. A more elaborate error handler might take other information from the calling routine to provide a more detailed message. It might also remind the user to record other relevant information such as the name of the form the user was viewing when the error occurred, what the user was doing, and so forth.

```vb
' Display an error message. If the help file
' and context are available, allow the user to
' click the Help button.
Public Sub ShowErrorMessage(routine_name As String)
Dim txt As String

    ' Create the error message.
    txt = MakeErrorMessage(routine_name)

    ' Display with or without the help button
    ' as is appropriate.
    If DEBUG_MODE And Len(Err.HelpFile) > 0 Then
        MsgBox txt, _
            vbOKOnly + vbMsgBoxHelpButton, _
            "Unexpected Error", _
            Err.HelpFile, Err.HelpContext
    Else
        MsgBox txt, vbOKOnly, "Unexpected Error"
    End If
End Sub


' Make an appropriate error message.
Public Function MakeErrorMessage(routine_name As String) As String
    MakeErrorMessage = _
        "Encountered an unexpected error." & _
        vbCrLf & _
        "Please forward the following " & _
        "information to the development team." & _
        vbCrLf & "----------" & vbCrLf & _
        "Error " & Format$(Err.Number) & _
        " in " & routine_name & "." & _
        vbCrLf & Err.Description
End Function
```

You can download the ShowErrorMessage code from the book's Web site at www.vb-helper.com/err.htm. Program ShowErr, also available at the Web site, demonstrates this method for reporting errors. Figure 13.1 shows the program displaying an error dialog.

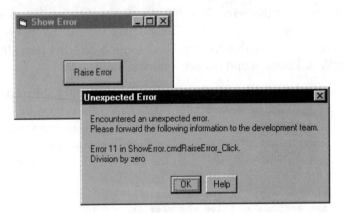

Figure 13.1   Program ShowErr displaying an error message.

Displaying an error message like this is extremely simple. It requires very few extra resources so it is likely to succeed. For example, if the file system is full, the program may be unable to write an error message into a log file or a database, but it will be able to present an error message.

This technique has some drawbacks, however. The user must record the error information faithfully and give it to the developers promptly. Because most users are not programmers, they do not know what information is important and do not always give relevant information to developers.

This method also tells users that there is a problem. If the program can continue execution, it may not need to bother the user. In that case, it would be better to record the error quietly and let the user continue working. Later sections in this chapter explain how to record errors quietly. Of course, if the program cannot perform as the user expects, it must present some message so the user knows what is happening.

Unwind the Stack

The error messages described in the previous section provide a minimum of information. An error handler could present lots of other information such as the values of variables when the error occurred. It can also raise a new error to be handled by the calling routine. A program can use this fact to generate a trace of the sequence of subroutine calls that led to the error. It can also display the values of the variables in each of the routines in the call sequence.

To make a trace, a subroutine that detects an error saves information about itself in an error collection. It then raises the error errStackDump. Control transfers to the routine that called this one. When that routine sees the error errStackDump, it adds information about itself to the error collection and again raises the errStackDump error. Control continues moving up the stack until it reaches a routine that was triggered by Visual Basic; usually, that is an event handler. That routine uses the information in the error collection to create the stack trace. It can display the trace to the user, save it to a file, and so forth.

Program StackDmp, shown in Figure 13.2, uses this method to display stack traces. Click the option button next to the name of the routine you want to raise an error. Then click the Execute button and the program will display an appropriate stack trace.

The following listing shows the error message displayed in Figure 13.2. The comments to the right indicate the meaning of the lines in the message. In this example, subroutine Sub_A_1 started the process with a subscript out of range error.

```
Error 9.                          ' The error code.
Subscript out of range            ' The error description.

Stack dump:
> cmdExecute                      ' Routine cmdExecute called Sub_A.
    txt = In cmdExecute           ' The value of txt in cmdExecute.
      > Sub_A                      ' Routine Sub_A called Sub_A_1.
          txt = In Sub_A          ' The value of txt in Sub_A.
            > Sub_A_1              ' Sub_A_1 raised the error.
                txt = In Sub_A_1  ' The value of txt in Sub_A_1.
```

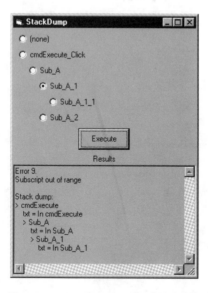

Figure 13.2   Program StackDmp displaying a stack trace.

Program StackDmp uses the RoutineInfo class to record information about routines. As errStackDump errors make control pass up the stack, each routine records information about itself using RoutineInfo objects.

The following code shows how the RoutineInfo class stores information about a routine. The TextValue function returns a textual representation of the information indented by a specified amount. The program uses this value to build the stack trace message.

```
' A class to hold information about a routine.
Option Explicit

Private RoutineName As String
Private VariableValues As New Collection

' Save the routine's name.
Public Sub SaveName(ByVal routine_name As String)
    RoutineName = routine_name
End Sub

' Add a variable value string.
Public Sub SaveValue(ByVal variable_name As String, _
    ByVal variable_value As String)

    VariableValues.Add variable_name & " = " & _
        variable_value
End Sub

' Return a textual representation of the stack.
Public Function TextValue(ByVal num_spaces As Integer) As String
Dim result As String
Dim spaces As String
Dim variable_value As Variant

    ' Start with the routine's name.
    result = Space(num_spaces) & "> " & _
        RoutineName & vbCrLf

    ' Build a string listing the variable values.
    spaces = Space(num_spaces + 4)
    For Each variable_value In VariableValues
        result = result & spaces & _
            variable_value & vbCrLf
    Next variable_value

    TextValue = result
End Function
```

The ErrorStack collection contains a series of RoutineInfo objects. When a routine encounters an error, it calls the AddToErrorStack routine to record information about itself. AddToErrorStack takes as parameters the name of the routine and the names and values of its variables. It creates a new RoutineInfo object and adds it to the ErrorStack collection. If the routine's reraise parameter is True, AddToErrorStack raises the errStackDump error. That makes control pass one routine higher up the call stack.

The ErrorStackText function in the StackInfo.bas module returns a textual representation of the stack trace. It then empties the stack so it will be ready for the next error.

```
' Manage an error stack.
Option Explicit

' Error code to represent a stack dump.
Public Const errStackDump = 41001

' The collection of routine information.
Private ErrorStack As Collection

' The error information that started it all.
Private ErrorNumber As Long
Private ErrorSource As String
Private ErrorDescription As String
Private ErrorHelpFile As String
Private ErrorHelpContext As Long

' Create a RoutineInfo object, save the values
' in it, and add it to the top of the ErrorStack
' collection.
Public Sub AddToErrorStack(ByVal reraise As Boolean, _
    ByVal routine_name As String, _
    ParamArray variable_values() As Variant)

Dim routine_info As New RoutineInfo
Dim variable_num As Integer

    ' Make sure we have an even number of
    ' variable_values items because variable
    ' names and values come in pairs.
    If (UBound(variable_values) + 1) Mod 2 <> 0 Then Stop

    ' If this is the first error in the stack,
    ' allocate the stack and save error information.
    If ErrorStack Is Nothing Then ClearErrorStack

    ' Save the RoutineInfo values.
    routine_info.SaveName routine_name
```

```
        For variable_num = 0 To UBound(variable_values) Step 2
            routine_info.SaveValue _
                variable_values(variable_num), _
                variable_values(variable_num + 1)
        Next variable_num

        ' Add the new RoutineInfo item to the top of
        ' the ErrorStack stack.
        If ErrorStack.Count = 0 Then
            ErrorStack.Add routine_info
        Else
            ErrorStack.Add routine_info, , 1
        End If

        ' If we should reraise the error, do so.
        If reraise Then _
            Err.Raise ErrorNumber, ErrorSource, _
                ErrorDescription, ErrorHelpFile, _
                ErrorHelpContext
End Sub

' Allocate the stack and save the current error
' information.
Public Sub ClearErrorStack()
        ' Start with a new stack collection.
        Set ErrorStack = New Collection

        ' Save the error values.
        ErrorNumber = Err.Number
        ErrorSource = Err.Source
        ErrorDescription = Err.Description
        ErrorHelpFile = Err.HelpFile
        ErrorHelpContext = Err.HelpContext
End Sub

' Return a textual representation of the stack.
Public Function ErrorStackText() As String
Dim routine_info As RoutineInfo
Dim result As String
Dim num_spaces As Integer

        ' Make sure there is stack info.
        If ErrorStack Is Nothing Then Stop

        ' Start with the error information.
        result = "Error " & Format$(ErrorNumber) & _
            "." & vbCrLf & Err.Description & vbCrLf & _
            vbCrLf & "Stack dump:" & vbCrLf

        ' Create the entries for each routine.
        For Each routine_info In ErrorStack
```

```
        ' Add this routine's information.
        result = result & routine_info.TextValue(num_spaces)
        num_spaces = num_spaces + 4
    Next routine_info

    ErrorStackText = result

    ' Empty the stack.
    Set ErrorStack = Nothing
End Function
```

All this elaborate preparation allows the actual error handlers in the main program to be relatively simple. If a routine that is called by another encounters an error, it simply calls AddToErrorStack to save its trace information. It sets the reraise parameter to True so AddToErrorStack raises the errStackDump error when it finishes. Control moves up the call stack until Visual Basic finds an installed error handler. Because the routine that called AddToErrorStack is already executing in an error handler, control moves past that routine to the routine that called it.

For example, in Figure 13.2, subroutine Sub_A calls subroutine Sub_A_1. When Sub_A_1 encounters an error, it calls AddToErrorStack. That routine raises the errStackDump error and control moves back up the stack. Because Sub_A_1 is already executing an error handler, control passes up the stack to Sub_A.

Then Sub_A also invokes AddToErrorStack. That records information about Sub_A and reraises the errStackDump error. Control continues up the call stack.

The following code shows how subroutine Sub_A_1 handles errors. If its option button is selected, it raises an error itself. If the button is not selected, it invokes subroutine Sub_A_1_1. In any case, if the routine encounters an error, it calls AddToErrorStack.

```
Private Sub Sub_A_1()
Dim txt As String

    On Error GoTo Sub_A_1_Error

    txt = "In Sub_A_1"

    If optError(errSub_A_1).Value Then Err.Raise 9

    Sub_A_1_1
    Exit Sub

Sub_A_1_Error:
    ' Save our information and start or continue
    ' a stack dump.
```

```
        AddToErrorStack True, "Sub_A_1", "txt", txt
End Sub
```

Eventually, control moves all the way up the call stack until it reaches the routine that started the code running; usually, that is an event handler. In program StackDmp, the event handler that starts it all is cmdExecute_Click.

When this routine encounters an error, it calls subroutine AddToErrorStack much as the other routines do. This time, however, it sets the reraise parameter to False so AddToErrorStack does not raise the errStackDump error. If it raised an error, control would pass beyond the program's code and the application would crash.

After calling AddToErrorStack, the event handler uses the ErrorStackText function to build and display the final stack trace message. In this case, the program displays the message in a TextBox. It could just as easily display it in a message box, save it to a file, write it to a database, or mail it to you and other developers as described in the following sections.

```
' Clear txtResults and execute Sub_A. If there is
' an error, display the results in txtResults.
Private Sub cmdExecute_Click()
Dim txt As String

    On Error GoTo ExecuteError

    txtResults.Text = ""

    txt = "In cmdExecute"

    If optError(errCmdExecute).Value Then Err.Raise 9

    Sub_A

    txtResults.Text = "Ok"
    Exit Sub

ExecuteError:
    ' Save our information but do not reraise
    ' the stack dump error.
    AddToErrorStack False, "cmdExecute", "txt", txt

    ' Display the stack dump. This resets the stack.
    txtResults.Text = ErrorStackText
    Exit Sub
End Sub
```

This system is a bit tricky, so you may want to step through program StackDmp a few times in the debugger to see how things work. All of the code is available at the Web site. The complicated code is contained in the Stackerr.bas module and the RoutineInfo class. The main program's error handling code is fairly straightforward.

Save Errors in a File

Instead of presenting error messages to the user, a program can append error messages to a file. You can periodically check this file to see what errors have occurred.

Program FileErr demonstrates this technique. When you click its Raise Error button, the program invokes the SaveErrorToFile subroutine as shown in the following code.

```
' Raise an error.
Private Sub cmdRaiseError_Click()
    On Error GoTo RaiseErrorError

    ' Raise a divide by zero error.
    Err.Raise 11

RaiseErrorError:
    SaveErrorToFile "FileError.cmdRaiseError_Click"
    Exit Sub
End Sub
```

Subroutine SaveErrorToFile begins by using the MakeErrorMessage function to create an appropriate error message. It then opens a log file, writes the error information into the file, and closes the file. In this example, the program writes to the file errors.log in the current directory. You could modify it to write to a file in a fixed location, possibly on a shared network hard drive.

If SaveErrorToFile has trouble saving information to the log file, it falls back to the more elementary strategy of displaying the error to the user. It uses MakeErrorMessage to create a new message describing the problem with the error log file. It then displays both messages to the user.

```
' Append mail to an error log file.
Public Sub SaveErrorToFile(ByVal routine_name As String)
Dim txt1 As String
Dim txt2 As String
Dim file_name As String
Dim fnum As Integer
Dim file_open As Boolean
```

```vb
' Create the error message.
txt1 = MakeErrorMessage(routine_name)

On Error GoTo SaveErrorToFileError

' Open the file.
fnum = FreeFile
file_name = App.Path
If Right$(file_name, 1) <> "\" _
    Then file_name = file_name & "\"
file_name = file_name & "errors.log"
Open file_name For Append As #fnum

' Remember that the file is open.
file_open = True

' Write the date and time, and the error message.
Print #fnum, Now
Print #fnum, txt1
Print #fnum, "**********"

' Close the file.
Close #fnum
Exit Sub

SaveErrorToFileError:
    ' There was an error saving to the file.
    ' Just present the message.
    txt2 = MakeErrorMessage("SaveErrorToFile")
    MsgBox "Error saving error message to file." & _
        vbCrLf & _
        "Please record the following information " & _
        "and send it to the development team:" & _
        vbCrLf & vbCrLf & txt2 & _
        vbCrLf & vbCrLf & txt1

    ' Close the file if we opened it.
    If file_open Then Close #fnum
    Exit Sub
End Sub

' Make an appropriate error message.
Public Function MakeErrorMessage(ByVal routine_name As String) As String
    MakeErrorMessage = _
        "Unexpected error " & _
        Format$(Err.Number) & _
        " in " & routine_name & "." & _
        vbCrLf & Err.Description
End Function
```

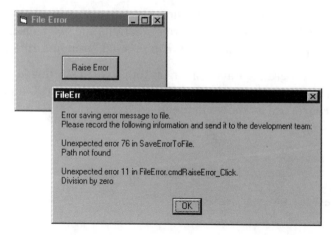

Figure 13.3   Program FileErr displays an error message when it cannot write to the error log file.

When subroutine SaveErrorToFile works, it adds messages like the ones shown here to the error log file.

```
6/30/98 4:33:36 PM
Unexpected error 11 in ProcessRequests.PrintReports.
Division by zero
**********
6/27/98 1:57:36 PM
Unexpected error 9 in ProcessRequests.AlignArrays.
Subscript out of range
**********
```

When SaveErrorToFile has a problem, it displays an error message like the one shown in Figure 13.3.

Save Errors in a Database

If a program saves error messages in a file, you can cut and paste them into reports, error management systems, or other documentation. If the messages are saved in a database, you can also write programs to manipulate them.

For example, you could develop an incident tracking system. For each incident, the database would record such items as description, status (New, Assigned, Fixed, Tested, etc.), person assigned, actions taken, date reported, date fixed, and so forth. With this system in place, a program can write error messages directly into the incident tracking database. It can automatically enter values like the description and creation date, and it can set the error's status to New. These errors will automatically appear in new incident reports.

Program DBErr, available at the Web site, shows how to save simple error information to a database. It saves only the record's creation time and a description. A real incident management system would require much more information.

When you click the program's Raise Error button, it raises a divide by zero error. The program's error handler calls subroutine SaveErrorToDatabase to create the new error record as shown in the following code.

```
' Raise an error.
Private Sub cmdRaiseError_Click()
    On Error GoTo RaiseErrorError

    ' Raise a divide by zero error.
    Err.Raise 11

RaiseErrorError:
    SaveErrorToDatabase "FileError.cmdRaiseError_Click"
End Sub
```

Subroutine SaveErrorToDatabase, shown in the following code, calls the MakeErrorMessage function to generate an appropriate error message. It then opens the error database, uses an SQL statement to create the new error record, and closes the database.

In this example, the program uses the Access database errors.mdb in the current directory. You could modify it to use a database in a different directory. You could also use a different kind of database, such as Oracle or Informix.

If SaveErrorToDatabase encounters an error while creating the new error record, it falls back to the less-complicated strategy of displaying an error message. It uses MakeErrorMessage to create a new message describing the problem with the database and it displays both messages to the user.

```
' Create a new error record in the error database.
Public Sub SaveErrorToDatabase(ByVal routine_name As String)
Dim txt1 As String
Dim txt2 As String
Dim error_database As Database
Dim database_open As Boolean
Dim database_name As String

    ' Create the error message.
    txt1 = MakeErrorMessage(routine_name)

    On Error GoTo SaveErrorToDatabaseError

    ' Open the database.
    database_name = App.Path
    If Right$(database_name, 1) <> "\" _
```

```
        Then database_name = database_name & "\"
    database_name = database_name & "errors.mdb"
    Set error_database = OpenDatabase(database_name)

    ' Remember that the database is open.
    database_open = True

    ' Save the new information.
    error_database.Execute _
        "INSERT INTO AutoErrors VALUES(" & _
        "Now, '" & txt1 & "')"

    ' Close the database.
    error_database.Close
    Exit Sub


SaveErrorToDatabaseError:
    ' There was an error saving to the file.
    ' Just present the message.
    txt2 = MakeErrorMessage("SaveErrorToFile")
    MsgBox "Error saving error message to database." & _
        vbCrLf & _
        "Please record the following information " & _
        "and send it to the development team:" & _
        vbCrLf & vbCrLf & txt2 & _
        vbCrLf & vbCrLf & txt1

    ' Close the database if we opened it.
    If database_open Then error_database.Close
    Exit Sub
End Sub


' Make an appropriate error message.
Public Function MakeErrorMessage(ByVal routine_name As String) As String
    MakeErrorMessage = _
        "Unexpected error " & _
        Format$(Err.Number) & _
        " in " & routine_name & "." & _
        vbCrLf & Err.Description
End Function
```

Figure 13.4 shows Visual Basic 5's Visual Data Manager, available in the Add-Ins menu, displaying a record from the simple error database used by program DBErr. Visual Basic 6's Visual Data Manager is similar. The Data Manager in Visual Basic 4 is significantly different, but it provides similar features for viewing and modifying database files.

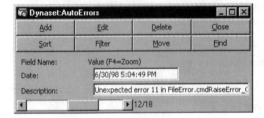

Figure 13.4 Visual Data Manager displaying error records.

Send Email

Writing error messages into files or databases are passive techniques. You must look in the file or database to find new errors. Few developers realize they can make bug notification more active by automatically sending messages to developers using electronic mail.

Program MailErr uses Microsoft's messaging application program interface (MAPI) to send mail when it encounters an error. To send mail, the program uses the MAPISession and MAPIMessages controls. Because these are controls, they must reside on a form. The program's MailErrorForm contains both of these controls and the SendErrorMail subroutine that uses them.

When you click the main program's Raise Error button, the code raises a divide by zero error. An error handler catches the error and invokes the MailError-Form's SendErrorMail subroutine as shown in the following code.

```
' Raise an error.
Private Sub cmdRaiseError_Click()
    On Error GoTo RaiseErrorError

    ' Raise a divide by zero error.
    Err.Raise 11

RaiseErrorError:
    MailErrorForm.SendErrorMail "MailError.cmdRaiseError_Click"
End Sub
```

Subroutine SendErrorMail sets the MAPISession control's UserName and Password properties, and then signs on to the mail system. You will need to modify the UserName and Password values for your system.

The routine then fills in the MAPIMessages control's properties to define the message's recipient, subject, and body text. You could modify this code to send the mail to more than one recipient.

The program then sends the mail with the Send command. It gives this command the parameter False to indicate that the control should not display a status message to the user. Finally, the subroutine signs off the mail session.

If SendErrorMail encounters an error while sending the mail, it falls back to the strategy of displaying an error message to the user. It uses MakeErrorMessage to create a new message describing the problem with the mail system and it displays both messages.

```
' Send mail to the bugs account.
Public Sub SendErrorMail(ByVal routine_name As String)
Dim txt1 As String
Dim txt2 As String

    ' Create the error message.
    txt1 = MakeErrorMessage(routine_name)

    On Error GoTo SendErrorMailError

    mpsErrorMail.UserName = "user@user_computer"
    mpsErrorMail.Password = "user_password"
    mpsErrorMail.SignOn

    mpmErrorMail.SessionID = mpsErrorMail.SessionID
    mpmErrorMail.Compose
    mpmErrorMail.RecipDisplayName = "Automatically Reported Bugs"
    mpmErrorMail.RecipAddress = "bugs@development_computer"
    mpmErrorMail.AddressResolveUI = False
    mpmErrorMail.MsgSubject = "Automatic Error Report"
    mpmErrorMail.MsgNoteText = txt1
    mpmErrorMail.Send False

    mpsErrorMail.SignOff

    ' Make sure this form is not loaded.
    Unload Me
    Exit Sub

SendErrorMailError:
    ' There was an error saving to the file.
    ' Just present the message.
    txt2 = MakeErrorMessage("SendErrorMail")
    MsgBox "Error mailing automatic error message." & _
        vbCrLf & _
        "Please record the following information " & _
        "and send it to the development team:" & _
        vbCrLf & vbCrLf & txt2 & _
        vbCrLf & vbCrLf & txt1
```

```
    ' Make sure this form is not loaded.
    Unload Me
    Exit Sub
End Sub

' Make an appropriate error message.
Public Function MakeErrorMessage(ByVal routine_name As String) As String
    MakeErrorMessage = _
        "Unexpected error " & _
        Format$(Err.Number) & _
        " in " & routine_name & "." & _
        vbCrLf & Err.Description
End Function
```

By sending you mail, this method bring errors to your attention promptly. If you act quickly, you may be able to diagnose and solve the problem before users are aware it exists.

Self-Test

Program Bad13, shown in Figure 13.5, uses another strategy for handling errors. It writes error messages into separate files. When the program encounters an error, subroutine SaveErrorToFile examines the files in the directory specified by the FILE_PREFIX constant. It adds successive values to the prefix filename until it finds a filename that does not yet exist. For example, the program looks for C:\Temp\err1.txt, C:\Temp\err2.txt, C:\Temp\err3.txt, and so forth until if finds a file that does not exist. The routine then opens that file and saves the error information in it.

Program Bad13 calculates the ratio of two numbers. Enter values in the two TextBoxes and click the Calculate button. The program displays the ratio of the first value to the second. Enter nonnumeric values or the value 0 for the second variable to generate errors.

The following code shows how the program calculates ratios and displays errors when it catches them. It has several problems that make it less than ideal

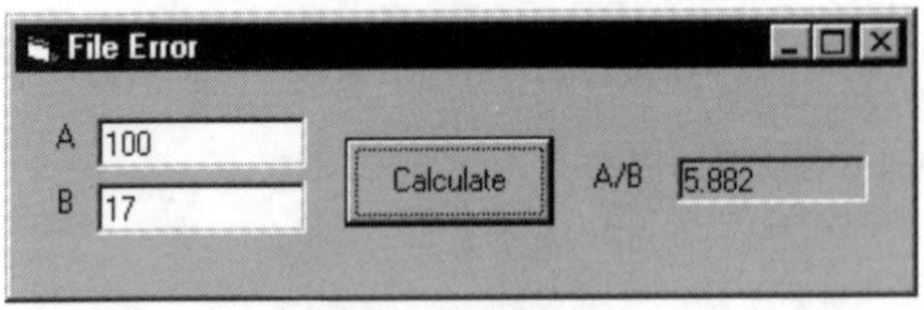

Figure 13.5   Program Bad13.

at error handling. Look over the code and try to find ways to improve it. Appendix A, "Self-Test Solutions," contains a better version of the program that handles errors more safely.

```
' Calculate the ratio of A / B.
Private Sub cmdCalculate_Click()
Dim A As Single
Dim B As Single
Dim A_over_B As Single

    On Error GoTo RaiseErrorError

    A = CSng(txtA.Text)
    B = CSng(txtB.Text)
    A_over_B = A / B
    lblAOverB.Caption = Format$(A_over_B, "0.000")

RaiseErrorError:
    SaveErrorToFile _
        "Error " & Format$(Err.number) & _
        " in FileError.cmdRaiseError_Click." & _
        vbCrLf & Err.Description
End Sub

' Append mail to an error log file.
Public Sub SaveErrorToFile(ByVal txt As String)
Const FILE_PREFIX = "C:\Errors\err"
Const FILE_SUFFIX = ".txt"
Dim file_name As String
Dim fnum As Integer
Dim trial As Integer

    On Error GoTo SaveErrorToFileError

    ' Find a file name we can use.
    trial = 1
    Do
        ' Compute the next name to try.
        file_name = FILE_PREFIX & _
            Format$(trial) & FILE_SUFFIX

        ' See if the file exists.
        If Dir(file_name) = "" Then Exit Do
        trial = trial + 1
    Loop

    ' Open the file.
    fnum = FreeFile
    Open file_name For Append As #fnum
```

```
' Write the date and time, and the error message.
Print #fnum, Now, txt, "**********"

' Close the file.
Close #fnum
Exit Sub

SaveErrorToFileError:
' There was an error saving to the file.
' Just display the message.
MsgBox txt
Exit Sub
End Sub
```

Summary

The following Bug Stoppers summarize the standard error management code described in this chapter. Combined with the concepts explained in Chapter 12, "Error Handling Fundamentals," these provide formidable protection against all sorts of unanticipated problems.

 BUG STOPPERS: Standard Error Handlers

Use a systematic approach.

Handle error events raised by controls.

Present error messages to the user.

Use stack unwinding error handlers.

Save errors in a file.

Save errors in a database.

Send electronic error mail.

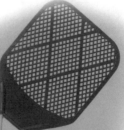

PART FIVE

Post-Coding Activities

Many developers think their jobs are finished when they have written enough code. Actually, there are several important tasks that should occur after the code is produced. The developer must test, debug, profile, and optimize the code. An independent tester should also evaluate the code to see if the developer missed anything. As the pieces of the system are finished, they must be assembled and tested. Finally, after the application is certified and packaged for end users, the developers should analyze the project to see if they can learn anything for future projects.

The chapters that follow discuss these post-coding activities in detail. They explain what these tasks are and how you can approach them to create the best applications possible.

CHAPTER 14

Testing

M ost programmers know, at least at a theoretical level, that a program must eventually be tested before it is packaged for sale. Unfortunately, most also regard testing as something that occurs quickly at the end of the project. A few fast tests, perhaps a bug fix or two, and the application is off to the end users.

That attitude is guaranteed to cause trouble. At best, the project will be significantly delayed or shipped with unfixed bugs. At worst, last-minute testing will discover design flaws so great that the entire project must be scrapped.

This chapter describes different kinds of testing that you should apply to your development efforts. It covers testing habits that can help you catch bugs as soon as possible, before they can corrupt other parts of the program. Following these techniques will help you reduce the chances of discovering nasty surprises just before the project's due date.

Use Many Tests

Testing is the process of working with a program to expose bugs. Bugs can be very difficult to find, so no single test is likely to find them all. To catch as many bugs as possible, you need to use a wide variety of tests so each can flush out some fraction of the program's bugs.

One way to classify tests is by method, scope, and development phase. The method is a specific testing technique. Scope indicates the amount of the system considered by the test. Development phase indicates the time at which the test is performed. These classifications are described in the following sections.

Testing Techniques

There are many different testing techniques, each of which may find some of the bugs in a program. You should use as many techniques as possible so you catch as many bugs as you can. The following list summarizes some of the more important testing methods you can use.

Code walkthrough. Mentally step through the code imagining what it will do at each step.

Code step through. Step through the code in the debugger and watch what it does.

Code review. Explain the code to other developers. This can take the form of a verbal code walkthrough.

Exhaustive input checking. Send every possible input to a routine and verify that it produces correct results.

Black box testing. Send a large number of randomly selected inputs to a routine and verify that it produces correct results.

White box testing. Send a carefully selected set of inputs to a routine and verify that it produces correct results.

Each of these techniques is explained in greater detail later in this chapter.

Test Scope

In addition to using different testing methods, you can test the code at different granularities. You can test individual subroutines and you can test the complete, assembled system. You should test at every level possible to ensure that you catch the greatest number of bugs.

The natural progression for test granularity is: routine, module, subsystem, system. Begin by testing individual routines. When you can find no bugs in the routines, test them together in their modules. For example, suppose you have a .bas module that contains routines for performing matrix multiplication. Study the module and examine the interactions among the routines it contains. Identify the public variables and routines exposed to the outside world and carefully define their characteristics. Write test programs to exercise the features provided by the module.

When you can find no more problems in modules, combine them into subsystems and test them. In Visual Basic, a subsystem might be an ActiveX control, or the client or server in a client/server application.

As you test the subsystems, combine them to form larger subsystems as necessary. Finally, when you have tested all the subsystems, assemble them into the finished application and test them together.

Development Phase

Many programmers think testing is something that occurs only at the end of the project. However, the longer a bug remains undetected, the harder it is to fix. If you defer testing to the end of the project, you are guaranteed to find the bugs as late as possible and many will be difficult to fix. Bugs found at the last minute can have repercussions that may delay the application's release or result in a buggy product.

Testing must occur throughout the entire development process. You should even test the initial requirements and high-level design. Obviously, you cannot step through the high-level design in the debugger because the design is not program code. You can still apply the other testing techniques, however. You can perform walkthroughs and design reviews to make sure the design makes sense. You can even perform limited forms of black box and white box testing. You and other developers can generate a collection of scenarios and perform walkthroughs to see how the design handles them.

Bugs that enter the project during the design phase can have profound consequences later in the project. They can be so hard to fix later that it is worth almost any amount of effort to fix them immediately.

Step through the Code

Visual Basic is blessed with an extremely powerful debugger. As soon as you finish writing a routine, you should use the debugger to verify that it does what you think it should. Stepping through the code in the debugger gives a very different impression than staring at the code does. Stepping through the routine allows you to find bugs that are easy to miss when you read the source code.

Begin testing by setting a breakpoint on the routine's first line. Click on the line and press F9 or select the Run menu's Toggle Breakpoint command. Then start the program. When the program reaches the line you marked, it will stop.

Use Shift-F8, the Run menu's Step Over command, or the Step Over button to let the program execute the next line of code. To step into subroutines, use F8, the Run menu's Step Into command, or the Step Into button.

Sometimes it is convenient to skip a series of statements. For example, the routine might contain a For loop that will execute thousands of times. In that case, first step through the loop a few times to make sure it seems to be doing its job properly. Then click on the first line after the loop and place a breakpoint there. Press F5 to make the program run until it reaches the breakpoint.

As you step through the routine, examine the variables. Make sure they contain the values you think they should. If a value seems strange, study the code until you understand how the value was generated. Do not accept the value until you have proven to yourself that it is correct.

Continue stepping through the code until you reach the end of the routine. Then start over again and follow a different path through the code. If an If statement's condition was True the first time you walked through the routine, make it False this time. Repeat the entire process, examining variables to make sure they have the correct values, until you reach the end of the routine.

Then do it again, and again, and again until you have executed every line of code in the routine. Do not skip any code assuming it is too simple to be wrong. Assume every line could be wrong. Be patient. Thoroughly walking through a subroutine can take quite a while. The time you spend now, however, will be more than repaid in reduced debugging time later.

Hold Code Reviews

After you have stepped through a routine in the debugger, you should hold a code review to discuss the routine with other programmers. The review should include the routine's author (you), at least one experienced programmer, and at least one inexperienced programmer. The three of you provide very different points of view that allow you to catch more bugs than any one of you would separately.

As the routine's author, you know how the code works, or at least how it is intended to work. Explaining the code to the others helps make your ideas concrete. Often the process of explaining the code verbally or in writing is enough to help you discover new bugs.

Advanced reviewers ask hard "what if" questions. They can probe the routine for weaknesses and look for special cases that are not handled properly. They should pay special attention to the routine's assumptions and error handling code.

Inexperienced reviewers ask questions that others will not. The answers to some of these questions seem obvious to you and more experienced reviewers. Sometimes the answers are so obvious that more experienced programmers will overlook the fact that they are wrong. If you explain the code to a beginner while a more experienced programmer listens, the two of them sometimes find bugs that none of you would find alone. At the same time, the beginner learns more about good programming practices and bugs that may arise in the future.

Test Exhaustively

To perform an exhaustive test, you send every possible input into a routine and verify that the result is correct. This kind of test is almost foolproof. If you test every input the routine might ever encounter, the routine cannot fail to produce correct results later. Note that you still need to protect the routine from unforeseen conditions, such as when a crucial file is missing or the system runs out of memory.

Unfortunately, it is almost never possible to test a routine exhaustively. Most routines must be able to handle so many different inputs that testing every possible combination is impossible. For example, suppose a routine is designed to sort a list of 10 numbers with values between 1 and 100. The number of possible arrangements of 10 numbers between 1 and 100 is $100^{10} = 10^{20}$. Even if you could test 1 million of these combinations per second, it would take more than 3 million years to test them all. Many routines used in real applications have far more possible inputs than this.

In cases when you cannot test exhaustively, you can turn to black box and white box testing.

Perform Black Box Testing

In a black box test, you treat a routine as if it were a black box. You dump inputs into the routine, see what comes out, and verify that the results are correct. You use no information about how the routine works or what goes on inside the box to pick the test cases.

If you can test every possible input, black box testing turns into exhaustive testing. Normally, however, you do not have time to test exhaustively. Instead, you can generate a large number of random inputs, dump them into the black box, and verify the results. If you test several million of the 10^{20} possible input combinations, you will have some chance of detecting the routine's most frequently occurring bugs.

Black box tests are usually much easier to run than either exhaustive or white box testing, so you should run them whenever possible.

Perform White Box Testing

When you perform a white box test, you are allowed to peek inside the box and see how the routine works. Using that information, you devise the most treacherous combinations of inputs that you can. You pick the nastiest special cases and the weirdest values to create inputs that are likely to cause problems for the routine. The following list presents some general guidelines you can follow to flush out bugs.

Do the unexpected. Pick inputs that will not generally be expected by the routine. Test unusual and impossible conditions. If the routine takes a person's age as an input, try passing it the ages 0, –1, and 90,000. If the routine assumes an input is nonzero, try to invoke it with that input set to 0. Make sure the routine verifies its arguments and catches any invalid values.

Follow all paths. Devise inputs that force the routine to execute every line of code. Consider all of the If, Select Case, and other statements that perform decisions. Then try to generate inputs that force every possible combination of those decisions.

Test boundaries. Use inputs that exercise the boundary conditions of arrays, collections, and other data structures used by the routine. If an array has dimensions 1 to 100, see what happens if you try to access entries 0, 1, 100, and 101. Try a few items somewhere in the middle, too.

Do nothing. Try to omit inputs to the routine. If the code takes optional parameters, omit some in every possible combination. If the routine works with a data structure, try passing it one that is empty or that has not been initialized.

In general, discovering the absolutely best possible set of inputs is difficult. The book, *The Art of Software Testing*, by Glenford Myers (John Wiley & Sons, 1979) provides an in-depth look at selecting the best possible test cases for white box testing. It shows how to design the smallest possible number of test cases that are still likely to find any bugs the routine contains.

Consider Global Variables

When you test a routine, remember that global variables may be part of a routine's inputs. If the routine uses global variables and data structures, you need to test their effects, too. Be sure to consider both module-global and system-global objects.

Plan Tests

Plan tests in advance and allow sufficient time for them. Make up a chart of all of the different combinations of test technique, scope, and development phase that make sense and plan tests for them.

Write the tests explicitly into the project schedule. If developers see that the tests are expected, they are more likely to perform them.

Follow each project activity immediately with the tests needed to find any bugs introduced by the activity. After you write a routine, test it. After you write a specification, test it. Try to catch the bugs as early as possible. They will only become harder to remove later.

Test Continuously

The previous sections have mentioned this, but it is so important that it is worth repeating: test continuously. If you leave testing to the end of the project, you guarantee unwelcome surprises. Every developer must test at every stage of the project. Frequent testing allows you to catch bugs before they can cause serious damage.

Have the Proper Attitude

Most programmers find testing a dull chore. They rush through it to get on to something more interesting. Many programmers find bug chasing even more repulsive than testing. If that is the case, you should not think of testing as a horrible task that you should avoid as much as possible. Instead, think of it as an easy way to get out of debugging later. Every hour you spend testing may save you several hours debugging. Tests that catch bugs early let you spend more time writing new code in the long run.

Admit to yourself that you must eventually find and fix all of the bugs. Postponing the inevitable will not make the bugs go away. Find the bugs now using well-focused tests, or find them later when they cause unexpected behavior that may be hard to find and correct.

Write Test Routines

When you test a routine, write test code that you can save for later use. Give test routines appropriate names and place them in test modules. For example, to test a subroutine named FillExpenseTable, write a subroutine named Test_FillExpenseTable. If FillExpenseTable is contained in the module Expenses, put subroutine Test_FillExpenseTable in a module named Test_Expenses.

If the test routine needs access to variables local to the Expenses module, put it in that module. Then use conditional compilation symbols to make it easy to remove the test routine before you compile the final project. Unfortunately, this can be a bit awkward in Visual Basic. If you place an #If statement before a routine and an #End If statement after it, the code editor may not display those statements together with the routine. It may display the #End If statement at the top of the following subroutine. There are two ways you can handle this. First, you can block out only the inside of the routine and leave its declaration and End statement in the file.

Alternatively, you can set the editor to full module view. Select the Tools menu's Options command. Click on the Editor tab and select the Full Module View (in Visual Basic 4) or Default to Full Module View (in Visual Basic 5 and 6) checkbox. This will let you see the #If Then and #End If statements at the same time as the routine they surround.

Save all of your test routines for later use. When you modify the original routine, you will need to retest it to make sure nothing has broken. If you keep the test routines, retesting the modified code will be easy. Remove the test modules from the project before you build the final system, but keep those modules around somewhere.

Create a special Test menu in the application's main menu. Put commands in this menu to run the test routines. Before compiling the program's final version, set this menu's Visible property to False so it is hidden from users.

Look for Bugs

It may seem silly to say this, but the purpose of testing is to find bugs, not to merely pass a test. If passing a test were the goal, you could write tests that did nothing and every routine would pass.

To be useful, a test must find bugs. Every time you find and eliminate a bug, you improve the code. If you do not find any bugs, the test is not helping. You should think of the test as a failure because it failed to improve the code.

Design tests to find bugs. Exercise the toughest special cases you can imagine. Try to flush the bugs out rather than avoiding them.

Test When You Are Alert

When you are inattentive, you are more likely to overlook bugs that you should be able to catch during testing. You will not question suspicious results as closely. You may invent reasons for odd behavior without proving you are correct. You may not think about all of the possible special cases and follow all of the paths through the code.

Test when you are alert. Take a short break between coding and testing. If your attention wanes, take another break. Stay sharp and catch as many bugs as you can while it is still relatively easy. If you miss them now because you are not paying attention, you will need to find them later.

Test a little bit at a time. Testing for too many continuous hours can make you lose your focus. If you have trouble concentrating on the task at hand, take a break, stretch, walk around, and clear your mind. Then come back refreshed and ready to concentrate.

Test It Anyway

If the code is too simple to be wrong, test it anyway. If you make only a tiny change that cannot possibly change the routine's results, test it anyway. If the code looks perfect, test it anyway. Even if you only change comments, test it anyway. It is very easy to intend to change comments and then make just one inconsequential change to the code at the same time. It is surprising how often a change that cannot possibly hurt the code causes a bug. Test to make sure.

Test any time you make changes to the code. Modifying code is much more likely to introduce bugs than writing new code is. Whenever you make a change, no matter how trivial, there is a reasonable chance that you have introduced a new bug. Test the code immediately to catch the bug now.

Running a test that finds no bugs may not be interesting, but it is better than searching for bugs later in code you thought was safe.

Test Ported Code

Test code when you port it from one platform or version of Visual Basic to another. Usually, the code will work, but occasionally, subtle differences will make working code fail.

For example, both Windows 95 and Windows NT declare 32-bit API functions using long integers. The device context handle (hDC) required by many API functions is declared as a long integer. However, Windows 95 uses numbers for hDCs that are less than 32,768. The program can get away with saving hDC values in normal 2-byte integers. If you move this code to Windows NT, it will crash. Windows NT uses hDC values that are too big to fit in 2-byte integers. When the code tries to assign a big long integer value into a short integer, it generates an overflow error.

Test code when you port it. If you have followed the advice of the previous sections, you have saved the test routines you used to test the original code. In that case, testing the code will be easy.

Start from the Immediate Window

Instead of running the entire program, you can test a single subroutine from within the Immediate window. First, set a breakpoint at the beginning of the subroutine. Set another at the beginning of the program and press F5. The program will start and then stop almost immediately.

Now in the Immediate window, enter the name of the subroutine together with any parameters it needs. If the routine modifies any of its parameters, you must create temporary test variables in the main program so you will have variables to pass to the routine. Then press the carriage return key. Visual Basic will invoke the subroutine and stop at your breakpoint.

Executing a function from the Immediate window is generally similar. Type a question mark followed by the function's name, including any arguments it needs. Press the carriage return key to make Visual Basic execute the function and display its return value.

Examine Variables

As you step through a routine, you can easily view the routine's variables. In Visual Basic 4, click on the variable in the source code window. Then click the Instant Watch button or press Shift-F9. In Visual Basic 5 and 6, you can also let the mouse float over the variable to see its value.

You can make the Immediate window display the variable's value by typing a question mark, followed by the variable's name, followed by a carriage return. For example, the following command makes the Immediate window display the value of the variable X.

```
?X
```

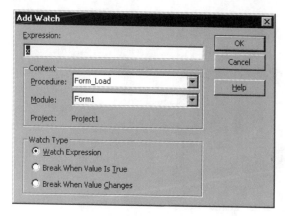

Figure 14.1 Adding a watch for a variable.

You can make the code itself print values to the Immediate window using the Debug.Print statement. For instance, the following code makes the program display the string "X" followed by the value of variable X.

```
Debug.Print "X" & Str$(X)
```

If you want to view the value of a variable frequently, you can set a watch on it. In Visual Basic 4, click on the variable's name and select the Tools menu's Add Watch command. In Visual Basic 5 and 6, click on the variable and select the Debug menu's Add Watch command. You will then see the dialog shown in Figure 14.1. Click the OK button to add the watch.

The Watch window shows the values of watched variables whenever the program stops. Figure 14.2 shows the Watch window attached to the Immediate window. In this example, the variable x has the value 0. The statement ?x in the Immediate window made Visual Basic display the value there as well as in the Watch window.

Expression	Value	Type	Context
66 x	0	Integer	Form1.Form_Load

```
?x
 0
```

Figure 14.2 The Watch and Immediate windows.

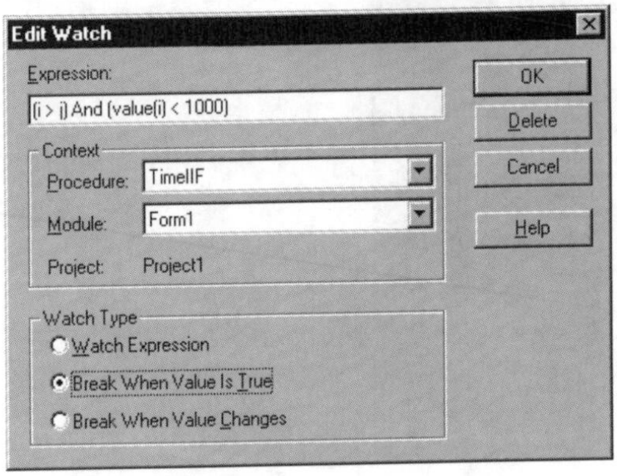

Figure 14.3 Watching for a condition.

You can right-click on the Watch window to display a popup menu allowing you to add, edit, or delete watches. When you edit a watch, Visual Basic displays a dialog like the one shown in Figure 14.3. Using this dialog, you can modify the value Visual Basic displays. If you click the Break When Value Changes option, Visual Basic will stop the program when the variable's value changes. If you click the Break When Value Is True option, the program will stop when the watch expression is True.

Figure 14.3 shows the watch editing dialog preparing a watch expression. In this example, the program will stop whenever the condition (i > j) And (value(i) < 1000) is True. Watch expressions like this one can make finding bugs much easier. If you know a variable is being set to an incorrect value, enter a Boolean expression that says the variable has that value in the watch window. Then run and let the program stop when the variable is set.

Modify Variables

The Immediate window allows you to modify values in addition to displaying them. Simply enter the variable name, an equals sign, and the variable's new value. Then press the carriage return key. For instance, the following line of code sets the variable X to the value 1324.

```
X = 1324
```

Assignments in the Immediate window can include the values of other variables and even function return values. The following statement sets entry number i in the day_name array to the current day's name (Monday, Tuesday, etc.).

```
day_name(i) = Format$(Date, "dddd")
```

Use Ctrl-F9

While running code in the debugger, you can click on a line of code and press Ctrl-F9 to make control jump to that line. This is a remarkably powerful feature provided by few other development environments. It allows you to quickly test different paths through a routine. Test one path. Then use Ctrl-F9 to jump back to the beginning of the routine to test another path.

Sometimes it is hard to make an If statement's condition have the value you want. In that case, you can use Ctrl-F9 to jump into the right part of the If statement's code to see what would happen if the condition has the proper value.

You can even use Ctrl-F9 to skip certain specific statements or jump out of loops. Use caution when you jump into a loop, however. If you jump into the middle of a For loop, the value of the control variable and the loop's status is unclear. For example, suppose when the following code stops, you use Ctrl-F9 to jump to the Debug statement. Visual Basic executes Debug.Print with the variable i set to 0, and then ends the For loop. This is probably not what you would expect. The moral is to jump into loops cautiously or not at all.

```
Private Sub BadJump()
Dim i As Integer

    Stop                            ' Stop here.
    For i = 1 To 10
        Debug.Print i               ' Use Ctrl-F9 to jump to here.
    Next i
End Sub
```

Examine Decision Statements

Decision statements determine the path of execution that the program follows. Decisions made by If and Select statements are more likely to send the program off course than simple calculations are. Because they may mark the beginning of a bad decision, you should pay special attention to If statements while you are testing.

For and While loops make decisions implicitly. Every time the program passes through a loop, it evaluates the loop's stopping conditions to see if it should stop. The logic used by these tests can be confusing, particularly if the code uses Exit statements to break out of the middle of the loop.

As you test a routine, concentrate on the statements that make decisions. Exercise all of the possible decision results so you follow each possible path of execution.

Anticipate Outputs

Some programmers begin a test and then look at the results. If they do not know what to expect, they are likely to convince themselves that the results look correct even if they are not.

Before you begin a test, know what outputs to expect. Compare your predicted outputs with the actual results carefully. If there is a discrepancy, figure out why. Sometimes you will have a simple difference in formatting. Be absolutely certain that is all that is wrong before you declare the results correct. It is easy to convince yourself that a small difference is unimportant when actually a bug is at work.

Fake Errors

Use the Err.Raise statement to simulate error conditions and test a routine's error handling. Test obvious errors such as division by zero (11) in arithmetic expressions and file not found (53). Also test some errors that are unlikely to occur, such as out of memory (7) and object already loaded (360).

If a routine calls other routines or library functions, or uses control properties, simulate errors in those calls. For example, the GetStockObject API function returns 0 if it fails. If a routine uses this function, you should execute the code until you get to the call to GetStockObject. Use Ctrl-F9 to skip that statement and then use the Immediate window to set the return value to 0 to simulate an error.

```
        :
' Set a break point on the following line.
brush_handle = GetStockObject(BLACK_BRUSH)

' Skip to the following line and set
' brush_handle = 0 in the Immediate window.
If brush_handle = 0 Then
    ' Error getting the brush handle.
        :
```

Find Your Own Bugs

Many development projects use separate testers to look for bugs in the code. Part of the reason for having separate testers is that they do not know the code as intimately as the developers do. Because they are unfamiliar with the code's internals, they do not have preconceptions that might stop them from finding cases the code cannot handle. They will hopefully try things the developers will not think of because the developers know what inputs the code expects.

On the other hand, testers cannot design test cases specifically designed to uncover problems in the code. Because they do not understand the code, they cannot perform white box tests. If you wrote a routine, only you understand it well enough to effectively run white box tests.

A tester who finds a bug knows very little about where the bug is or exactly what the problem might be. All he can tell you is that an error occurred. On the other hand, when you find a bug in your own routine, you can usually locate it relatively quickly.

For example, suppose you are building an application that dispatches firefighters. A tester might be able to tell you that the program dispatched a supervisor to a simulated sulfuric acid spill when it should have dispatched a hazardous materials unit. This tells you very little about the cause and location of the error.

On the other hand, suppose you have just finished writing the code that determines which units have the skills to work a particular incident. If you test the routine thoroughly, you may discover that the routine incorrectly gives supervisors every skill. Now you know precisely where the bug is and you can fix it easily.

Do not rely on testers to find your bugs. Catch them yourself before testers even see your code.

Have Someone Else Test Your Code

While you should perform the initial testing on your code, someone else should test it, too. If you understand the assumptions made internally by the code, you may not test those assumptions. Suppose your routine takes as parameters the start and end times for a person's work day. If you work a fairly typical day, you may test the routine only using hours that might actually apply to you. You may not think that some people who work late-night shifts may have a start time (10 P.M.) that comes later than their start time (6 A.M.) the next day. A different tester who is unfamiliar with the code may make a different set of assumptions and uncover weaknesses in the code.

A different person can also take a more objective approach to testing. You naturally do not want your code to fail. Subconsciously you want the tests to fail to find any bugs. A separate tester can attack the code aggressively and wholeheartedly.

Don't Shoot the Messenger

Do not take out your frustrations on the testers who find your bugs. They are just doing their part to improve the program. Testers do not cause bugs, they just find existing bugs that you should have found earlier. They are doing you a favor in exposing your bugs before customers find them. Testers deserve your thanks, not your anger. Do not blunt their enthusiasm for exposing bugs by treating them badly.

Fix Your Own Code

Once a tester identifies a bug in your code, you should fix it yourself. You know your code better than anyone else does, so it will be easier and safer for you to fix the bug.

Modifying code is a risky business. Changes introduce a greater number of bugs per line of code than original coding does. Understanding the entire routine and not just the bug makes changes much less risky. If you originally wrote the routine, you are most likely to understand it in its entirety. Someone else would be tempted to make the change without going to the trouble of mastering the complete routine.

Thank the tester who finds a bug in your code and then fix the bug yourself.

Simulate User Actions

To test large parts of the completed system, you can simulate many user actions using simple Visual Basic code. For example, to simulate a button click, you can invoke the button's Click event handler. To simulate a change in a TextBox, set the TextBox's Text property to a new value.

Using similar techniques, you can build test subroutines that exercise much of the system. To run the tests, you just need to invoke them and verify that the results are correct. In many cases, you can even verify the results automatically. For example, you can compare a TextBox's new text contents to the value you know it should have.

The following code tests the ExpenseReporter application shown in Figure 14.4. It fills in a number of text values and verifies that the program calculates the correct totals in the TotalText, DueEmpText, and DueCompText fields.

Next, the routine invokes a menu command to present a preview of the printed expense report. The preview form, shown in Figure 14.5, is presented modally

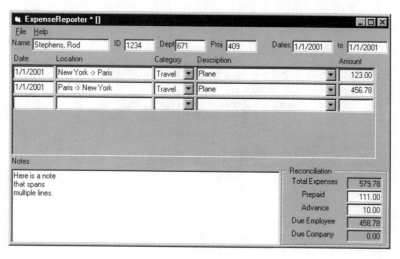

Figure 14.4 The ExpenseReporter application.

so the tester must verify that it is correct and then close it. The routine finishes by verifying that the preview process applied correct styles to the Amount-Text(0) field. That field was entered as "123." The preview command should have changed it to "123.00" before displaying the preview form.

```
Private Sub MainFormTest_001()
    ' Set basic information.
    NameText.Text = "Stephens, Rod"
    IDText.Text = "1234"
    DeptText.Text = "671"
    ProjText.Text = "409"
```

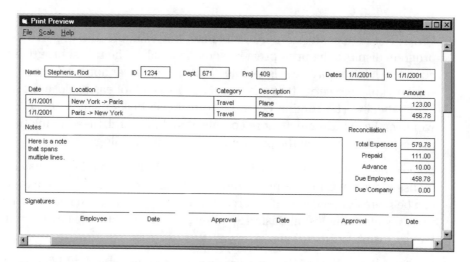

Figure 14.5 The ExpenseReporter program's preview screen.

```
    FromDateText.Text = "1/1/2001"
    ToDateText.Text = "1/1/2001"
    PrepaidText.Text = "111.00"
    AdvanceText.Text = "10.00"
    NotesText.Text = "Here is a note" & _
        vbCrLf & "that spans" & _
        vbCrLf & "multiple lines."

    ' Set expense detail line 0 information.
    DateText(0).Text = "1/1/2001"
    LocationText(0).Text = "New York -> Paris"
    CategoryCombo(0).Text = "Travel"
    DescrCombo(0).Text = "Plane"
    AmountText(0).Text = "123"

    ' Set expense detail line 1 information.
    DateText(1).Text = "1/1/2001"
    LocationText(1).Text = "Paris -> New York"
    CategoryCombo(1).Text = "Travel"
    DescrCombo(1).Text = "Plane"
    AmountText(1).Text = "456.78"

    ' Verify totals.
    If TotalText.Text <> "579.78" Then Stop
    If DueEmpText.Text <> "458.78" Then Stop
    If DueCompText.Text <> "0.00" Then Stop

    mnuFilePrintPreview_Click

    ' Verify number formats modified before
    ' the preview displays.
    If AmountText(0).Text <> "123.00" Then Stop
End Sub
```

Other user actions are harder to simulate. For example, the ExpenseReporter program displays the print preview screen modally. The test subroutine has no control while the preview is visible. That means it cannot easily examine the screen's image to verify that it is correct. It also cannot easily close the preview automatically. The routine could perform these tasks using a timer, but that would make the test much more complicated. In general, these simulation techniques work best when the program uses no modal dialogs.

Some other more exotic operations are also difficult to simulate in Visual Basic. Mouse movement, mouse press and release, and key press and release events can be more complicated. If you really want to, you can even simulate many of these events using Visual Basic's SendKeys statement, and the keybd_event and mouse_event API functions.

Finally, a Visual Basic 5 or 6 program can install a nonstandard WindowProc to read Windows messages directly. To test some of the more exotic messages this program might receive, you may need to send messages directly using the SendMessage API function.

Not all tests are simple enough that simulating them in this way is practical. However, it is worth the effort to simulate as many as possible. Simulations let you quickly and easily perform tests that otherwise might be quite time consuming. If the tests are easy to use, you and other developers are more likely to run them, while you might skip slower, manual tests.

Check Code Coverage

Use the code profiler that comes with Visual Basic to check the program's code coverage. For more information on the profiler, see Chapter 15, "Code Profiler."

In addition to giving performance statistics, the profiler can show you which lines of code are unused. Start the profiler and thoroughly exercise the program. Then examine any lines of code that were not executed. If it is possible to reach a line of code, expand your tests so they execute that line. If it is impossible to reach a line of code, remove it. Unused code indicates a possible bug.

Keep Testing

When you can find no more errors using your current tests, build some more tests using a different approach. If you still cannot find any bugs after trying all the techniques and strange special cases you can think of, stop.

Do not stop testing simply because you are sick of it, you have used up your test cases, or because you have reached the scheduled end date for testing. Remember, the longer a bug stays in the program, the harder it will be to fix. Fixing bugs is easier during testing than it is after you have put the finishing touches on the application. It is also less embarrassing than letting your customers find bugs and telling all their friends and business associates that you write buggy software.

Stop testing when testing is no longer profitable; in other words, when it no longer finds bugs.

Estimate the Number of Bugs

If you can accurately estimate the number of bugs remaining, and if you can predict the speed with which you will find and fix the bugs, you can guess how long you will need to continue testing. Unfortunately, neither of these estimates is easy.

Estimating the number of bugs remaining is hard. Often in programming classes a student has asked me for help, saying, "I just have one more bug." The student assumes there is only one bug due to lack of experience. Really there are usually several bugs; the student just knows about one.

There are several ways you can estimate the number of bugs remaining in a program. One method is to guess based on previous experience or industry averages. If this project team produced three errors per hundred lines of code in the past, and if this project is similar to the previous ones, then the current project will probably contain about three errors per hundred lines of code.

Another method is to examine a large piece of code extremely closely and count the number of bugs it contains. You then assume the rest of the project has a similar number of bugs per line of code. For this method to be useful, you need to be relatively certain you have found most of the bugs in the test code. Pieces of the code must also have been written by the developers in proportion to their contributions to the project as a whole. If one programmer wrote 10 percent of the project's code, 10 percent of the sample should come from that programmer. Finally, the sample code should be representative of the project as a whole. If only 5 percent of the project is mail processing code, the sample must not contain 95 percent mail processing code.

One intriguing technique for bug estimation is to seed the code with artificial bugs. After a certain amount of testing, you compute the fraction of the seed bugs that have been found. If the testers have found half of the seed bugs, they have hopefully found roughly half of the other bugs, too. Of course, if the seed bugs do not resemble the real bugs, the estimate will be inaccurate. If the code contains a lot of bugs involving Internet communications but the seed bugs contain none, those bugs will not be counted.

These techniques cannot guarantee accurate predictions, but they can give you a rough estimate with which to work. If you estimate the project contains around 470 bugs and you have found only 125, you need to continue testing. If your current testing methods are not finding bugs, you should design some new tests. You should not rest with an estimated 345 bugs outstanding until you have made an extraordinary effort to find them. Chances are they are there waiting for your customers to find them.

Estimate Bug Finding Time

Once you have a guess for the number of bugs remaining, you need to estimate the speed with which the testers can find the bugs. This is not easy, either. Some bugs are harder to find than others. As the number of bugs remaining decreases, it will probably become harder to find new bugs. The bugs that

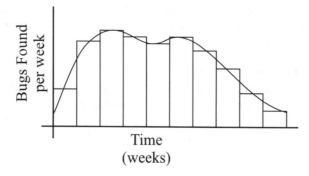

Figure 14.6 A graph of bugs found per week.

remain will also have been in the code the longest so they will be the hardest to fix and the most likely to cause new bugs.

If the tests do not expose all of the possible kinds of bugs, you may not know others exist until late in the testing process. For example, if none of the tests you used to predict the bug count exercises the electronic mail interface, lots of bugs may be hidden in that part of the code.

One simple method for estimating bug catching time is to graph the number of bugs found per unit time in the past. The graph may reveal an obvious trend. In Figure 14.6, the number of bugs found per week wobbles around a bit, drops quickly, and then starts to level out. If this trend continues, the team will not find many bugs in the next few weeks. At this point, the effectiveness of the tests is declining. If you have not found a substantial fraction of the bugs estimated, you should design a new set of tests to locate the hidden bugs.

Test User Interfaces from the Top Down

Visual Basic makes top-down development easy. Once you have a solid design, you can quickly put together the application's main forms. You can then incrementally add controls, menus, and code behind them. The system develops in a top-down fashion. The high-level objects like forms are created first and the low-level coding details are added later.

As the project develops, you can test it in a top-down fashion. When you add a command button to a form, test it. Initially write a dummy event handler that just presents a message box saying it is there. As you fill in the details, test them.

In order to test some routines, you may need to write other dummy routines. If a subroutine calls three functions, you will need to write dummies for each of them. These dummies must take reasonable inputs and produce correct outputs so you can test the calling routine. It does not matter how the dummies produce their results, however. For example, they may look up results that have been computed by hand and stored in a text file or database.

Because of the need for extensive test cases and dummy routines that can simulate them, it is hard to analyze elaborate code subsystems using top-down testing. On the other hand, testing user interfaces is relatively easy. You can create the forms, buttons, and menus. Add the code that displays different kinds of forms and dialogs. Provide simple dummies for code that does not deal directly with the user interface.

Using this technique, you can test the user interface code quickly and verify that the program behaves properly on the surface. You can also show this interface to your customers early in the project and get feedback before you have written a huge amount of code.

Test Code from the Bottom Up

Intricate code systems are hard to test using a top-down approach. A bottom-up strategy can make testing them much easier.

First, test the routines that do not call any other routines. Once they are thoroughly tested, test routines that call only routines that have been tested. Continue the process, testing more complex routines using only tested routines, until you have tested all of the code.

At this point, integrate the code that was tested from the bottom up with the user interface that was tested from the top down. Now you can test the complete application. If you have properly tested the user interface code and the more complex application code, you should not find many bugs at this stage.

Perform a Postmortem

An important but often neglected part of development is a thorough dissection of the project after its completion. You can learn a lot from the bugs encountered during development, but only if you pay close attention. Making mistakes does not automatically make you wiser. You must study the errors carefully to learn from them.

During this postmortem analysis, you should determine why things went wrong and how they were fixed. Using that information, you can hopefully make fewer mistakes in the future. The following list summarizes questions you should ask about each bug.

What was the bug? Be sure you understand what the bug was.

At what stage in project development was the bug introduced? It is a well-known fact that the longer a bug remains in a project, the harder it is to fix. Pay special attention to bugs introduced during the design phase and other early stages.

Who caused the bug? You do not need to be judgmental about this, but you need to find out who caused the bug. Someone who caused a large number of bugs might benefit from some extra training. If someone proves better at one aspect of the project than another, he might concentrate on that area. For example, some people are great at high-level design and documentation but weak at coding. Use everyone's strengths in the future.

When and how was the bug detected? Can that method of detection be used intentionally to look for similar errors in the future? You may be able to use the method to devise new tests to catch similar bugs earlier.

Could the bug have been detected sooner? If you can figure out ways to find similar bugs sooner, you can use them to improve tests and increase early detection.

How could the bug have been prevented in the first place? The easiest bugs to fix are those that do not occur. If you can think of ways to make the bug less likely to occur, use them in the future. This does not include statements like, "Pay better attention to detail." Answers must be concrete to be useful. For example, "Finalize database design before designing user management module."

Of course, not all of this information will be available at the end of the project unless you do a little bookkeeping during development. If a bug was introduced during design and fixed during early development, no one may remember it by the time the project is finished.

Developers should keep track of the bugs as they are found and fixed. The process must be easy enough that it does not become a burden to the developers. Otherwise, they may not bother to record the bugs, or their productivity will suffer.

To minimize the amount of extra work required, developers should record only bugs that make it into the project's master code. A bug that a developer writes into a new subroutine and then immediately fixes does not count.

The developer should record the minimum amount of information needed to analyze the bug later. This includes where the bug is located, its description, and when it was detected. For example:

Module: Validate.BAS
Routine: IntOk

What: Overflow when the user enters a 5-digit value greater than 32767.

Detected: Coding

Knowing the module and routine that contains the bug, you can probably deduce who caused the bug and when, even at the end of the project.

Gather this information and study it. Pay special attention to bugs that took a long time to detect or fix. Share your results with other projects. You may not be able to prevent every problem from reoccurring in another project, but you guarantee problems if you refuse to learn from past mistakes.

Self-Test

Because testing is a bit different from the topics covered in previous chapters, this section does not present source code for you to evaluate. Instead, it describes an application for you to test. Figure 14.7 shows a simple calculator program named Calc. This program allows the user to enter numbers with up to 12 characters including a decimal point, plus an optional negative sign. The user can click on the buttons to perform simple arithmetic calculations. In addition to clicking buttons, the user can enter values and operators using the keyboard.

The program displays the result of the calculation if the result will fit in 12 characters. If the result is too large, the program displays the string Overflow. If the value is too large a negative number, the program displays Underflow. If the user tries to divide by 0, the program displays #INF.

For this self-test, design a set of black box tests for this program. Because you do not know how the application works internally, you cannot build white box tests. However, knowing the program's specification, you can probably create a set of gray box tests that search for strange special cases that might give the

Figure 14.7   The Calc program.

program trouble. For example, these tests should divide by 0, cause an overflow and underflow, and so forth.

Write the tests in English. There is little point in writing tests in Visual Basic code until you have looked at the program's source code. Appendix A, "Self-Test Solutions," contains a description of tests used to find bugs in this program. You can find the source code for the program including its tests at the book's Web site at www.vb-helper.com/err.htm.

Summary

Testing may not be much fun, but it is certainly better than endless bug chasing. Test properly and often to catch bugs as quickly as possible. In the long run, testing will let you spend less time in pursuit of bugs and more time doing more interesting things, such as coding. The following Bug Stoppers summarize the testing concepts described in this chapter.

 ## BUG STOPPERS: Testing

Use lots of different kinds of tests.

Test using different techniques.

Test at routine, module, subsystem, and system levels.

Test during all phases of development.

After you finish a routine, step through it using the debugger.

Hold code reviews.

Test exhaustively if possible.

Use black box testing.

Use white box testing.

Don't forget, global variables are inputs, too.

Plan tests ahead of time.

Test continuously throughout the project.

Test right away.

Have the attitude that testing is intended to catch bugs.

Write test routines and save them for later.

Look for bugs. Don't just check tests off a list.

Test when you are alert.

(Continues)

Retest code any time you make changes.

Test when you port code.

Start routines from the Immediate window.

Examine variables using quick watches and the Immediate window.

Modify variables using the Immediate window.

Use Ctrl-F9 to jump to other parts of the code.

Examine decision statements carefully.

Know what outputs to expect before you perform a test.

Simulate errors.

Find your own bugs.

Have someone else test your code, too.

Don't shoot the messenger. Testers do not cause bugs, they only find them.

Fix your own code.

Simulate user actions to automate testing.

Check code coverage and examine unused code.

Keep testing until you cannot find any more bugs.

Estimate the number of bugs.

Estimate bug finding time.

Test user interfaces from the top down.

Test complex code from the bottom up.

Perform a postmortem to learn from your mistakes.

CHAPTER 15

Profiling

The Professional and Enterprise editions of Visual Basic 4 and 5 come with Visual Basic Code Profiler (VBCP). VBCP lets you generate performance and usage statistics for your programs. These statistics allow you identify slow pieces of code and code that is not executed.

After you locate unused code, you can examine it to decide if there is a bug. If the program should use the code but does not, you can modify the program so it uses the code properly. If the program already uses the code but your test cases did not exercise it, you can update the tests so they give the program a more vigorous workout. Finally, if the unused code is unnecessary, you can remove it.

VBCP can also tell you which code takes most of the program's time. You can then optimize that code to improve overall performance. By telling you which code takes the most time, the profiler lets you concentrate your optimization efforts on just that code. You do not waste time optimizing code that is already fast enough. You also do not add bugs by needlessly complicating that code.

Installing VB Code Profiler

In Visual Basic 4, VBCP comes in the Tools\Vbcp directory on the Visual Basic CD-ROM. It runs as an add-in within the Visual Basic development environment. To install VBCP in Visual Basic 4, follow these steps:

1. Copy the file Vbcp16.exe (16-bit) or Vbcp32.exe (32-bit) from the CD-ROM to your hard disk. You can also copy the help file Vbcp.hlp if you like.

2. Execute the .exe file you copied. This will register VBCP so you can run it from the Add-Ins menu.

3. Run the Visual Basic development environment. In the Add-Ins menu, select the Add-In Manager command. Check the VB Code Profile and click the Ok button.

In Visual Basic 5, VBCP comes in the Tools\Unsupprt\Vbcp directory on the Visual Basic CD-ROM. To install VBCP in Visual Basic 5, follow these steps:

1. Copy the file Vbcp.dll from the CD-ROM to your System directory. In Windows 95, that directory is Windows\System. In Windows NT, the System directory is Winnt\System.

2. Register the DLL using RegSvr32.exe by executing the following command:

```
RegSvr32 vbcp.dll
```

If you do not already have RegSvr32 installed, you can find it in the Tools\RegUtils directory on the Visual Basic CD-ROM.

3. Edit the file Vbaddin.ini in the Windows directory. In Windows 95, this directory is Windows. In Windows NT, the Windows directory is Winnt. Find the Add-Ins32 section of the file and add the line VBCP.VBCPClass=0 like this:

```
[Add-Ins32]
VBCP.VBCPClass=0
```

4. Run the Visual Basic development environment. In the Add-Ins menu, select the Add-In Manager command. Check the VB Code Profile and click the Ok button.

Visual Basic 6 does not include VBCP. Instead the Enterprise Edition includes the Application Performance Explorer (APE). Unfortunately APE is designed to test the performance of the components in multi-tier client/server applications rather than the performance of code within a simple application. You can learn more about APE in the online help.

The following sections explain how to use VBCP in Visual Basic 5. The concepts apply to the Visual Basic 4 version, and even to Visual Basic 6 programs. For example, you could insert profiling code of your own in a Visual Basic 6 program. This would be a fairly involved project, though, so it is not described here.

How VBCP Works

VBCP adds profiling code to your Visual Basic project. It does nothing magical. It simply inserts statements between each of the statements in your code. The VBCP statements record timing and hit information in a database for later analysis. With enough time and effort, you could do something similar yourself.

The following code shows function TestFormat. This routine formats a double value so it has at most 12 characters, plus an optional sign.

```
Private Const TEXT_FORMAT = "0.############"
    :
' Return a textual representation of the value.
Private Function TestFormat(ByVal value As Double, _
    ByVal is_signed As Boolean) As String
Dim txt As String

    txt = Format$(Abs(value), TEXT_FORMAT)
    txt = Left$(txt, 12)
    If is_signed And value < 0 Then txt = "-" & txt
    TestFormat = txt
End Function
```

The following code shows how VBCP modifies this function. The calls to VBCP_Update and VBCP_UpdateIf record timing and hit count information when they are called.

```
' Return a textual representation of the value.
Private Function TestFormat(ByVal value As Double, _
    ByVal is_signed As Boolean) As String
  VBCP_Update 1, "TestFormat", 1
Dim txt As String

    txt = Format$(Abs(value), TEXT_FORMAT)
  VBCP_Update 1, "TestFormat", 2
    txt = Left$(txt, 12)
  VBCP_Update 1, "TestFormat", 3
    If is_signed And value < 0 And _
VBCP_UpdateIf(1, "TestFormat", 4) Then txt = "-" & txt
    TestFormat = txt
  VBCP_Update 1, "TestFormat", 5
End Function
```

Using VBCP

To use the code profiler, follow these steps:

1. Save the project. VBCP requires that you save the project before profiling the code. If you have not saved the project, VBCP complains that the code is dirty.

2. From the Add-Ins menu, select the VB Code Profiler command. This displays VBCP as shown in Figure 15.1.

3. Select the modules you want profiled. You must include the startup form or module.

4. Select the kind of information to profile. The choices are:

    Line Timing. VBCP records the amount of time spent executing each line of code.

    Function Timing. VBCP records the amount of time spent executing each routine.

    Line Hit Count. VBCP records the number of times each line is executed.

    Function Hit Count. VBCP records the number of times each routine is executed.

5. Click the Add Profiler Code button. At this point, VBCP adds the profile code between your Visual Basic statements.

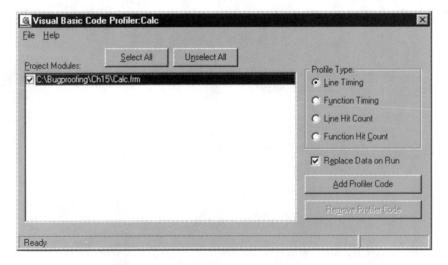

Figure 15.1   Visual Basic Code Profiler.

6. Run the program and exercise the code you want to study. You may need to execute fast code several times to get meaningful statistics.

7. Analyze the results. This is described in more detail later.

8. Click the Remove Profiler Code button. This makes VBCP remove the code it added to the project.

9. Save the project. VBCP made changes so it will not profile the code again until you save it.

Analyzing Results

After you have run a profiled application but before you remove the profiler code, you can examine the results of the profile run. In VBCP, open the File menu and select the View Results command. The display you see and the things you can learn from the display depend on the type of profile data you collected.

Line Timing

Figure 15.2 shows the result display for a line timing test. The display shows the total time spent running each line of code. It also shows the number of times each line was executed, the average amount of time taken each time the lines were executed, and the percentage of the program's time spent running each line.

For instance, line 5 in the AddCharacter subroutine is

```
txt = txtDisplay.Text
```

This line was executed 197 times during the test. It took 0.08 seconds for all 197 executions, or roughly 0.0004 seconds each time the line was executed. That was approximately 1.73 percent of the program's total time.

ModName	FuncName	CodeLine	TotalTime	AvgTime	PctTime	Hits	PctHits	LineText
C:\Bugproofing\Ch15\Calc.frm	AddCharacter	1	0	0	0.00%	220	4.11%	>>Entry Point<<
C:\Bugproofing\Ch15\Calc.frm	AddCharacter	2	0	0	0.00%	220	4.11%	If NewEntry Then
C:\Bugproofing\Ch15\Calc.frm	AddCharacter	3	0	0	0.00%	23	0.43%	txtDisplay.Text = ch
C:\Bugproofing\Ch15\Calc.frm	AddCharacter	4	0.0100	0.0004	0.22%	23	0.43%	NewEntry = False
C:\Bugproofing\Ch15\Calc.frm	AddCharacter	5	0.0800	0.0004	1.73%	197	3.68%	txt = txtDisplay.Text
C:\Bugproofing\Ch15\Calc.frm	AddCharacter	6	0.0100	0.0001	0.22%	197	3.68%	If Left$(txt, 1) = "." Then txt = Mic
C:\Bugproofing\Ch15\Calc.frm	AddCharacter	7	0.0300	0.0002	0.65%	197	3.68%	If Len(txt) >= MAX_CHARS Then
C:\Bugproofing\Ch15\Calc.frm	AddCharacter	8	0	0	0.00%	0	0.00%	Beep
C:\Bugproofing\Ch15\Calc.frm	AddCharacter	9	0.0100	0.0001	0.22%	197	3.68%	ElseIf ch = "." And InStr(txt, ".") >
C:\Bugproofing\Ch15\Calc.frm	AddCharacter	10	0	0	0.00%	0	0.00%	Beep
C:\Bugproofing\Ch15\Calc.frm	AddCharacter	11	0.0200	0.0001	0.43%	197	3.68%	txtDisplay.Text = txt & ch

Figure 15.2 Line timing statistics.

Notice that lines 8 and 10 of the AddCharacter routine have hit counts of 0 each. That shows these lines were not executed during the test. This could indicate a bug in the program if those lines should have been executed. In this case, the code executed a white box test that checked only a small part of the program. A more complete coverage test would be expanded to exercise lines 8 and 10.

By clicking on a column heading, you can make VBCP sort the results using that column. Figure 15.3 shows the same data in Figure 15.2 sorted by total time. You can use this display to quickly identify code that you should consider optimizing.

As you examine the statistics, keep user interactions in mind. In Figure 15.3, the line that took the most time was the statement

```
MsgBox "No errors found."
```

This single line took more than 3 seconds and accounted for almost 72 percent of the program's total time. The reason this statement was so slow is that it had to wait for the user to click the message box's Ok button. The call to MsgBox is quick, but the user is relatively slow. Because the profiler gives this line credit for so much of the program's time, the other more interesting times seem small. The line that uses the second most time is given credit for only 14 percent of the total time. If you subtract out the time spent waiting for the user to close the message box, however, this line accounts for more than half of the program's time.

You can also use this display to look for lines of code that are never used. Click on the Hits column heading to sort the results by number of hits. The lines that were never executed are listed at the top with hit counts of 0. You should examine each of these lines and determine which of three cases applies. First, if the line should have been executed but was not, fix the bug in the code. Second, if the tests were not thorough enough to exercise the code, expand the tests. Third, if the code is unnecessary, remove it.

ModName	FuncName	CodeLine	TotalTime	AvgTime	PctTime	Hits	PctHits	LineText
C:\Bugproofing\Ch15\Calc.frm	TestSendOperar	15	0.0200	0.0009	0.43%	22	0.41%	new_value = CDbl(txtDisplay.Tex
C:\Bugproofing\Ch15\Calc.frm	TestSendOperar	6	0.0200	0.0001	0.43%	196	3.66%	Form_KeyPress Asc(ch)
C:\Bugproofing\Ch15\Calc.frm	AddCharacter	11	0.0200	0.0001	0.43%	197	3.68%	txtDisplay.Text = txt & ch
C:\Bugproofing\Ch15\Calc.frm	TestCalculated	26	0.0200	0.0033	0.43%	6	0.11%	actual_result = CDbl(txtDisplay.Te
C:\Bugproofing\Ch15\Calc.frm	TestWhiteBox	11	0.0300	0.0300	0.65%	1	0.02%	DoEvents
C:\Bugproofing\Ch15\Calc.frm	AddCharacter	7	0.0300	0.0002	0.65%	197	3.68%	If Len(txt) >= MAX_CHARS Then
C:\Bugproofing\Ch15\Calc.frm	Form_KeyPress	2	0.0500	0.0002	1.08%	231	4.32%	ch = Chr$(KeyAscii)
C:\Bugproofing\Ch15\Calc.frm	AddCharacter	5	0.0800	0.0004	1.73%	197	3.68%	txt = txtDisplay.Text
C:\Bugproofing\Ch15\Calc.frm	TestFormat	2	0.2200	0.0051	4.75%	43	0.80%	txt = Format$(Abs(value), TEXT_F
C:\Bugproofing\Ch15\Calc.frm	txtDisplay_Chan	2	0.6610	0.0027	14.26%	241	4.51%	txtDisplay.SelStart = Len(txtDispla
C:\Bugproofing\Ch15\Calc.frm	TestWhiteBox	22	3.3350	3.3350	71.94%	1	0.02%	MsgBox "No errors found."

Figure 15.3   Line timing statistics sorted by total time.

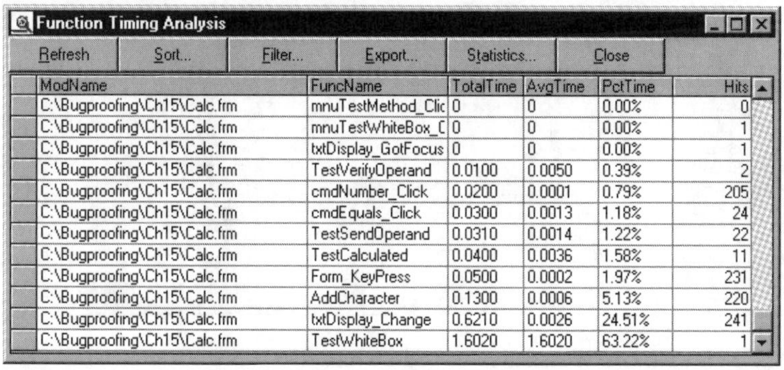

ModName	FuncName	TotalTime	AvgTime	PctTime	Hits
C:\Bugproofing\Ch15\Calc.frm	mnuTestMethod_Clic	0	0	0.00%	0
C:\Bugproofing\Ch15\Calc.frm	mnuTestWhiteBox_C	0	0	0.00%	1
C:\Bugproofing\Ch15\Calc.frm	txtDisplay_GotFocus	0	0	0.00%	1
C:\Bugproofing\Ch15\Calc.frm	TestVerifyOperand	0.0100	0.0050	0.39%	2
C:\Bugproofing\Ch15\Calc.frm	cmdNumber_Click	0.0200	0.0001	0.79%	205
C:\Bugproofing\Ch15\Calc.frm	cmdEquals_Click	0.0300	0.0013	1.18%	24
C:\Bugproofing\Ch15\Calc.frm	TestSendOperand	0.0310	0.0014	1.22%	22
C:\Bugproofing\Ch15\Calc.frm	TestCalculated	0.0400	0.0036	1.58%	11
C:\Bugproofing\Ch15\Calc.frm	Form_KeyPress	0.0500	0.0002	1.97%	231
C:\Bugproofing\Ch15\Calc.frm	AddCharacter	0.1300	0.0006	5.13%	220
C:\Bugproofing\Ch15\Calc.frm	txtDisplay_Change	0.6210	0.0026	24.51%	241
C:\Bugproofing\Ch15\Calc.frm	TestWhiteBox	1.6020	1.6020	63.22%	1

Figure 15.4 Function timing statistics sorted by total time.

Function Timing

Figure 15.4 shows the display for a function timing test sorted by total time. This display shows the total time spent in each routine. It also shows the number of times each routine ran, the average time used by the routine calls, and the percentage of the program's total time due to each routine.

In this example, it might seem as if the TestWhiteBox subroutine is a good candidate for optimization. Actually, TestWhiteBox includes a call to MsgBox, so its speed is determined by how quickly the user dismisses the message box. This is also a test routine, so spending a lot of effort optimizing it probably makes little sense.

Line Hit Counting

Figure 15.5 shows the results of a line hit count test sorted by hits. You can use this display to see which lines of code are executed the most. If you scroll to the top of the display, you can see the lines that are never executed. The information presented here is also included in the line timing test shown in Figure 15.2. Collecting only the hit count information may be faster.

These statistics do not tell you whether an allocated variable is ever used. They also do not distinguish between the test and action parts in a single-line If statement. If the program reaches the If statement, the profiler counts the line as hit, whether the If statement's test is True or False. Conversely, in a multiline If statement, the profiler does not count hits on lines that are not executed because the If statement's condition is False.

In the following code, the hit count for the first DoSomething statement is 1 even though DoSomething is never called. The hit count for the DoSomethingElse statement is 0 because the multiline If statement surrounding it prevented it from executing.

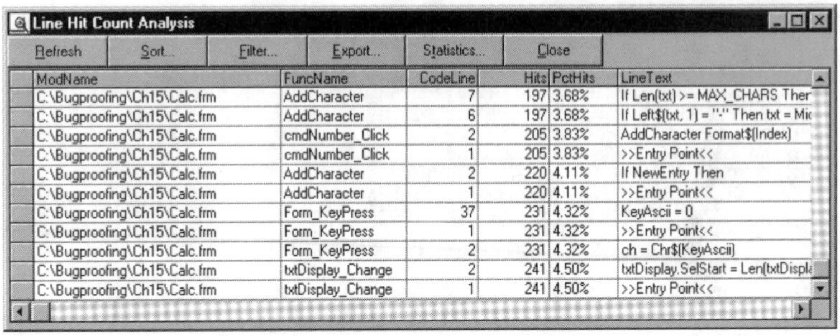

ModName	FuncName	CodeLine	Hits	PctHits	LineText
C:\Bugproofing\Ch15\Calc.frm	AddCharacter	7	197	3.68%	If Len(txt) >= MAX_CHARS Ther
C:\Bugproofing\Ch15\Calc.frm	AddCharacter	6	197	3.68%	If Left$(txt, 1) = "-" Then txt = Mi
C:\Bugproofing\Ch15\Calc.frm	cmdNumber_Click	2	205	3.83%	AddCharacter Format$(Index)
C:\Bugproofing\Ch15\Calc.frm	cmdNumber_Click	1	205	3.83%	>>Entry Point<<
C:\Bugproofing\Ch15\Calc.frm	AddCharacter	2	220	4.11%	If NewEntry Then
C:\Bugproofing\Ch15\Calc.frm	AddCharacter	1	220	4.11%	>>Entry Point<<
C:\Bugproofing\Ch15\Calc.frm	Form_KeyPress	37	231	4.32%	KeyAscii = 0
C:\Bugproofing\Ch15\Calc.frm	Form_KeyPress	1	231	4.32%	>>Entry Point<<
C:\Bugproofing\Ch15\Calc.frm	Form_KeyPress	2	231	4.32%	ch = Chr$(KeyAscii)
C:\Bugproofing\Ch15\Calc.frm	txtDisplay_Change	2	241	4.50%	txtDisplay.SelStart = Len(txtDispl
C:\Bugproofing\Ch15\Calc.frm	txtDisplay_Change	1	241	4.50%	>>Entry Point<<

Figure 15.5 Line hit count statistics sorted by hits.

```
If False Then DoSomething      ' Hit count = 1.

If False Then                  ' Hit count = 1.
    DoSomethingElse            ' Hit count = 0.
End If
```

If you want really precise hit counts for the lines in your program, use multiline If statements.

Function Hit Counting

Figure 15.6 shows the results of a function hit count test sorted by hits. This shows the routines that ran the most. The function timing statistics shown in Figure 15.4 also include function hit information, although they do not show the percentage of hits due to each routine.

Function hit test statistics provide a useful sanity check. If you discover that one routine is being called far more often than you expected it to be, you should look at the code and figure out why. You should also examine routines that are never called. Either modify the code so they are called properly, expand your test cases so they exercise these routines, or remove them if they are unnecessary.

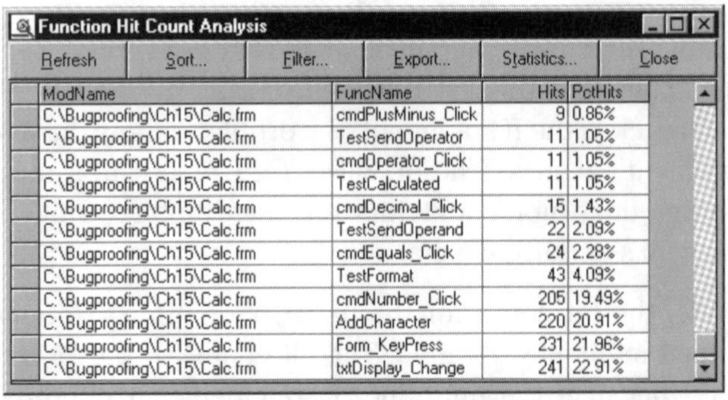

ModName	FuncName	Hits	PctHits
C:\Bugproofing\Ch15\Calc.frm	cmdPlusMinus_Click	9	0.86%
C:\Bugproofing\Ch15\Calc.frm	TestSendOperator	11	1.05%
C:\Bugproofing\Ch15\Calc.frm	cmdOperator_Click	11	1.05%
C:\Bugproofing\Ch15\Calc.frm	TestCalculated	11	1.05%
C:\Bugproofing\Ch15\Calc.frm	cmdDecimal_Click	15	1.43%
C:\Bugproofing\Ch15\Calc.frm	TestSendOperand	22	2.09%
C:\Bugproofing\Ch15\Calc.frm	cmdEquals_Click	24	2.28%
C:\Bugproofing\Ch15\Calc.frm	TestFormat	43	4.09%
C:\Bugproofing\Ch15\Calc.frm	cmdNumber_Click	205	19.49%
C:\Bugproofing\Ch15\Calc.frm	AddCharacter	220	20.91%
C:\Bugproofing\Ch15\Calc.frm	Form_KeyPress	231	21.96%
C:\Bugproofing\Ch15\Calc.frm	txtDisplay_Change	241	22.91%

Figure 15.6 Function hit count statistics sorted by hits.

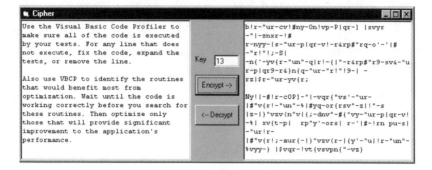

Figure 15.7   Program Bad15 showing text and its encryption.

Self-Test

Program Bad15, shown in Figure 15.7, uses some relatively slow code to perform simple encryption. Enter some text in the left text box and a numeric value in the Key field. Then click the Encrypt button to make the program encrypt the text.

Enter encrypted text in the right text box and the key that was used to encrypt the text in the Key field. Then click the Decrypt button to make the program decrypt the text.

This program is reasonably responsive for moderate amounts of text. If you enter a lot of text, however, the program slows down considerably. If you enter 1000 characters, the program takes 6 or 7 seconds to encrypt or decrypt the text. It should be able to run much faster.

The code for program Bad15 follows. Enter the code or download it from the book's Web page at www.vb-helper.com/err.htm. Run it using the Visual Basic Code Profiler to see where the program spends most of its time. Then make the fewest changes possible to improve the program's performance. You should be able to make the program much faster with only a few changes.

```
Option Explicit

' Encrypt the text by adding the key number
' to each character's ASCII code.
Private Sub cmdEncrypt_Click()
    txtCiphertext.Text = ""
    MousePointer = vbHourglass
    DoEvents

    Crypt txtPlaintext, txtCiphertext, Int(txtKey.Text)
```

```
        MousePointer = vbDefault
End Sub


' Encrypt the text by subtracting the key number
' from each character's ASCII code.
Private Sub cmdDecrypt_Click()
    txtPlaintext.Text = ""
    MousePointer = vbHourglass
    DoEvents

    Crypt txtCiphertext, txtPlaintext, -Int(txtKey.Text)

    MousePointer = vbDefault
End Sub


' Encrypt the input text.
Private Sub Crypt(ByVal txtIn As TextBox, ByVal txtOut As TextBox, _
    ByVal key As Integer)
Const MIN_ASC = 32  ' ASCII code for space.
Const MAX_ASC = 126 ' ASCII code for ~.
Const NUM_ASC = MAX_ASC - MIN_ASC + 1

Dim i As Integer
Dim ch As String
Dim ch_num As String

    txtOut.Text = ""
    For i = 1 To Len(txtIn.Text)
        ch = Mid$(txtIn.Text, i, 1)
        ch_num = Asc(ch)
        ' Translate only printable characters.
        If ch_num >= MIN_ASC And ch_num <= MAX_ASC Then
            ch_num = ch_num + key - MIN_ASC
            ch_num = (ch_num Mod NUM_ASC)
            If ch_num < 0 Then ch_num = ch_num + NUM_ASC
            ch_num = ch_num + MIN_ASC
        End If
        ch = Chr$(ch_num)
        txtOut.Text = txtOut.Text & ch
    Next i
End Sub
```

Summary

Use the Visual Basic Code Profiler to make sure all of the code is executed by your tests. For any line that does not execute, fix the code, expand the tests, or remove the line.

Also use VBCP to identify the routines that would benefit most from optimization. Wait until the code is working correctly before you search for these routines. Then optimize only those that will provide significant improvement to the application's overall performance.

The following list of Bug Stoppers summarizes the tests you can perform using VBCP.

BUG STOPPERS: Profiling

Use line timing statistics to see which lines take the longest.

Use function timing statistics to see which routines take the longest. These are candidates for optimization.

Use line hit statistics to find code that is never executed. Fix the code, extend the tests, or remove the lines.

Use function hit statistics to get an idea of which routines are used the most and which are never used.

CHAPTER 16

Debugging Habits

I f you debug carefully, fully understanding the implications of any changes you make, you can fix bugs and move on with confidence. On the other hand, if you use the debugger to find the specific line of code where an error occurred and implement a quick patch, you are as likely to cause problems as you are to fix them.

To debug as effectively as possible, you should follow certain guidelines. This chapter describes some of the techniques you can use to make debugging safer and more efficient.

Think First

Think before you act. Do not just try things. Study the routine you are debugging so you understand what it is supposed to do before you start experimenting.

Be certain you understand the entire routine, not just the piece of code that contains the bug. The surrounding code may depend on the behavior of the buggy code. If you fix the bug without considering the rest of the code, other parts of the routine may break.

Programmers who read through a routine's code looking for a bug tend to be more successful than those who just use the debugger to step through the code. If you do not know what to expect, you cannot tell if the debugger is showing you the correct behavior anyway. Study the code first, then act.

Debug When You Are Alert

There is no question that debugging is hard. Understanding what the program is supposed to do, what it actually does, and how you can fix the error takes concentration and creativity. If you debug when you are inattentive, you are unlikely to do an effective job. At best, you will take longer than necessary to find the bug. At worst, you will accidentally introduce new bugs while trying to fix the old ones.

Debug when you are alert. When you are not, perform other chores that require less attention to detail. Fill out paperwork, write progress reports, or just take a break. Return to debugging when you are more alert.

Code Properly While Debugging

All of the coding and testing guidelines described in earlier chapters apply equally to bug fixing. Use proper coding, commenting, and testing practices when you debug.

Code written during debugging is more likely to contain bugs than code written in the program's initial implementation. Since bugs are more likely while debugging, you should be more careful than ever to code thoughtfully and test thoroughly. Unfortunately, many programmers rush through debugging to get back to more interesting tasks. In particular, they often do not test their changes thoroughly. At best, they test only the particular bug they have fixed and they do not detect new bugs they have introduced. At worst, they do no testing and do not even fix the bug they were originally chasing.

Use correct programming techniques so you can fix bugs once and you will not need to fix them again.

Fix Your Own Bugs

Fix the bugs in your code. You know your code better than anyone else does, so you should be able to fix it most effectively. It will be easier for you to understand the entire body of code that contains the bug, so you will be less likely to make mistakes.

Making programmers fix their own code also puts responsibility where it belongs. If someone causes a lot of bugs, that person will spend a lot of time debugging. Not only does that seem fair, it also keeps bug-prone individuals busy so they cannot contaminate more code. Hopefully, they will eventually adopt better design and coding techniques so they make fewer mistakes.

Fix It Now

Fix bugs as soon as you find them. Do not let the schedule or other pressures make you delay fixing a bug. Bugs are easiest to fix when they are fresh in your mind. Procrastination only gives you more time to forget key details about the code that might help find the bug. Remember, sooner or later you must find and fix every bug. You might as well get it over with right away.

On the other hand, concentrate on one thing at a time. If you are looking for a bug and you find another one, make a quick note about the new bug and continue looking for the first one. Keep working on the original bug until you find and fix it. Then go back and fix the other bug.

Come Back Later

You should fix bugs as soon as you find them partly because you are more likely to remember how the code works. At the same time, if you spend too much time on one bug, your concentration may wane. You need to balance the need to keep the bug at the top of your attention with the need to work when you are most alert and effective.

If you find you are stuck on a bug and are making no progress, take a break and return to the problem later. Give yourself a chance to clear your mind of any preconceptions that may be blocking your progress. Then return with a fresh approach.

Comment Repairs

Do not remove incorrect code. Instead, comment it out and add a note indicating who made the change, when it was made, and why. Later you can use these comments to analyze the project's bugs. For example, knowing how many bugs the project contained per line of code can help you predict bug counts in future projects. Discovering which code contained the most bugs can help you determine which routines to rewrite later. It may also identify developers who could benefit from additional training.

Leaving the original code in also lets you see it later if there is another problem with this code. You can easily change the code back if it turns out that the original code was correct and some other routine was responsible for the bug. If the bug resurfaces, the comment lets you see what other solutions have been tried so you do not accidentally change the code back to its previous incorrect form.

The following code shows a typical bug fix comment. The keyword BUGFIX makes searching for the bugs easy. This example also includes an incident number used by the project to track bugs.

```
'       BUGFIX: 5/27/98 by Rod Stephens. Incident #129.
'       The following line placed duplicate nodes in the
'       AVL tree when nodes were deleted.
'       Set target = replacement
        Set target = replacement.NextNode
```

See What Changed

While bugs may sometimes seem to spontaneously appear in properly working code, they really do not. Something must change for the code to stop working. If a program that worked before suddenly fails, think about what has changed. Compare a previous version of the code to the new version and see which lines are different. Of course, to make this comparison, you need to keep previous versions of the software. Use a version control system or make frequent backups.

Sometimes when I am about to make a large change that I consider risky, I make a new copy of the code. I then modify that code and leave the original untouched. When something goes wrong, I can compare the new code to the original. In extreme cases, I throw the new code away and start from scratch.

Also consider recent changes to the operating system and other software you may have just upgraded. You may not be able to change the behavior of the system, but knowing what changed may help you determine the parts of your program that you need to examine. For example, if you have recently upgraded a custom control, look for places where the program uses the control's properties, events, and methods.

Think about data that may have changed. Even if the code has not changed, if the data manipulated by the code changes, it may make bugs appear. The apparent bugs may be correct behavior that you do not recognize because you have not used the new data before. They may also be real bugs that did not surface with the previous data.

Finally, consider the possibility that the bug was always there and that you simply failed to notice it before. Sometimes when you notice a bug, it seems so obvious that you wonder how it could ever have escaped detection.

Don't Believe in Magic

Just as bugs do not spontaneously appear, they do not spontaneously fix themselves. If a bug seems to have disappeared, it is almost surely still there, but hiding. Remember that you will eventually need to find and fix every bug. Assuming a bug fixed itself will just make it harder to find later. Continue chasing the bug while it is fresh in your mind. Do not stop until you find the bug, even if it appears to have gone away by itself.

Once in a great while, fixing one bug also fixes another. While working through your list of bugs, one may disappear. Do not assume a previous bug fix has removed this bug unless you can prove it. It is just as likely that another bug fix hid the bug rather than removing it.

Study the modified code until you figure out how the previous change removed the bug. Add a new comment explaining how the other repair worked its magic.

Fix Routines, Not Lines

Do not use the debugger to pinpoint the single line that caused a bug and fix it. Instead, study the entire routine so you understand what it is supposed to do and what it actually does. Unless you understand the context in which the bug appears, you cannot safely fix it.

It is also possible that the bug involves more than one line of code. Looking for a single incorrect line can distract you from finding the whole problem.

Note that understanding the entire routine means it will be easier to debug short routines. It is also easier to debug a routine that performs one well-defined task instead of one that performs several poorly described unrelated tasks. It is easier to keep the entire purpose of a short, well-focused routine in mind all at once. Make debugging easier by keeping that in mind when you program. Keep routines tightly focused on the task at hand so they are easier to fix later.

Fix Bugs, Not Symptoms

Be sure you have uncovered the true bug before you modify the source code. Sometimes one routine will fail because of a condition caused by another routine. If the other routine is wrong, the condition is a symptom of a bug in that other routine. Fix the real bug. Do not simply modify the first routine so it can recover when the erroneous condition occurs.

It is not always obvious whether a particular routine's behavior is its own fault or the fault of an auxiliary routine. In that case, ask yourself whether other routines will also be confused by the results of the auxiliary routine. If so, you should rewrite that routine so it makes sense to all of the routines instead of merely covering up the problem in this one instance.

For example, suppose the NumNonBlanks function returns the number of non-blank characters selected in a text box and the NumWords function returns the number of words selected. The following function uses those two functions to calculate the average length of the selected words.

```
Private Function AverageWordLength() As Single
    AverageWordLength = NumNonBlanks / NumWords
End Function
```

Now suppose you test the program and trace a bug to this function. The AverageWordLength function crashes when no words are selected in the text box and NumWords is 0. In this example, you should ask yourself if the bug is in AverageWordLength or in the NumWords function. If the bug is in NumWords, other routines may be confused by its behavior. In this case, NumWords is returning a sensible value. When no words are selected, it makes sense to return the value 0. If NumWords is not at fault, the bug must be in the Average-WordLength function.

For another example, suppose the BestStudent function returns the index of the student who received the highest score on a test if any student received a score greater than 90. If no student scored more than 90, the routine returns –1 indicating that no student deserves special honors. Now suppose another routine displays the names of the highest-scoring students for each test using the following code:

```
For test_num = 1 To NumTests
    lblHonorsStudent(test_num).Caption = _
        StudentNames(BestStudent(test_num))
Next test_num
```

This code fails if there is some test for which no student scored better than 90. In that case, BestStudent returns –1 and the routine fails trying to access the –1 entry in the StudentNames array. For this code, you should ask whether the bug is in this display routine or in the BestStudent function.

In this case, the BestStudent function returns a misleading result. It does not return the index of the best student. Instead, it returns the index of the student most deserving of honors but only if some student scored high enough to deserve honors. The display routine is not really the source of the error. Any other routine that uses BestStudent can suffer from the same confusion. The problem is in BestStudent, not in the display routine.

There are two good ways to fix this bug. First, you can make BestStudent return the index of the best student even if that student did not do very well. If the best student scores a 50, he is still the best student. The meaning of the function matches its name.

Second, you could change the name of BestStudent to HonorsStudent so it correctly reflects the function's return value.

Note that both of these fixes could cause problems in other parts of the program. Another routine that uses BestStudent may already be using special code to protect itself from the value –1. Changing BestStudent so it always returns a valid index may make that code fail. This underscores the importance of fixing the real bug and not the symptom. If the programmer writing that other routine had fixed BestStudent instead of patching the other routine to accommodate the –1 value, this problem would never have arisen.

Similarly, if another routine relies on the fact that BestStudent never returns the index of a student with a score less than 90, it may break when you fix BestStudent. This emphasizes the importance of finding and fixing errors as early as possible. If BestStudent had been fixed before the other routine was written, it would have relied on the correct behavior and there would have been no problem.

Look for Multiple Bugs

Sometimes more than one bug contributes to a single incorrect behavior. You may find a bug and think it is the sole cause of the problem. Before you declare the problem solved, look for other bugs that may have contributed to the incorrect behavior.

Also look for other bugs that may have been hidden by the bug you found. The bug you found may have prevented another bug from becoming obvious. Look for it now, before you declare the code fixed.

Even completely correct bug fixes may create new bugs. If a routine has contained a bug for a long time, other routines may have been written that depend on its buggy behavior. When you finally repair the bug, those other routines may fail. Look for this sort of bug now. If you find the bug now, you will know exactly why the other routine failed. If you experience a problem later, you may have no idea why the code no longer works.

Do Not Experiment

Do not experiment with the code. Do not try making a change to see what happens. This is one of the worst ways to debug. It is much better to examine the routine as a whole and figure out what it is supposed to do. Then you can analyze what it actually does and find the problem.

Many programmers begin debugging by stepping through a routine in the debugger. As soon as they see the code start to diverge from what they expect, they stop, change the code, and then run the program again. Without a complete understanding of the routine, the change is as likely to break the routine as to fix it.

Know what you are doing before you make changes. Do not guess.

Test Fixes

Changes to existing code produce more bugs per line of code than originally writing the code does. There are several reasons for this. When you write a routine originally, you must understand the whole routine. When you debug, you may be lazy and try to fix the code without fully understanding it all.

Code changed during debugging also tends to involve the most complicated statements. Simple assignment statements and variable declarations occasionally contain bugs, but complicated If Then statements and While loops are far more likely to be wrong. Because the statements most likely to contain errors are complex, you are more likely to make a mistake while changing them.

Since the odds of making a mistake are greater when you fix bugs, you must thoroughly test your changes. Test the code even if you are absolutely positive the change cannot have caused any other problems. The most obviously correct code often hides the bugs that are hardest to find.

Simplify

As is mentioned in the previous section, code changed during debugging tends to involve the most complicated statements. When you debug a very complex statement, simplify it. That will help you make the change correctly and will make debugging easier in the future if you do make a mistake.

For example, the following If statement is complicated and confusing. It is supposed to determine whether a game program should display intermediate moves while the computer is calculating a move. Unfortunately, it contains a bug that makes it call DisplayMove only when the Winner object does not have the value Nothing. That only happens when the game is over and the computer cannot be moving. Therefore, the program never displays intermediate moves.

```
' If we are showing intermediate moves, and the computer
' is moving, and the game is in progress, show the move.
If chkShowMoves.Value = vbChecked And _
    PlayerMoving Is PlayerComputer And _
    Not (Winner Is Nothing) Then _
        DisplayMove
```

The following version fixes the bug and makes the If statement easier to understand. If there is a problem with this statement in the future, it will be easier to understand and fix.

```
Dim show_moves As Boolean
Dim computer_moving As Boolean
Dim game_continuing As Boolean

    ' If we are showing intermediate moves, and the computer
    ' is moving, and the game is in progress, show the move.
    show_moves = (chkShowMoves.Value = vbChecked)
    computer_moving = (PlayerMoving Is PlayerComputer)
    game_continuing = (Winner Is Nothing)

    If show_moves And _
        computer_moving And _
        game_continuing _
    Then DisplayMove
```

While you should simplify statements that contain bugs, resist the urge to modify code that works. When you fix a bug, you need to thoroughly test the code to see if the change works and to catch any new bugs you may have created or uncovered. Simplifying the code while you fix a bug will not add much time to the task because you need to test the code anyway.

On the other hand, if you make changes to working code, you should spend extra time testing the changes or you run the risk of introducing new bugs in code that worked before. Save time and effort by leaving the working code alone. If it isn't broken, don't fix it, or it soon will be.

Examine Decisions Closely

When you review a routine that contains a bug, pay special attention to the places where the code makes decisions. If the program makes a decision, it can make the wrong decision.

If, Select, For, and While statements contain program logic that may contain bugs. Simple calculations and variable declarations are less likely to contain errors. Concentrate on the more complex decision statements.

Look for Bugs Where There Are Bugs

Intuition may lead you believe that a routine that contained many bugs in the past would contain few bugs now. After all, if a lot of bugs have been fixed, there cannot be many left.

Actually, the opposite is true. Code that contained many bugs in the past will probably contain more bugs in the future. This is due partly to the fact that repairing a bug is likely to introduce a new bug. It also reflects the fact that a buggy routine is probably not well designed. It may not perform a well-defined, tightly focused task. It may be fragmented with related code scattered throughout. It may be too complex to fit into one routine or it may simply have misleading comments. For whatever reason, programmers have had trouble understanding and fixing this routine in the past and they probably will in the future.

Look for bugs where there have been bugs in the past. Keep track of which routines are buggy so it is easy to tell which ones are causing problems. If you insert comments into the code as you fix the bugs, you can use them to determine which routines have held bugs in the past.

At some point, when a routine has wasted enough of your time, you should consider throwing it away and completely rewriting it. If you invest the time to properly design, implement, and test the routine, it may never give you trouble again.

Self-Test

This Self-Test section contains a debugging problem. The Bad16 program, shown in Figure 16.1, draws a histogram on a shaded background. The program works, but it takes roughly three seconds for the form to load on a 133-megahertz Pentium. This should take less than half a second.

Note that the background is smoothly shaded only on computers using high color graphics. If your computer is using 256 color mode, the background will be covered with large bands of color. It will still have the same bad performance, however.

Examine the code and figure out where it is spending all of its time. Use the Visual Basic Code Profiler (VBCP) if you like, or look at the timing results shown in Table 16.1. Then modify the code to improve the program's performance without introducing other bugs.

```
Option Explicit

Private Values(1 To 10) As Single
```

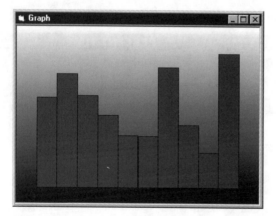

Figure 16.1   Program Bad16 displaying a bar chart.

```
' Generate some random data and draw the graph.
Private Sub Form_Load()
    ' Load some random data.
    LoadData

    ' Shade the background.
    ShadePicture

    ' Draw the graph.
    DrawGraph
End Sub

' Create some random data.
Private Sub LoadData()
Dim i As Integer
Dim min As Single
Dim max As Single

    Randomize

    min = picGraph.ScaleHeight * 0.1
    max = picGraph.ScaleHeight * 0.8
    For i = 1 To 10
        Values(i) = Int((max - min + 1) * Rnd + min)
    Next i
End Sub

' Shade picGraph from white at the top to
' black at the bottom.
Private Sub ShadePicture()
Const START_COLOR = 255
Const END_COLOR = 0
Dim Y As Single
```

Table 16.1 Function Timing Results for Program Bad16

FUNCTION	TOTAL TIME	PERCENT TIME
Form_Load	0.000	0.00
DrawGraph	0.040	1.34
ShadePicture	2.941	98.66

```
Dim clr As Single
Dim d_clr As Single

    d_clr = (END_COLOR - START_COLOR) / picGraph.ScaleHeight
    clr = START_COLOR
    For Y = 0 To picGraph.ScaleHeight
        picGraph.Line (0, Y)- _
            (picGraph.ScaleWidth, Y), _
            RGB(clr, clr, clr)
        clr = clr + d_clr
    Next Y
End Sub

' Draw the graph.
Private Sub DrawGraph()
Dim i As Integer
Dim dx As Single
Dim y0 As Single

    y0 = picGraph.ScaleHeight * 0.9
    dx = picGraph.ScaleWidth / 12

    ' Draw the bar chart.
    For i = 1 To 10
        picGraph.Line (i * dx, y0)-((i + 1) * dx, Values(i)), vbRed, BF
    Next i
    For i = 1 To 10
        picGraph.Line (i * dx, y0)-((i + 1) * dx, Values(i)), vbBlack, B
    Next i
End Sub
```

Table 16.1 shows the function timing results given by VBCP for program Bad16 on a 133-megahertz Pentium. The table shows that program Bad16 spends almost all of its time in subroutine ShadePicture.

Study these results and the code to see if you can figure out where the program is wasting so much time, but be warned: The solution does not lie entirely within the code shown here. If you are an experienced Visual Basic programmer, you should be able to deduce the problem. If you are a beginner, do not spend too much time looking at the code before you read the solution in Appendix A, "Self-Test Solutions."

Summary

Probably the most dangerous mistake programmers make when debugging is rushing through the job. They do not take the time to understand the context in which the code operates and they do not thoroughly test their changes.

Treat repair code just as you treat new code and follow the same guidelines. Use good coding practices and test the results. The Bug Stoppers that follow summarize the other debugging practices covered in this chapter.

 ## BUG STOPPERS: Debugging Habits

Think first, then act.

Debug when you are alert.

Debug using the same coding practices you use when writing any other code.

Fix your own bugs.

Fix bugs right away.

If you get stuck, take a break.

Add comments describing repairs.

If something suddenly breaks, see how the code has changed recently.

Don't believe in magic.

Fix routines, not lines.

Fix bugs, not symptoms.

Look for multiple bugs causing one behavior.

Look for bugs hidden by other bugs.

Do not experiment.

Test fixes thoroughly.

Simplify code when you fix it.

Examine decisions closely.

Look for bugs where there have been bugs in the past.

Self-Test Solutions

T his appendix contains improved versions of the code presented in the "Self-Test" section at the end of each chapter. These are not the only solutions possible. Many are not even the best solutions possible. Each demonstrates concepts presented in its chapter and generally ignores techniques presented in other parts of the book.

You can download the good and bad versions of these programs from the book's Web page at www.vb-helper.com/err.htm. This page will also contain updated versions of these programs and other examples as they are written.

The following sections include annotated versions of the original code examples contained in the book's "Self-Test" sections. Numbers in the comments far to the right correspond to text that explains problems in the code.

Chapter 1

This code has two main bad themes. First, it is not written for humans. It needs a lot of comments to explain to the reader what is happening. This absolutely must be fixed.

Second, it is over-optimized for the early stages of a project. Binary search is a fairly complex algorithm. Implementing it to search a list of only 50 items is overkill. A simpler linear search that looks through the list of values one at a time would be easier to implement, less likely to contain bugs, and more than fast enough to search such a small list.

On the other hand, if the binary search code was copied verbatim from another project that had already implemented and debugged it, the code might be relatively safe. In that case, it would be reasonable to reuse the existing code.

The original bad version of the code follows. See the notes after the code for explanations of the code's bad points.

```
Option Explicit

Private Values(1 To 50) As Integer

Private Sub Form_Load()
    Ready                                              ' 1
End Sub

Private Sub Ready()                                    ' 1
Dim i As Integer
Dim txt As String

    Randomize                                          ' 2
    Values(1) = Int(Rnd * 10 + 1)
    For i = 2 To 50
        Values(i) = Values(i - 1) + Int(10 * Rnd + 1)
    Next i
    For i = 1 To 50
        txt = txt & Format$(i, "@@") & _
            Format$(Values(i), "@@@@") & vbCrLf
    Next i
    txtValues.Text = txt
End Sub

Private Sub CmdSearch_Click()
Dim i As Integer                                       ' 3

    i = BinarySearch(Values, CInt(txtTarget.Text))     ' 4
    lblPosition.Caption = Format$(i, "@@") & _
            Format$(Values(i), "@@@@") & vbCrLf
End Sub

Public Function BinarySearch(list() As Integer, _
    target As Integer) As Integer                      ' 2
Dim a As Integer                                       ' 3
Dim b As Integer                                       ' 3
Dim c As Integer                                       ' 3

    a = 1                                              ' 5
    c = 50
    Do While a <= c
        b = (c + a) / 2
        If target = list(b) Then
            BinarySearch = b
            Exit Function
```

```
        ElseIf target < list(b) Then
            c = b - 1
        Else
            a = b + 1
        End If
    Loop
    BinarySearch = 0
End Function
```

1. The name Ready is not very descriptive. A human reader would get more information if the routine were named something like InitializeData or RandomizeValues.

2. This code needs comments to help the reader understand what it does.

3. This variable should have a more descriptive name to help the reader understand how the program uses it.

4. This routine does not program defensively or offensively. If the target value is not in the list, the search routine returns the value 0. When CmdSearch_Click tries to access Values(i), it crashes.

5. This is not covered in this chapter, but it is such a bad practice it deserves to be mentioned. The program should never use hard-coded numbers like 1 and 50. If you later changed the code so it used a 100-entry array, the binary search routine would stop working. Either these numbers should be defined as constants or the routine should calculate them using UBound and LBound.

The improved version of the code follows. Refer to the original version to see what has changed. This version uses a simpler linear searching routine instead of the more complex binary search. For more information on search routines and other algorithms, consult the book *Ready-to-Run Visual Basic Algorithms* by Rod Stephens (John Wiley & Sons, 1998).

```
Option Explicit

' The list of values.
Private Const NUM_VALUES = 50
Private Values(1 To NUM_VALUES) As Integer

' Initialize the data.
Private Sub Form_Load()
    InitializeData
End Sub

' Create some random data.
Private Sub InitializeData()
Dim i As Integer
Dim last_value As Integer ' The last value assigned.
Dim txt As String
```

```vb
    Randomize

    ' Initialize the random numbers with each
    ' value 1-11 bigger than the previous one.
    For i = 1 To NUM_VALUES
        last_value = last_value + Int(10 * Rnd) + 1
        Values(i) = last_value
    Next i

    ' Display the values.
    For i = 1 To NUM_VALUES
        txt = txt & Format$(i, "@@") & _
            Format$(Values(i), "@@@@") & vbCrLf
    Next i
    txtValues.Text = txt
End Sub

' Search for the target.
Private Sub CmdSearch_Click()
Dim position As Integer

    position = LinearSearch(Values, CInt(txtTarget.Text))
    If position < 1 Then
        lblPosition.Caption = "Not found"
    Else
        lblPosition.Caption = Format$(position)
    End If
End Sub

' Locate a target item using linear search. If the
' target is not found, return 1 less than the
' smallest array index.
Public Function LinearSearch(list() As Integer, _
    target As Integer) As Integer
Dim i As Integer

    For i = LBound(list) To UBound(list)
        ' See if we found the target.
        If list(i) = target Then
            LinearSearch = i
            Exit Function
        End If

        ' If the values are too big, we passed
        ' where it should be so it's not here.
        If list(i) = target Then Exit For
    Next i

    ' We didn't find the target.
    LinearSearch = LBound(list) - 1

End Function
```

Chapter 2

My daily schedule varies to some extent, but Table A.1 shows its general format. The tasks are not really as simple as they seem. For example, Email involves posting answers to email questions on the Web at www.vb-helper.com. Program, Proofread, and Write can involve one or more articles, columns, or books on any given day. Usually they involve more than one because I get tired if I program, write, and proofread the same material all in one day.

Generally, I am most creative first thing in the morning. I am alert most of the morning and in the mid-afternoon. Before and after lunch, and in the late afternoon, my attention starts to wander and I become both less creative and less attentive to detail.

This productivity profile has a couple of mismatches with the schedule shown in Table A.1. Some email from business associates requires attention to detail but not a lot of creativity. The majority of my email is from Web site visitors and usually includes beginners' questions that are easy to answer. Responding to simple questions should not take up my most productive time.

Writing takes a lot of creativity but not as much precision as writing code. This task would be easiest in the morning when I am most creative. Programming takes lots of precision and some creativity. It can probably move to one of my later precise time periods like the mid-afternoon.

The biggest problem with this schedule is that it wastes some of my most creative and productive hours in the early morning with routine email. The long stretch of uninterrupted programming that follows wears me down so my attention wanders and I read email for a break. Writing new text, which requires the most creativity, is deferred until late afternoon when I am not spectacularly creative.

Table A.1   A Typical Daily Schedule

6:30 A.M.–8:30 A.M.	Email
8:30 A.M.–11:00 A.M.	Program
11:00 A.M.–11:30 A.M.	Email
11:30 A.M.–12:30 P.M.	Lunch
12:30 P.M.–1:00 P.M.	Email.
1:00 P.M.–2:00 P.M.	Proofread
2:00 P.M.–2:30 P.M.	Email
2:30 P.M.–4:30 P.M.	Write
4:30 P.M.–5:30 P.M.	Email

Finally, reading email happens several times during the day. This breaks up big periods of time that I could use for larger tasks like long programming sessions. It also prevents me from seeing how much mail I have all at once. That makes it easy for me to spend a few extra minutes each time I read my email. A few minutes five times a day can really add up.

With these problems in mind, I switched to the schedule shown in Table A.2. Here, writing gets most of my productive hours from 7:00 A.M. to 9:00 A.M. and 1:00 P.M. to 3:00 P.M. Programming gets my remaining precision hours from 9:00 A.M. to 11:30 A.M. Proofreading gets my last productive hours from 3:00 P.M. to 4:00 P.M. Email that is not urgent gets my least-productive time.

This schedule gives me longer periods of uninterrupted time for the most important tasks. It also puts those tasks in the time slots most appropriate for their needs. Consolidating email sessions lets me reduce the total time I spend on email each day, mostly by making it is easier to realize how much time I am spending on it.

Switching to this schedule was not easy. At first I had to set my watch alarm to remind me to move on to the next task, particularly when I was reading email. It took about a week before it became comfortable and a few weeks before I got the new schedule's full benefit.

Chapter 3

An important design mistake in the original version of this code is that the routines ComputeTotal and Prepare use the global variable NumTxt to avoid repeatedly computing the number of controls named Text1. Subroutine Average takes a different approach and computes this value using a local variable.

The program should use one approach or the other, but not both. If it uses a global variable, it should explicitly declare a data type for NumTxt. If it uses

Table A.2   Revised Daily Schedule

6:30 A.M.–7:00 A.M.	Read urgent email only
7:00 A.M.–9:00 A.M.	Write
9:00 A.M.–11:30 A.M.	Program
11:30 A.M.–12:30 P.M.	Lunch
12:30 P.M.–1:00 P.M.	Read urgent email only
1:00 P.M.–2:30 P.M.	Write
2:30 P.M.–3:30 P.M.	Proofread
3:30 P.M.–5:00 P.M.	Read remaining email

local variables, it could make them static and then it would not need to recalculate the value every time each subroutine ran.

Of course, it would be much better to simply examine the controls in the Text1 control array as in the following code. That does not demonstrate the techniques presented in this chapter, however.

```
Dim ctl As TextBox

    For Each ctl In Text1
        :
    Next ctl
```

This code also uses variants extensively. It uses most of them as simple counters that should be declared as integers instead. The original bad version of the code follows. See the notes after the code for explanations of the code's bad points.

```
DefInt I-K                                              ' 1

Dim NumTxt                                              ' 2

Private Sub Command1_Click()                            ' 3
    ComputeTotal
End Sub

Private Sub Command2_Click()                            ' 3
    Average
End Sub

Private Sub Command3_Click()                            ' 3
    Prepare
End Sub

Public Sub Average()                                    ' 3
Dim NumTxt                                              ' 2, 4

    For Each ctl In Form1.Controls                      ' 5, 6
        If ctl.Name = "Text1" Then NumTxt = NumTxt + 1  ' 7
    Next ctl
    For i = 0 To NumTxt - 1                             ' 6
        Total = Total + CInt(Text1(i).Text)             ' 6
    Next i
    Text2.Text = Format$(Total / NumTxt)                ' 7
End Sub

Public Sub ComputeTotal()                               ' 3
Dim box As Object                                       ' 8

    If NumTxt = 0 Then                                  ' 5
        For Each box In Form1.Controls                  ' 9
            If box.Name = "Text1" Then NumTxt = NumTxt + 1  ' 7
```

```
        Next box
    End If
    For i = 0 To NumTxt - 1                          ' 6
        Total = Total + CInt(Text1(i).Text)          ' 6
    Next i
    Text2.Text = Format$(Total)                      ' 7
End Sub

Public Sub Prepare()                                 ' 3, 10
Dim box As Object                                    ' 8

    If NumTxt = 0 Then                               ' 5
        For Each box In Form1.Controls               ' 9
            If box.Name = "Text1" Then NumTxt = NumTxt + 1   ' 7
        Next box
    End If
    For i = 0 To NumTxt - 1                           ' 6
        Text1(i).Text = Format$(Int(100 * Rnd + 1))   ' 7
    Next i
End Sub
```

1. Do not use Deftype statements. Declare each variable separately and explicitly.

2. Explicitly declare each variable with its type even if it should be a variant.

3. This code is not written for humans. People need comments explaining what the code does.

4. This variable conflicts with a global variable of the same name. They should have different names.

5. This complicated code desperately needs comments to let the reader know what it is doing.

6. Variables ctl, i, and Total should be explicitly declared.

7. Text1 and Text2 are terrible names for controls. Never use Visual Basic's default control names. These should be changed to something like txtValue and txtResult.

8. The variable box should be declared using the most specific data type possible. In this case, that is Control instead of Object.

9. The form refers to its one form name, Form1. A form should never refer to its type name.

10. Prepare is not a meaningful name. This subroutine should have a descriptive name such as InitializeValues or RandomizeData.

The improved version of the code follows. Refer to the original version to see what has changed.

```
Option Explicit
```

```
Private mintNumControls As Integer

' Calculate and display the average.
Private Sub cmdAverage_Click()
    ComputeAverage
End Sub

' Randomize the values.
Private Sub cmdRandomize_Click()
    RandomizeValues
End Sub

' Calculate and display the total.
Private Sub cmdTotal_Click()
    ComputeTotal
End Sub

' Calculate and display the average of the values
' entered in the TextBoxes named txtValue.
Public Sub ComputeAverage()
Dim ctl As Control
Dim i As Integer
Dim total As Integer

    ' If the TextBoxes named txtValue have not yet
    ' been counted, count them.
    If mintNumControls = 0 Then
        For Each ctl In Controls
            If ctl.Name = "txtValue" Then _
                mintNumControls = mintNumControls + 1
        Next ctl
    End If

    ' Add up the values entered in txtValue controls.
    For i = 0 To mintNumControls - 1
        total = total + CInt(txtValue(i).Text)
    Next i

    ' Divide the total by the number of controls
    ' and display the result.
    txtResult.Text = Format$(total / mintNumControls)
End Sub

' Calculate and display the total of the values
' entered in the TextBoxes named txtValue.
Public Sub ComputeTotal()
Dim ctl As Control
Dim i As Integer
Dim total As Integer

    ' If the TextBoxes named txtValue have not yet
    ' been counted, count them.
    If mintNumControls = 0 Then
```

```
        For Each ctl In Controls
            If ctl.Name = "txtValue" Then _
                mintNumControls = mintNumControls + 1
        Next ctl
    End If

    ' Add up the values in txtValue controls.
    For i = 0 To mintNumControls - 1
        total = total + CInt(txtValue(i).Text)
    Next i

    ' Display the total.
    txtResult.Text = Format$(total)
End Sub

' Set the values of the TextBoxes named txtValue
' to random numbers between 1 and 100.
Public Sub RandomizeValues()
Dim ctl As Control
Dim i As Integer

    ' If the TextBoxes named txtValue have not yet
    ' been counted, count them.
    If mintNumControls = 0 Then
        For Each ctl In Controls
            If ctl.Name = "txtValue" Then _
                mintNumControls = mintNumControls + 1
        Next ctl
    End If

    ' Generate a random value for each control.
    For i = 0 To mintNumControls - 1
        txtValue(i).Text = Format$(Int(100 * Rnd + 1))
    Next i
End Sub
```

Chapter 4

The original bad version of the code follows. Its most obvious problem is that it uses hard-coded numbers when it should use defined constants. A more subtle problem is that it really should not use constants either. Instead, it should use the txtInput control array's LBound and UBound properties to determine the proper dimensions for the Values array at runtime. Then you can make the program manipulate more or fewer values simply by creating or removing controls from the form.

The bad version also passes the dimensions of the Values array into the Load-Values, RandomizeValues, and DisplayValues subroutines. Those routines should use Visual Basic's LBound and UBound functions to determine the array's bounds directly. See the notes after the code for explanations of the code's specific bad points.

```
Option Explicit

Private Values(0 To 9) As String                         ' 1

' Randomize the values entered by the user.
Private Sub cmdRandomize_Click()
    LoadValues Values, 0, 9                              ' 1, 2
    RandomizeValues Values, 0, 9                         ' 1, 2
    DisplayValues Values, 0, 9                           ' 1, 2
End Sub

' Load the values from the txtInput TextBoxes.
Private Sub LoadValues(list() As String, _
    min As Integer, max As Integer)                     ' 2
Dim i As Integer

    For i = min To max
        list(i) = txtInput(i).Text                      ' 3
    Next i
End Sub

' Randomize the values in the array.
Private Sub RandomizeValues(list() As String, _
    min As Integer, max As Integer)                     ' 2
Dim i As Integer
Dim new_index As Integer
Dim temp_string As String

    Randomize
    For i = min To max - 1
        ' Randomly pick an entry with index between
        ' i and max to go in position i.
        new_index = Int((max - i + 1) * Rnd + i)

        ' Swap that entry with the one in position i.
        temp_string = Values(i)
        Values(i) = Values(new_index)
        Values(new_index) = temp_string
    Next i
End Sub

' Display the values in the lblOutput Labels.
Private Sub DisplayValues(list() As String, _
    min As Integer, max As Integer)                     ' 2
Dim i As Integer

    For i = min To max
        lblOutput(i).Caption = list(i)                  ' 3
    Next i
End Sub
```

1. The program should use defined constants, not magic numbers.

2. The program should not pass array bounds into these routines. They should figure out the bounds directly using Visual Basic's LBound and UBound functions.

3. This code assumes the txtInput and lblOutput control arrays have indexes ranging from 0 to 9. The program should use the control arrays' LBound and UBound properties to learn the true ranges.

The program should use the LBound and UBound properties provided by the txtInput and lblOutput control arrays to determine the indexes they span. However, there is little need to carry this idea to extremes. The program's purpose is to randomize a list of values and display the result. It would make no sense for the program to have different numbers of controls in the txtInput and lblOutput arrays.

The program could perform elaborate checks to verify that these arrays hold the same number of controls, but that would be a waste of time. If the arrays contain different numbers of items, the program will crash with an error message that says a control array element does not exist. The message is descriptive enough that you could easily determine the exact problem and fix it.

Similarly, someone could remove one of the controls from the middle of the control arrays. In that case, Visual Basic will again tell you that a control array element does not exist, and you can easily fix the problem.

The following code shows the revised program without magic numbers.

```
Option Explicit

' This array is dimensioned in Form_Load.
Private Values() As String

' See how many txtInput controls there are and
' redimension the Values array.
Private Sub Form_Load()
Dim min_index As Integer
Dim max_index As Integer

    min_index = txtInput.LBound
    max_index = txtInput.UBound
    ReDim Values(min_index To max_index)
End Sub

' Randomize the values entered by the user.
Private Sub cmdRandomize_Click()
    LoadValues Values
    RandomizeValues Values
    DisplayValues Values
```

```
End Sub

' Load the values from the txtInput TextBoxes.
Private Sub LoadValues(list() As String)
Dim i As Integer

    For i = LBound(list) To UBound(list)
        list(i) = txtInput(i).Text
    Next i
End Sub

' Randomize the values in the array.
Private Sub RandomizeValues(list() As String)
Dim max_index As Integer
Dim i As Integer
Dim new_index As Integer
Dim temp_string As String

    Randomize
    max_index = UBound(list)
    For i = LBound(list) To max_index - 1
        ' Randomly pick an entry with index between
        ' i and max to go in position i.
        new_index = Int((max_index - i + 1) * Rnd + i)

        ' Swap that entry with the one in position i.
        temp_string = Values(i)
        Values(i) = Values(new_index)
        Values(new_index) = temp_string
    Next i
End Sub

' Display the values in the lblOutput Labels.
Private Sub DisplayValues(list() As String)
Dim i As Integer

    For i = LBound(list) To UBound(list)
        lblOutput(i).Caption = list(i)
    Next i
End Sub
```

Chapter 5

The original version of program Bad5 follows. Its two most obvious problems are that it uses constants and hard-coded values when it could use LBound and UBound, and that it does not verify its data or results. See the notes after the code for explanations of the code's specific bad points.

```
Option Explicit
```

```vb
' Declare the list of values.
Const NUM_VALUES = 50
Private Values(1 To NUM_VALUES) As Integer

' Randomly initialize some values.
Private Sub Form_Load()                                    ' 1
    InitValues
End Sub

' Randomly initialize some values.
Private Sub InitValues()
Dim i As Integer
Dim txt As String

    ' Pick the random values.
    Randomize
    Values(1) = Int(10 * Rnd + 1)
    For i = 2 To NUM_VALUES                                ' 2
        Values(i) = Values(i - 1) + Int(10 * Rnd + 1)     ' 3
    Next i

    ' Display the values.
    For i = 1 To NUM_VALUES
        txt = txt & Format$(i, "@@") & _
            Format$(Values(i), "@@@@") & vbCrLf
    Next i
    txtValues.Text = txt
End Sub

' Search using the selected method.
Private Sub CmdSearch_Click()
Dim position As Integer
Dim num_searches As Integer

    If optSearchMethod(0).Value Then                       ' 4
        ' Linear search.
        position = LinearSearch(Values, _
            CInt(txtTarget.Text), num_searches)            ' 5
    ElseIf optSearchMethod(1).Value Then
        ' Binary search.
        position = BinarySearch(Values, _
            CInt(txtTarget.Text), num_searches)            ' 5
    End If

    ' Display the results.
    If position = 0 Then
        lblPosition.Caption = "Not found"
    Else
        lblPosition.Caption = Format$(position)
    End If
    lblSearches.Caption = Format$(num_searches)
End Sub
```

```
' Use linear binary search to find the target.
Public Function LinearSearch(list() As Integer, _
    target As Integer, num_searches As Integer) As Integer
Dim i As Integer

    For i = 1 To NUM_VALUES                               ' 2
        num_searches = num_searches + 1
        If Values(i) = target Then Exit For
    Next i

    If i <= NUM_VALUES Then
        LinearSearch = i
    Else
        LinearSearch = 0
    End If
End Function

' Use binary search to find the target. For details
' of the algorithm, see Ready-to-Run Visual Basic
' Algorithms, ISBN 0-471-24268-3.
Public Function BinarySearch(list() As Integer, _
    target As Integer, num_searches As Integer) As Integer
Dim min_index As Integer
Dim max_index As Integer
Dim mid_index As Integer

    min_index = 1                                         ' 2
    max_index = NUM_VALUES
    Do While min_index <= max_index
        num_searches = num_searches + 1
        mid_index = (min_index + max_index) / 2
        If target = list(mid_index) Then
            BinarySearch = mid_index
            Exit Function
        ElseIf target < list(mid_index) Then
            max_index = mid_index - 1
        Else
            min_index = mid_index + 1
        End If
    Loop
    BinarySearch = 0                                      ' 2
End Function
```

1. This routine should validate the randomly generated data to determine whether it makes sense.

2. The program should use LBound and UBound to find array bounds.

3. The minimum and maximum increments between numbers should be constants, not hard coded.

4. This If statement should have an Else clause.

5. This routine should validate its results.

The following code shows a better version of the program. This version does not validate its data when it unloads because that data is never modified after it is initially generated.

```vb
Option Explicit

' Enabled debugging tests.
#Const DEBUG_MODE = True

' Declare the list of values.
Const NUM_VALUES = 50
Private Values(1 To NUM_VALUES) As Integer

' Randomly initialize some values.
Private Sub Form_Load()
    InitValues

    ' Validate the data.
    ValidateList
End Sub

' Randomly initialize some values.
Private Sub InitValues()
Const MIN_INCREMENT = 1
Const MAX_INCREMENT = 10
Dim i As Integer
Dim last_value As Integer
Dim txt As String

    ' Pick the random values.
    Randomize
    For i = LBound(Values) To UBound(Values)
        last_value = last_value + _
            Int((MAX_INCREMENT - MIN_INCREMENT + 1) * _
                Rnd + MIN_INCREMENT)
        Values(i) = last_value
    Next i

    ' Display the values.
    For i = LBound(Values) To UBound(Values)
        txt = txt & Format$(i, "@@") & _
            Format$(Values(i), "@@@@") & vbCrLf
    Next i
    txtValues.Text = txt
End Sub

' Verify that the list is arranged in increasing order.
Private Sub ValidateList()
```

```
Dim i As Integer

    For i = LBound(Values) + 1 To UBound(Values)
        If Values(i - 1) >= Values(i) Then Stop
    Next i
End Sub

' Search using the selected method.
Private Sub CmdSearch_Click()
Dim target As Integer
Dim position As Integer
Dim num_searches As Integer

    target = CInt(txtTarget.Text)

    If optSearchMethod(0).Value Then
        ' Linear search.
        position = LinearSearch(Values, _
            target, num_searches)
    ElseIf optSearchMethod(1).Value Then
        ' Binary search.
        position = BinarySearch(Values, _
            target, num_searches)
    Else
        ' This should never happen.
        Stop
    End If

    ' Display the results.
    If position = 0 Then
        lblPosition.Caption = "Not found"
    Else
        lblPosition.Caption = Format$(position)
    End If
    lblSearches.Caption = Format$(num_searches)

    ' If DEBUG_MODE is true, verify the result.
    #If DEBUG_MODE Then
        If position <> 0 Then _
            VerifyResult target, position
    #End If
End Sub

' Use linear binary search to find the target.
Public Function LinearSearch(list() As Integer, _
    target As Integer, num_searches As Integer) As Integer
Dim i As Integer

    For i = LBound(Values) To UBound(Values)
        num_searches = num_searches + 1
        If Values(i) = target Then Exit For
    Next i
```

```
        If i <= UBound(Values) Then
            LinearSearch = i
        Else
            LinearSearch = LBound(Values) - 1
        End If
End Function

' Use binary search to find the target. For details
' of the algorithm, see Ready-to-Run Visual Basic
' Algorithms, ISBN 0-471-24268-3.
Public Function BinarySearch(list() As Integer, _
    target As Integer, num_searches As Integer) As Integer
Dim min_index As Integer
Dim max_index As Integer
Dim mid_index As Integer

    min_index = LBound(list)
    max_index = UBound(list)
    Do While min_index <= max_index
        num_searches = num_searches + 1
        mid_index = (min_index + max_index) / 2
        If target = list(mid_index) Then
            BinarySearch = mid_index
            Exit Function
        ElseIf target < list(mid_index) Then
            max_index = mid_index - 1
        Else
            min_index = mid_index + 1
        End If
    Loop
    BinarySearch = LBound(list) - 1
End Function

' Verify a search result.
Private Sub VerifyResult(target As Integer, index As Integer)
    If Values(index) <> target Then Stop
End Sub
```

Chapter 6

The original version of the Bad6 program follows. It contains several pieces of code that are more difficult to understand than necessary. See the notes after the code for explanations of the code's specific bad points.

```
Option Explicit

' Make txtOutput as large as possible.
Private Sub Form_Resize()
    txtOutput.Move 0, 0, ScaleWidth, ScaleHeight
```

```
End Sub


' Read the data from the data file.
Private Sub Form_Load()                                        ' 1
Dim fnum As Integer

    ' Open the file.
    fnum = FreeFile
    Open App.Path & "\types.dat" For Input As fnum

    ' Read the data.
    LoadData fnum
End Sub


' Read the data file and close it.
Sub LoadData(fnum As Integer)                                  ' 1, 7
Const FORMAT_SPECIFIER = "!@@@@@@@@@@@@@@@@@@@"

Dim output_txt As String
Dim all_data As String                                         ' 2
Dim next_line As String
Dim token As String

    ' Read all the data.
    all_data = Input(LOF(fnum), #fnum)                         ' 3

    ' Start with column headers.
    output_txt = _
        Format("Data Type", FORMAT_SPECIFIER) & _
        Format("Size", FORMAT_SPECIFIER) & _
        Format("Approx Min", FORMAT_SPECIFIER) & _
        Format("Approx Max", FORMAT_SPECIFIER)
    output_txt = output_txt & vbCrLf & _
        Format("---------", FORMAT_SPECIFIER) & _
        Format("----", FORMAT_SPECIFIER) & _
        Format("----------", FORMAT_SPECIFIER) & _
        Format("----------", FORMAT_SPECIFIER) & _
        vbCrLf

    ' Read the lines from the file.
    Do While Len(all_data) > 0
        ' Get the next line.
        next_line = GetToken(all_data, vbCrLf)                 ' 4

        ' Break the line into pieces.
        Do While Len(next_line) > 0
            token = GetToken(next_line, ";")                   ' 4, 5
            If Len(token) > 0 Then output_txt = output_txt & Format(toke
        Loop
        output_txt = output_txt & vbCrLf
    Loop

    ' Display the result.
```

```
        txtOutput = output_txt                               ' 6
    End Sub


    ' Get the next delimited token from the string txt.
    Function GetToken(txt As String, delimiter As String) As String    ' 4, 7
    Dim p As Integer                                         ' 8

        ' Find the delimiter.
        p = InStr(txt, delimiter)

        ' Get the token.
        If p = 0 Then p = Len(txt) + 1                       ' 9
        GetToken = Left(txt, p - 1)                          ' 3

        ' See what's left of the string txt.
        p = Len(txt) - p + 1 - Len(delimiter)               ' 10
        If p <= 0 Then
            txt = ""
        Else
            txt = Right(txt, p)                              ' 3
        End If
    End Function
```

1. Opening the file in one routine and closing it in another is confusing. In fact, this program never closes the file.

2. The all_data, next_line, and token variables perform similar functions so they should have similar names.

3. These calls to Input, Left, and Right assign values to strings so they should be Input$, Left$, and Right$ instead.

4. Function GetToken has a side effect. It returns a token but it also modifies the txt_buffer parameter. It should be rewritten as a subroutine so the side effect is not as subtle.

5. The following line is too long. It should be broken with a line continuation character or converted into a multiline If statement.

6. This statement should explicitly reference the control's Text property.

7. Parameters that are not modified should be declared ByVal. Parameters that are modified should be declared ByRef.

8. This variable has a meaningless name. It should be called something like delimiter_position.

9. This is an unexplained trick that makes the Left statement that follows work. It should be explained or rewritten so it is not tricky.

10. Variable p is reused. At this point, it no longer represents a position within the text buffer. Instead, it represents the text buffer's new length. The program should use a new variable.

The following code shows a better version of the program. To conserve space, this version still does not contain error handling code.

```
Option Explicit

' Make txtOutput as large as possible.
Private Sub Form_Resize()
    txtOutput.Move 0, 0, ScaleWidth, ScaleHeight
End Sub

' Read the data from the data file.
Private Sub Form_Load()
Dim fnum As Integer

    ' Open the file.
    fnum = FreeFile
    Open App.Path & "\types.dat" For Input As fnum

    ' Read the data.
    LoadData fnum

    ' Close the file.
    Close fnum
End Sub

' Read the data file.
Private Sub LoadData(ByVal fnum As Integer)
Const FORMAT_SPECIFIER = "!@@@@@@@@@@@@@@@@@@@@"

Dim output_txt As String
Dim all_data As String
Dim line_data As String
Dim token_data As String

    ' Read all the data.
    all_data = Input$(LOF(fnum), #fnum)

    ' Start with column headers.
    output_txt = _
        Format("Data Type", FORMAT_SPECIFIER) & _
        Format("Size", FORMAT_SPECIFIER) & _
        Format("Approx Min", FORMAT_SPECIFIER) & _
        Format("Approx Max", FORMAT_SPECIFIER)
    output_txt = output_txt & vbCrLf & _
        Format("---------", FORMAT_SPECIFIER) & _
        Format("----", FORMAT_SPECIFIER) & _
        Format("----------", FORMAT_SPECIFIER) & _
        Format("----------", FORMAT_SPECIFIER) & _
        vbCrLf

    ' Read the lines from the file.
    Do While Len(all_data) > 0
        ' Get the next line.
```

```
            GetToken all_data, line_data, vbCrLf

        ' Break the line into tokens.
        Do While Len(line_data) > 0
            GetToken line_data, token_data, ";"
            If Len(token_data) > 0 Then
                output_txt = output_txt & _
                    Format(token_data, _
                    FORMAT_SPECIFIER)
            End If
        Loop
        output_txt = output_txt & vbCrLf
    Loop

        ' Display the result.
        txtOutput.Text = output_txt
    End Sub


' Get the next delimited token from the text buffer.
' Remove the token from the buffer.
Private Sub GetToken(ByRef txt_buffer As String, _
    ByRef token As String, ByVal delimiter As String)
Dim delimiter_position As Integer
Dim new_length As Integer

        ' Find the delimiter.
        delimiter_position = InStr(txt_buffer, delimiter)

        ' Get the token and see what's left of txt_buffer.
        If delimiter_position = 0 Then
            ' The delimiter is not present.
            ' Use all of txt_buffer as the token.
            token = txt_buffer
            txt_buffer = ""
        Else
            ' The delimiter is present.
            ' Compute token and see what's left
            ' of txt_buffer.
            token = Left$(txt_buffer, delimiter_position - 1)
            new_length = Len(txt_buffer) - _
                delimiter_position + 1 - Len(delimiter)
            txt_buffer = Right$(txt_buffer, new_length)
        End If
    End Sub
```

Chapter 7

The bad version of the comments included at the end of Chapter 7 follows. In
general, these comments do not provide much useful information. They tell the

reader little that an experienced Visual Basic programmer could not learn by looking at the code. They also do not tell what the routine actually does. See the notes after the example for explanations of specific bad points.

```
Option Explicit

' True when the user is drawing.
Private Drawing As Boolean

' Save mouse position.                                    ' 1
Private LastX As Single
Private LastY As Single

' **********************************************
' Purpose: Start drawing.                                 ' 2
'
' Method:  Use the X and Y coordinates to see where       ' 3
'          the mouse currently is.
' **********************************************          ' 4, 7
Private Sub picDrawingArea_MouseDown(Button As Integer, _
        Shift As Integer, X As Single, Y As Single)

    ' Set Drawing to true.                                ' 8
    Drawing = True

    ' Record this point's location.                       ' 8
    LastX = X
    LastY = Y
End Sub

' **********************************************
' Purpose: Process the user's mouse move event in         ' 4
'          the drawing area.
'
' Method:  Use the X and Y coordinates to see where       ' 2
'          the mouse currently is.
'
' Errors:                                                 ' 5
'    If the user draws outside the drawing area,
'    raise error OUT_OF_BOUNDS.
' **********************************************          ' 6
Private Sub picDrawingArea_MouseMove(Button As Integer, _
        Shift As Integer, X As Single, Y As Single)

    ' If we are not drawing, BAIL OUT.                    ' 9
    If Not Drawing Then Exit Sub

    If X < 0 Or _
       Y < 0 Or _
       X > picDrawingArea.ScaleWidth Or _
       Y > picDrawingArea.ScaleHeight _
```

```
        Then       ' Make sure we are in the drawing area.              ' 10
            Err.Raise OUT_OF_BOUNDS, _
                "picDrawingArea", _
                "Cannot draw outside the drawing area."
        End If

        ' Draw a line from (LastX, LastY) to (X, Y).                    ' 8
        picDrawingArea.Line (LastX, LastY)-(X, Y)

        ' Save X and Y.                                                 ' 8
        LastX = X
        LastY = Y
    End Sub


    ' *************************************************
    ' Purpose: Finish drawing.                                          ' 1
    '
    ' Method:  Set Drawing to False.
    ' *************************************************                  ' 6
    Private Sub picDrawingArea_MouseUp(Button As Integer, _
            Shift As Integer, X As Single, Y As Single)

        Drawing = False
    End Sub
```

1. This phrase is awkward to read and harder to understand than necessary. It also does not say enough to explain the variables. It should say something like, "The last mouse position while drawing."

2. This comment is true but weak. It should say what caused the event, what the routine does in response, and why that is important.

3. This does not explain how the routine works. It merely restates what should be obvious to any experienced Visual Basic developer: the X and Y parameters give the current mouse coordinates.

4. This routine modifies the module-global variables Drawing, LastX, and LastY. An inputs section in the comments should say so.

5. This does not give the routine's logical purpose. It merely states the obvious: this is a mouse move event handler. It should explain why the event occurred, what the routine does in response, and why that is important.

6. Event handlers must never raise errors because the program cannot trap them.

7. The comments should include a history listing the programmers who worked on the code and explaining what they did.

8. These comments restate the obvious. They should explain why something is happening, not merely that it is happening.

9. This comment uses improper capitalization that lends undue emphasis to the phrase "BAIL OUT." The expression "bail out" is also not ordinary language and some readers may not understand it. It should say "do nothing" instead.

10. This comment should precede the lines it explains instead of sitting on the last line in a continued statement.

The following code shows an improved version of this code.

```
Option Explicit

' True when the user is drawing.
Private Drawing As Boolean

' The last mouse position while drawing.
Private LastX As Single
Private LastY As Single

' ************************************************
' Purpose: The user pressed the mouse to start
'          scribbling in the drawing area. Start
'          drawing.
'
' Method:  Set Drawing = True so we process future
'          MouseMove events to scribble.
'
' Outputs: Sets Drawing = True.
'          Saves the mouse coordinates in LastX
'          and LastY.
'
' Asserts: None.
'
' Developer           Date     Comments
' ──         ───  ───
' Josh Philps          9/ 6/99 Initial creation.
' ************************************************
Private Sub picDrawingArea_MouseDown(Button As Integer, _
        Shift As Integer, X As Single, Y As Single)

    ' We are starting to draw.
    Drawing = True

    ' Save the mouse position so we can draw
    ' to it later.
    LastX = X
    LastY = Y
End Sub


' ************************************************
' Purpose: The user is moving the mouse. If we are
```

```
'           scribbling, continue drawing.
'
' Method:  If Drawing = True, draw a line from the
'          previous point to this one.
'
' Outputs: Saves the new mouse coordinates in
'          LastX and LastY.
'
' Asserts: None.
'
' Developer         Date      Comments
' ----------        --------  --------
' Josh Philps           9/ 6/99 Initial creation.
' ************************************************
Private Sub picDrawingArea_MouseMove(Button As Integer, _
        Shift As Integer, X As Single, Y As Single)

    ' If we are not drawing, do nothing.
    If Not Drawing Then Exit Sub

    ' Draw a line from the last mouse position.
    picDrawingArea.Line (LastX, LastY)-(X, Y)

    ' Save the new mouse position so we can draw
    ' to it later.
    LastX = X
    LastY = Y
End Sub

' ************************************************
' Purpose: The user released the mouse to stop
'          scribbling. If we are scribbling, stop.
'
' Method:  Set Drawing to False so we ignore
'          future MouseMove events.
'
' Outputs: Sets Drawing = False.
'
' Asserts: None.
'
' Developer         Date      Comments
' ----------        --------  --------
' Josh Philps           9/ 6/99 Initial creation.
' ************************************************
Private Sub picDrawingArea_MouseUp(Button As Integer, _
        Shift As Integer, X As Single, Y As Single)

    Drawing = False
End Sub
```

Chapter 8

The broken version of program Bad8 is show in the following code. Its main problems are that it does not properly control the data types it uses. This causes worthless comparisons between strings and doubles and gives rounding errors that make the program fail to find target numbers in almost every case. See the notes after the code for explanations of specific bad points.

```
Option Explicit

' The list of values.
Private Const NUM_VALUES = 50
Private Values(1 To NUM_VALUES) As Variant                   ' 1

' Initialize the data.
Private Sub Form_Load()
    InitializeData
End Sub

' Create some random data.
Private Sub InitializeData()
Dim i As Integer
Dim last_value As Integer ' The last value assigned.         ' 2
Dim txt As String

    Randomize

    ' Initialize the random numbers with each
    ' value slightly bigger than the previous one.
    last_value = 10
    For i = 1 To NUM_VALUES
        Values(i) = last_value + Rnd + 0.01                 ' 3
        last_value = Values(i)
    Next i

    ' Display the values.
    For i = 1 To NUM_VALUES
        txt = txt & Format$(i, "@@") & ": " & _
            Format$(Values(i), "0.000") & vbCrLf             ' 4
    Next i
    txtValues.Text = txt
End Sub

' Search for the target.
Private Sub CmdSearch_Click()
Dim position As Integer

    position = LinearSearch(Values, txtTarget.Text)          ' 5
    If position < 1 Then
```

```
          lblPosition.Caption = "Not found"
     Else
          lblPosition.Caption = Format$(position)
     End If
End Sub


' Locate a target item using linear search. If the
' target is not found, return 1 less than the
' smallest array index.
Public Function LinearSearch(list() As Variant, _
     target As Variant) As Integer
Dim i As Integer

     For i = LBound(list) To UBound(list)
         ' See if we found the target.
         If list(i) = target Then                        ' 6
             LinearSearch = i
             Exit Function
         End If

         ' If the values are too big, we passed
         ' where it should be so it's not here.
         If list(i) > target Then Exit For               ' 7
     Next i
End Function                                             ' 8
```

1. The program uses variants to manipulate its most important pieces of data. It should use a specific data type. Using variants allows Visual Basic to use double precision floating-point numbers in some places and strings in others. This has disastrous consequences (see 4).

2. The code uses this integer to initialize variant values. This causes problems later (see 3). The Value array and this variable should have the same data type.

3. To add the integer last_value, the single precision value returned by Rnd, and the double precision value 0.01, Visual Basic promotes the result to a double. That makes the variant Values(i) a double. This causes several problems later.

4. This format statement displays values with only three decimal places. That gives a false impression of their true precision. The user cannot hope to later know what value to enter as a target. For example, the program displays the value 10.2870501971245 as 10.287. The user cannot hope to guess the correct value with enough precision to find it.

5. The program passes a string here for the target value. Function LinearSearch declares the target as a variant so Visual Basic passes the routine a string. That causes trouble later. At this point, the program should use a data type conversion function to force txtTarget.Text into the proper data type.

6. Here the program is comparing a string representation of a low precision number with a double precision numeric value. It should compare like data types and it should use an inequality, not an equality, statement.

7. Believe it or not, this comparison is always False. For some reason, Visual Basic defines numeric variants to always be less than string variants, even if they could both be converted into numbers or strings.

8. The function does not define a return value before ending.

The following code shows a better version of the program. Because the numbers are shown with a precision of three decimal places, the program checks whether the target value differs from a list value by no more than 0.0005. If so, the list value is identical to the target to within three decimal places.

```
Option Explicit

' The list of values.
Private Const NUM_VALUES = 50
Private Values(1 To NUM_VALUES) As Single

' Initialize the data.
Private Sub Form_Load()
    InitializeData
End Sub

' Create some random data.
Private Sub InitializeData()
Dim i As Integer
Dim last_value As Single ' The last value assigned.
Dim txt As String

    Randomize

    ' Initialize the random numbers with each
    ' value slightly bigger than the previous one.
    last_value = 10
    For i = 1 To NUM_VALUES
        Values(i) = last_value + Rnd + 0.01
        last_value = Values(i)
    Next i

    ' Display the values.
    For i = 1 To NUM_VALUES
        txt = txt & Format$(i, "@@") & ": " & _
            Format$(Values(i), "0.000") & vbCrLf
    Next i
    txtValues.Text = txt
End Sub

' Search for the target.
```

```
Private Sub CmdSearch_Click()
Dim position As Integer

    position = LinearSearch(Values, CSng(txtTarget.Text))
    If position < 1 Then
        lblPosition.Caption = "Not found"
    Else
        lblPosition.Caption = Format$(position)
    End If
End Sub

' Locate a target item using linear search. If the
' target is not found, return 1 less than the
' smallest array index.
Public Function LinearSearch(list() As Single, _
    target As Single) As Integer
Dim i As Integer

    For i = LBound(list) To UBound(list)
        ' See if we found the target.
        If Abs(list(i) - target) <= 0.0005 Then
            LinearSearch = i
            Exit Function
        End If

        ' If the values are too big, we passed
        ' where it should be so it's not here.
        If list(i) > target Then Exit For
    Next i

    ' We didn't find the target.
    LinearSearch = LBound(list) - 1
End Function
```

Chapter 9

The code for program Bad9 follows. This program's main failing is that it was designed in a nonuniform way. The design treats the bold property differently than the italic, underlined, and strikethrough properties even though they are conceptually very similar. It also treats the dissimilar commands Find, Find Relative, bold, unbold, and color uniformly even though they represent very different concepts. These mistakes give the program a confusing user interface and the underlying code is confused to match. See the notes following the code for more specific comments.

```
Option Explicit

Private Const cmd_FIND = 0
Private Const cmd_FIND_RELATIVE = 1
```

```
Private Const cmd_BOLD = 2
Private Const cmd_UNBOLD = 3
Private Const cmd_COLOR = 4

Private Const chk_UNDERLINE = 0
Private Const chk_ITALIC = 1
Private Const chk_STRIKETHROUGH = 2

' True when the program is changing display values.
Private SettingValues As Boolean

' Apply the selected command.
Private Sub cmdApply_Click()                                       ' 1
    If optCommand(cmd_FIND) Then                                   ' 2
        ' Find and select the indicated text.
        FindText
    ElseIf optCommand(cmd_FIND_RELATIVE) Then
        ' Find and select the indicated text.
        FindTextRelative
    ElseIf optCommand(cmd_BOLD) Then
        ' Color the selection bold.
        ColorSelection "Bold"
    ElseIf optCommand(cmd_UNBOLD) Then
        ' Unbold the selection.
        rchMainText.SelBold = False
    ElseIf optCommand(cmd_COLOR) Then
        ' Color the selection.
        ColorSelection cboSelColor.Text
    End If

    rchMainText.SetFocus
End Sub

' Find and select the indicated text.
Private Sub FindText()
Dim txt As String
Dim pos As Integer

    txt = rchMainText.Text
    pos = InStr(txt, txtFindText.Text)
    If pos = 0 Then
        Beep
    Else
        rchMainText.SelStart = pos - 1
        rchMainText.SelLength = Len(txtFindText.Text)
    End If
End Sub

' Find and select the indicated text skipping the
' indicated number of copies.
Private Sub FindTextRelative()                                     ' 3
Dim txt As String
Dim target As String
```

```
Dim targetlen As Integer
Dim pos As Integer
Dim skip As Integer
Dim trials As Integer

    txt = rchMainText.Text
    target = txtFindText.Text
    skip = CInt(txtSkip.Text)

    ' If skip >= 0, search forward from here.
    If skip >= 0 Then
        pos = rchMainText.SelStart + 1
        For trials = 0 To skip
            pos = InStr(pos + 1, txt, target)
            If pos = 0 Then Exit For
        Next trials
        If pos = 0 Then
            Beep
        Else
            rchMainText.SelStart = pos - 1
            rchMainText.SelLength = Len(txtFindText.Text)
        End If
    Else
        ' Skip < 0. Search backwards.
        targetlen = Len(target)
        trials = 0
        skip = -skip
        For pos = rchMainText.SelStart To 1 Step -1
            If Mid$(txt, pos, targetlen) = target Then
                trials = trials + 1
                If trials >= skip Then Exit For
            End If
        Next pos

        If pos <= 0 Then
            ' We didn't find it.
            Beep
        Else
            rchMainText.SelStart = pos - 1
            rchMainText.SelLength = targetlen
        End If
    End If
End Sub

' Color the selected text.
Private Sub ColorSelection(color As String)          ' 4
    Select Case color                                ' 2
        Case "Red"
            rchMainText.SelColor = vbRed
        Case "Green"
            rchMainText.SelColor = vbGreen
        Case "Blue"
```

```
            rchMainText.SelColor = vbBlue
        Case "Black"
            rchMainText.SelColor = vbBlack
        Case "Bold"
            rchMainText.SelBold = True
    End Select
End Sub


' Switch the value of the font's property.
Private Sub chkFontOption_Click(Index As Integer)
Dim value As Integer

    ' Ignore the event if the program is making the change.
    If SettingValues Then Exit Sub

    value = (chkFontOption(Index).value = vbChecked)
    Select Case Index
        Case chk_UNDERLINE
            rchMainText.SelUnderline = value
        Case chk_ITALIC
            rchMainText.SelItalic = value
        Case chk_STRIKETHROUGH
            rchMainText.SelStrikeThru = value
    End Select

    rchMainText.SetFocus
End Sub


' Update the check boxes.
Private Sub rchMainText_SelChange()                                ' 5
    ' Do not trigger a click event.
    SettingValues = True

    ' Check the SelUnderline property.
    Select Case rchMainText.SelUnderline
        Case True
            chkFontOption(chk_UNDERLINE).value = vbChecked
        Case False
            chkFontOption(chk_UNDERLINE).value = vbUnchecked
        Case Else ' More than one value.
            chkFontOption(chk_UNDERLINE).value = vbGrayed
    End Select

    ' Check the SelItalic property.
    Select Case rchMainText.SelItalic
        Case True
            chkFontOption(chk_ITALIC).value = vbChecked
        Case False
            chkFontOption(chk_ITALIC).value = vbUnchecked
        Case Else ' More than one value.
            chkFontOption(chk_ITALIC).value = vbGrayed
    End Select
```

```
' Check the SelStrikeThru property.
Select Case rchMainText.SelStrikeThru
    Case True
        chkFontOption(chk_STRIKETHROUGH).value = vbChecked
    Case False
        chkFontOption(chk_STRIKETHROUGH).value = vbUnchecked
    Case Else ' More than one value.
        chkFontOption(chk_STRIKETHROUGH).value = vbGrayed
End Select

SettingValues = False
End Sub
```

1. This subroutine is nonuniform and inelegant. It treats the different option button choices differently. It invokes subroutines for some and executes code itself for others. It should handle each case using the same style.

2. This statement should end with an Else clause to handle cases where none of the preceding tests is true. In that case, the Else clause should use a Stop statement to make the bug obvious.

3. This routine illustrates nonuniformity and featuritis. It is a powerful command that allows the user to search forward and backward while skipping any number of occurrences of the target text. It is unlikely that an application would actually need this functionality, though. Find and Find Next commands are more than adequate in most applications. It is also easy enough to unify Find and Find Next and make them share the same routine.

4. This routine performs two tasks that are only vaguely related: it colors text and it makes text bold. One hint that the routine is performing two unrelated tasks is that most of the cases modify SelColor, but one changes Sel-Bold. The routine also uses the single parameter color to represent two conceptually different values: text color and whether the text is bold.

5. This routine treats the different text properties uniformly. It could be simplified by moving the code executed for each of the three properties into a subroutine.

Figure A.1 shows an improved version of the program. This program treats bold, italic, underline, strikethrough, and color all uniformly as text attributes. The form has been modified to make that clear to the user. The resulting program has a simpler interface and simpler code.

The following code shows the improved version of this program.

```
Option Explicit

Private Const chk_UNDERLINE = 0
```

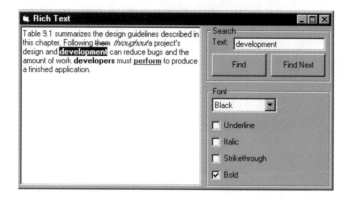

Figure A.1   Program Good9 uses a simplified user interface.

```
Private Const chk_ITALIC = 1
Private Const chk_STRIKETHROUGH = 2
Private Const chk_BOLD = 3

' True when the program is changing display values.
Private SettingValues As Boolean

' Find and select the indicated text starting from
' the beginning of the text.
Private Sub cmdFind_Click()
    FindText 1
End Sub

' Find and select the indicated text starting from
' the selected position + 1.
Private Sub cmdFindNext_Click()
    FindText rchMainText.SelStart + 2
End Sub

' Find and select the indicated text.
Private Sub FindText(start_pos As Integer)
Dim txt As String
Dim pos As Integer

    txt = rchMainText.Text
    pos = InStr(start_pos, txt, txtFindText.Text)
    If pos = 0 Then
        Beep
    Else
        rchMainText.SelStart = pos - 1
        rchMainText.SelLength = Len(txtFindText.Text)
    End If
    rchMainText.SetFocus
End Sub
```

```vb
' Set the selected text's color.
Private Sub cboSelColor_Click()
    If SettingValues Then Exit Sub

    Select Case cboSelColor.Text
        Case "Red"
            rchMainText.SelColor = vbRed
        Case "Green"
            rchMainText.SelColor = vbGreen
        Case "Blue"
            rchMainText.SelColor = vbBlue
        Case "Black"
            rchMainText.SelColor = vbBlack
        Case Else
            ' This should never happen.
            Stop
    End Select
    rchMainText.SetFocus
End Sub


' Switch the value of the font's property.
Private Sub chkFontOption_Click(Index As Integer)
Dim property_value As Integer

    ' Ignore the event if we are doing it.
    If SettingValues Then Exit Sub

    property_value = (chkFontOption(Index).Value = vbChecked)
    Select Case Index
        Case chk_UNDERLINE
            rchMainText.SelUnderline = property_value
        Case chk_ITALIC
            rchMainText.SelItalic = property_value
        Case chk_STRIKETHROUGH
            rchMainText.SelStrikeThru = property_value
        Case chk_BOLD
            rchMainText.SelBold = property_value
        Case Else
            ' This should never happen.
            Stop
    End Select

    rchMainText.SetFocus
End Sub


' Update the check boxes.
Private Sub rchMainText_SelChange()
    ' Do not trigger a click event.
    SettingValues = True

    ' Check the correct text style check boxes.
    CheckProperty rchMainText.SelUnderline, chkFontOption(chk_UNDERLINE)
```

```
CheckProperty rchMainText.SelItalic, chkFontOption(chk_ITALIC)
CheckProperty rchMainText.SelStrikeThru, _
    chkFontOption(chk_STRIKETHROUGH)
CheckProperty rchMainText.SelBold, chkFontOption(chk_BOLD)

' Display the correct color.
CheckColor

SettingValues = False
End Sub

' Set an option's checked value based on a text
' property value.
Private Sub CheckProperty(property_value As Variant, chk As CheckBox)
    Select Case property_value
        Case True
            chk.Value = vbChecked
        Case False
            chk.Value = vbUnchecked
        Case Else ' More than one value.
            chk.Value = vbGrayed
    End Select
End Sub

' Display the color of the selected text.
Private Sub CheckColor()
    Select Case rchMainText.SelColor
        Case vbRed
            cboSelColor.Text = "Red"
        Case vbGreen
            cboSelColor.Text = "Green"
        Case vbBlue
            cboSelColor.Text = "Blue"
        Case vbBlack
            cboSelColor.Text = "Black"
        Case Else ' More than one color.
            ' Select nothing.
            cboSelColor.ListIndex = -1
    End Select
End Sub
```

Chapter 10

Program Bad10's biggest problem is that it does not encapsulate the data that represents the items in the stack. The data values are stored directly in arrays within the main program. That means every routine that uses the stack must understand how the stack works. Later, if you decide to store the stack in a linked list instead of an array, you need to modify all of the routines that use the stack. This will be a lot of work and will give you lots of chances to make mistakes and create bugs.

The program also violates some other encapsulation guidelines in smaller ways. See the notes following the code for more specific comments.

```
Option Explicit

' The data for a person.
Private NumPeople As Integer
Private LastNames() As String                                    ' 1
Private FirstNames() As String

' Add an item to the stack.
Private Sub cmdPush_Click()
    ' Create space for the new person.
    ReDim Preserve LastNames(1 To NumPeople + 1)                 ' 2
    ReDim Preserve FirstNames(1 To NumPeople + 1)

    ' Save the new person's data.
    LastNames(NumPeople + 1) = txtLastName.Text
    FirstNames(NumPeople + 1) = txtFirstName.Text
    txtLastName.Text = ""
    txtFirstName.Text = ""

    ' Enable the Pop button.
    cmdPop.Enabled = True

    ' Update the number of people.
    NumPeople = NumPeople + 1

    ' Display the list.
    DisplayList
End Sub

' Remove the top item from the stack.
Private Sub cmdPop_Click()
    ' Display the person's values.
    txtLastName.Text = LastNames(NumPeople)
    txtFirstName.Text = FirstNames(NumPeople)

    ' Remove the last person.
    If NumPeople - 1 > 0 Then
        ReDim Preserve LastNames(1 To NumPeople - 1)             ' 3
        ReDim Preserve FirstNames(1 To NumPeople - 1)
    Else
        Erase LastNames
        Erase FirstNames
    End If

    ' Enable this button only if there are
    ' people left.
```

```
        cmdPop.Enabled = (NumPeople - 1 > 0)

        ' Save the new number of people.
        NumPeople = NumPeople - 1

        ' Display the list.
        DisplayList
    End Sub

' Display the people in the stack.
Private Sub DisplayList()
Dim i As Integer
Dim txt As String

    For i = 1 To NumPeople
        txt = LastNames(i) & ", " & _
            FirstNames(i) & _
            vbCrLf & txt
    Next i
    txtList.Text = txt

        ' The last name field is where the user will
        ' start editing the new data.
        txtLastName.SetFocus
    End Sub
```

1. The program uses parallel arrays LastNames and FirstNames to represent data for people. It should use a user-defined type containing LastName and FirstName fields instead. In this program, two arrays are manageable. In a larger program with a dozen or so fields for each person, the parallel array technique would be extremely awkward.

2. This routine calculates the expression NumPeople + 1 five times. It should calculate the value only once and save it in a variable for later use.

3. This routine calculates the expression NumPeople – 1 four times. It should calculate the value only once and save it in a variable for later use.

The following version of this program encapsulates the stack operations in the PersonStack class. Making the stack a class lets the program create new person stacks quickly and easily. In the previous version of the program, creating a new stack would be quite difficult. The program would need separate arrays and separate routines to manipulate the arrays for each stack. Using a class, creating a new stack is a simple matter of creating a new PersonStack object.

The PersonStack class encapsulates person data in the Person user-defined type. This UDT is used only by the PersonStack class to manage the stack. Because the rest of the program does not need to use the Person UDT, it is declared privately in the PersonStack class module.

```
' ****************
' File: Good10.frm
' ****************
Option Explicit

' The stack object.
Private TheStack As New PersonStack

' Add an item to the stack.
Private Sub cmdPush_Click()
    ' Save the new person's data.
    TheStack.Push txtLastName.Text, txtFirstName.Text
    txtLastName.Text = ""
    txtFirstName.Text = ""

    ' Enable the Pop button.
    cmdPop.Enabled = True

    ' Display the list.
    txtList.Text = TheStack.TextRepresentation
    txtLastName.SetFocus
End Sub

' Remove the top item from the stack.
Private Sub cmdPop_Click()
Dim last_name As String
Dim first_name As String

    ' Display the person's values.
    TheStack.Pop last_name, first_name
    txtLastName.Text = last_name
    txtFirstName.Text = first_name

    ' Enable this button only if there are
    ' people left.
    cmdPop.Enabled = (TheStack.NumPersons > 0)

    ' Display the list.
    txtList.Text = TheStack.TextRepresentation
    txtLastName.SetFocus
End Sub



' ****************
' File: Person.cls
' ****************
Option Explicit

' UDT to represent a person.
Private Type Person
    perLastName As String
```

```
        perFirstName As String
End Type


' The stack array.
Private NumPeople As Integer
Private People() As Person


' Add a person to the stack.
Public Sub Push(ByVal last_name As String, ByVal first_name As String)
    ' Update the number of people.
    NumPeople = NumPeople + 1

    ' Create space for the new person.
    ReDim Preserve People(1 To NumPeople)

    ' Save the new person's data.
    With People(NumPeople)
        .perLastName = last_name
        .perFirstName = first_name
    End With
End Sub


' Remove the top person from the stack. Return
' that person's data through parameters.
Public Sub Pop(last_name As String, first_name As String)
    ' Get the last person's data.
    With People(NumPeople)
        last_name = .perLastName
        first_name = .perFirstName
    End With

    ' Update the number of people.
    NumPeople = NumPeople - 1

    ' Remove the last person.
    If NumPeople > 0 Then
        ReDim Preserve People(1 To NumPeople)
    Else
        Erase People
    End If
End Sub


' Return the number of people in the stack.
Public Property Get NumPersons() As Integer
    NumPersons = NumPeople
End Property


' Return a textual representation of the stack.
Public Function TextRepresentation() As String
Dim i As Integer
Dim txt As String

    For i = 1 To NumPeople
```

```
                With People(i)
                    txt = .perLastName & ", " & _
                        .perFirstName & _
                        vbCrLf & txt
                End With
        Next i

        TextRepresentation = txt
    End Function
```

Chapter 11

The problem with program Bad11 is that it may sometimes try to access array elements with indexes outside the array's bounds. Even though integer overflow checks are disabled, overflow is not a problem because the CInt function raises overflow errors even if integer overflow checks are disabled. See the notes following the code for more specific comments.

```
Option Explicit

Private Values(1 To 100) As Single

Private Sub cmdGet_Click()
Dim index As Integer

    On Error GoTo GetError
    index = CLng(txtIndex.Text)                              ' 1
    txtValue.Text = Format$(CellValue(index))
    Exit Sub

GetError:
    MsgBox "Error" & Str$(Err.Number) & _
        " getting value." & vbCrLf & _
        Err.Description
End Sub

Private Sub cmdSet_Click()
    On Error GoTo SetError
    CellValue(txtIndex.Text) = txtValue.Text                 ' 2
    Exit Sub

SetError:
    MsgBox "Error" & Str$(Err.Number) & _
        " setting value." & vbCrLf & _
        Err.Description
End Sub

' Return the indicated array cell value.
Public Property Get CellValue(ByVal index As Integer) As Single
```

```
        CellValue = Values(index)                          ' 3
    End Property


    ' Set the indicated array cell value.
    Public Property Let CellValue(ByVal index As Integer, _
        new_value As Single)                               ' 4

        Values(index) = new_value                          ' 3
    End Property
```

1. If the value in txtIndex is too large, CInt will cause an overflow. However, the CInt function is not a numeric calculation, so it still raises an overflow error even if integer overflow errors are disabled. That means this statement does not make this optimization unsafe and the error is correctly trapped.

2. To call the CallValue property let procedure, Visual Basic must convert txtIndex.Text into an integer. This has the same consequences as using CInt (see note 1). In addition, if txtValue.Text is too large, it will cause a single precision overflow. Again, this error is raised properly even if floating-point error checks are disabled.

3. If index is less than 1 or greater than 100, it falls outside of the bounds of the Values array. If array bound checks are disabled, the program crashes.

4. The parameter new_value is passed by reference so it may be aliased. It is not clear whether that can cause a problem here because the parameter is never modified and the online documentation is vague. It would be safer to believe the worst and suppose that assuming no aliasing could cause problems. Alternatively, the parameter could be passed by value instead of by reference.

The following version of the code has been modified so it is safe for all of the optimizations. Note that the changes may slow the program enough to remove any advantage given by the optimizations.

```
Option Explicit

Private Values(1 To 100) As Single

Private Sub cmdGet_Click()
Dim index As Integer
Dim value As Single

    On Error GoTo GetError
    index = CInt(txtIndex.Text)
    txtValue.Text = Format$(CellValue(index))
    Exit Sub
```

```
GetError:
    MsgBox "Error" & Str$(Err.Number) & _
        " getting value." & vbCrLf & _
        Err.Description
End Sub

Private Sub cmdSet_Click()
    On Error GoTo SetError
    CellValue(txtIndex.Text) = txtValue.Text
    Exit Sub

SetError:
    MsgBox "Error" & Str$(Err.Number) & _
        " setting value." & vbCrLf & _
        Err.Description
End Sub

' Return the indicated array cell value.
Public Property Get CellValue(ByVal index As Integer) As Single
    ' Make sure the index is valid.
    If index < 1 Or index > 100 Then _
        Err.Raise 9, "Good11.CellValue", _
            "Subscript out of range"

    CellValue = Values(index)
End Property

' Set the indicated array cell value.
Public Property Let CellValue(ByVal index As Integer, _
    ByVal new_value As Single)

    ' Make sure the index is valid.
    If index < 1 Or index > 100 Then _
        Err.Raise 9, "Good11.CellValue", _
            "Subscript out of range"

    Values(index) = new_value
End Property
```

Chapter 12

Program Bad12 includes no error handling whatsoever. That makes it vulnerable to a couple kinds of errors. When the user resizes the form, the program tries to make its controls as big as possible. If the form is minimized or reduced to a very small height, the program tries to give some controls negative heights and crashes. The program also crashes if it is asked to display a nongraphic file.

The original bad version of the code follows. See the notes after the code for more specific comments.

```
Option Explicit

' Load cboPatterns with file selection patterns.
Private Sub Form_Load()                                        ' 1
    cboPatterns.AddItem "Bitmaps (*.bmp)"
    cboPatterns.AddItem "GIF (*.gif)"
    cboPatterns.AddItem "JPEG (*.jpg)"
    cboPatterns.AddItem "Graphic (*.bmp;*.gif;*.jpg)"
    cboPatterns.AddItem "All Files (*.*)"

    ' Start with the first choice (bitmaps) selected.
    cboPatterns.ListIndex = 0
End Sub

' Make the controls as big as possible.
Private Sub Form_Resize()                                      ' 1
Const GAP = 60

Dim wid As Integer
Dim hgt As Integer

    ' Put drvDrives at the top.
    wid = drvDrives.Width
    drvDrives.Move GAP, GAP, wid

    ' Put cboPatterns at the bottom.
    cboPatterns.Move GAP, ScaleHeight - cboPatterns.Height, wid

    ' Make dirDirectories and filFiles split the
    ' rest of the available height.
    hgt = (cboPatterns.Top - drvDrives.Top - _
        drvDrives.Height - 3 * GAP) / 2                        ' 2
    dirDirectories.Move GAP, drvDrives.Top + _
        drvDrives.Height + GAP, wid, hgt
    filFiles.Move GAP, dirDirectories.Top + _
        dirDirectories.Height + GAP, wid, hgt
End Sub

' The user selected a new pattern.
' Make filFiles use the selected pattern to list files.
Private Sub cboPatterns_Click()                                ' 1
Dim choice As String
Dim file_pattern As String
Dim start_pos As Integer
Dim end_pos As Integer

    ' Find the pattern between parentheses.
    choice = cboPatterns.List(cboPatterns.ListIndex)
    start_pos = InStr(choice, "(")
    end_pos = InStr(choice, ")")
    file_pattern = Mid$(choice, start_pos + 1, _
        end_pos - start_pos - 1)
```

```
        filFiles.Pattern = file_pattern
End Sub


' The user has picked a new drive.
' Update the directory list.
Private Sub drvDrives_Change()                            ' 1
    dirDirectories.Path = drvDrives.Drive                 ' 3
End Sub


' The user has picked a new directory.
' Update the file list.
Private Sub dirDirectories_Change()                       ' 1
    filFiles.Path = dirDirectories.Path
End Sub


' The user has picked a file.
' Display it.
Private Sub filFiles_Click()                              ' 1
Dim fname As String

    ' Display the selected file's full name
    ' in the form's caption.
    fname = filFiles.Path + "\" + filFiles.filename
    Caption = "Picture Viewer [" & fname & "]"

    ' Display the picture.
    MousePointer = vbHourglass
    DoEvents
    imgView.Picture = LoadPicture(fname)                  ' 4
    MousePointer = vbDefault
End Sub
```

1. All event handler code should have error handlers no matter how safe it seems.

2. If hgt <= 0, the program crashes. This occurs if the form is too short or if it is minimized. An error handler would detect this error, but the code should really protect itself with an If statement.

3. This routine crashes if the drive is not available; for example, if the user selects an empty floppy or CD-ROM drive.

4. This statement crashes if the file is not a graphic file.

The following code has been modified so it checks for all known and unknown errors. The program will continue to run even if an unexpected situation arises.

```
Option Explicit

' Set to False in the compiled version.
Private Const DEBUG_MODE = True
```

```
' Load cboPatterns with file selection patterns.
Private Sub Form_Load()
    On Error GoTo LoadError

    cboPatterns.AddItem "Bitmaps (*.bmp)"
    cboPatterns.AddItem "GIF (*.gif)"
    cboPatterns.AddItem "JPEG (*.jpg)"
    cboPatterns.AddItem "Graphic (*.bmp;*.gif;*.jpg)"
    cboPatterns.AddItem "All Files (*.*)"

    ' Start with the first choice (bitmaps) selected.
    cboPatterns.ListIndex = 0
    Exit Sub

LoadError:
    ' There are no known ways this routine can fail.
    ' At design time, stop so we can fix the bug.
    ' In the compiled version, continue.
    If DEBUG_MODE Then Stop
    Resume Next
End Sub

' Make the controls as big as possible.
Private Sub Form_Resize()
Const GAP = 60

Dim wid As Integer
Dim hgt As Integer

    On Error GoTo ResizeError

    ' Do nothing if the form is minimized.
    If WindowState = vbMinimized Then Exit Sub

    ' Put drvDrives at the top.
    wid = drvDrives.Width
    drvDrives.Move GAP, GAP, wid

    ' Put cboPatterns at the bottom.
    cboPatterns.Move GAP, ScaleHeight - cboPatterns.Height, wid

    ' Make dirDirectories and filFiles split the
    ' rest of the available height.
    hgt = (cboPatterns.Top - drvDrives.Top - _
        drvDrives.Height - 3 * GAP) / 2
    If hgt < 100 Then hgt = 100
    dirDirectories.Move GAP, drvDrives.Top + _
        drvDrives.Height + GAP, wid, hgt
    filFiles.Move GAP, dirDirectories.Top + _
        dirDirectories.Height + GAP, wid, hgt
    Exit Sub
```

```
ResizeError:
    ' There are no known ways this routine can fail.
    ' At design time, stop so we can fix the bug.
    ' In the compiled version, continue.
    If DEBUG_MODE Then Stop
    Resume Next
End Sub


' The user selected a new pattern.
' Make filFiles use the selected pattern to list files.
Private Sub cboPatterns_Click()
Dim choice As String
Dim file_pattern As String
Dim start_pos As Integer
Dim end_pos As Integer

    On Error GoTo NewPatternError

    ' Find the pattern between parentheses.
    choice = cboPatterns.List(cboPatterns.ListIndex)
    start_pos = InStr(choice, "(")
    end_pos = InStr(choice, ")")
    file_pattern = Mid$(choice, start_pos + 1, _
        end_pos - start_pos - 1)

    filFiles.Pattern = file_pattern
    Exit Sub

NewPatternError:
    ' There are no known ways this routine can fail.
    ' At design time, stop so we can fix the bug.
    ' In the compiled version, continue.
    If DEBUG_MODE Then Stop
    Resume Next
End Sub

' The user has picked a new drive.
' Update the directory list.
Private Sub drvDrives_Change()
    On Error GoTo DriveError

    dirDirectories.Path = drvDrives.Drive
    Exit Sub

DriveError:
    If MsgBox("Drive " & drvDrives.Drive & _
        " is unavailable. Try again?", _
        vbRetryCancel, "Drive Unavailable") _
        = vbRetry _
    Then
        ' Try again. The user may have inserted
        ' a missing floppy disk or CD-ROM.
```

```
        Resume
    End If


    ' Keep the previously selected drive.
    drvDrives.Drive = dirDirectories.Path
    Exit Sub
End Sub

' The user has picked a new directory.
' Update the file list.
Private Sub dirDirectories_Change()
    On Error GoTo DirectoryError

    filFiles.Path = dirDirectories.Path
    Exit Sub

DirectoryError:
    ' There are no known ways this routine can fail.
    ' At design time, stop so we can fix the bug.
    ' In the compiled version, continue.
    If DEBUG_MODE Then Stop
    Resume Next
End Sub

' The user has picked a file.
' Display it.
Private Sub filFiles_Click()
Dim fname As String

    On Error GoTo LoadPictureError

    ' Display the selected file's full name
    ' in the form's caption.
    fname = filFiles.Path
    If Right$(fname, 1) <> "\" Then fname = fname & "\"
    fname = fname & filFiles.filename
    Caption = "Picture Viewer [" & fname & "]"

    ' Display the picture.
    MousePointer = vbHourglass
    DoEvents
    imgView.Picture = LoadPicture(fname)
    MousePointer = vbDefault
    Exit Sub

LoadPictureError:
    If Err.Number = 481 Then
        ' The picture failed to load. This is an
        ' expected error but not a bug. Let the user know
        ' the file could not be loaded and continue.
        Beep
        Caption = "Picture Viewer [Invalid picture]"
        Set imgView.Picture = Nothing
```

```
        Else
            ' This is an unknown error.
            ' There are no other known ways this routine can fail.
            ' At design time, stop so we can fix the bug.
            ' In the compiled version, continue.
            If DEBUG_MODE Then Stop
        End If

        ' Among other things, the Resume Next lets the
        ' code continue until it resets the cursor with:
        '    MousePointer = vbDefault
        Resume Next
    End Sub
```

Chapter 13

Program Bad13 has a few problems. The main program's code that follows does not exit before the error handlers. The program enters the error handling code even if it is successful. It also does not let the user know anything is wrong when an error occurs.

While the main program has problems when it succeeds, the error management code has problems when it fails. It does not tell the user if there is a problem saving the error information.

One particularly troublesome case occurs if the prefix directory C:\Errors does not exist. In that case, the first call to the Dir function finds a filename that is not used; unfortunately, it is not used because it is invalid. When the program tries to create the file, it fails. If this directory does not exist, no error messages will ever be saved. For specific comments, see the notes that follow the code.

```
' Calculate the ratio of A / B.
Private Sub cmdCalculate_Click()
Dim A As Single
Dim B As Single
Dim A_over_B As Single

    On Error GoTo RaiseErrorError

    A = CSng(txtA.Text)
    B = CSng(txtB.Text)
    A_over_B = A / B
    lblAOverB.Caption = Format$(A_over_B, "0.000")

RaiseErrorError:                                            ' 1
    SaveErrorToFile _
        "Error " & Format$(Err.number) & _
        " in FileError.cmdRaiseError_Click." & _
        vbCrLf & Err.Description                            ' 2
```

```
End Sub

' Append mail to an error log file.
Public Sub SaveErrorToFile(ByVal txt As String)
Const FILE_PREFIX = "C:\Errors\err"                            ' 3
Const FILE_SUFFIX = ".txt"
Dim file_name As String
Dim fnum As Integer
Dim trial As Integer

    On Error GoTo SaveErrorToFileError

    ' Find a file name we can use.
    trial = 1
    Do
        ' Compute the next name to try.
        file_name = FILE_PREFIX & _
            Format$(trial) & FILE_SUFFIX

        ' See if the file exists.
        If Dir(file_name) = "" Then Exit Do
        trial = trial + 1
    Loop

    ' Open the file.
    fnum = FreeFile
    Open file_name For Append As #fnum                         ' 4

    ' Write the date and time, and the error message.
    Print #fnum, Now, txt, "**********"                        ' 5

    ' Close the file.
    Close #fnum
    Exit Sub

SaveErrorToFileError:
    ' There was an error saving to the file.
    ' Just display the message.
    MsgBox txt                                                 ' 6
    Exit Sub
End Sub
```

1. The program should use Exit Sub before the error handling code.

2. The program should blank the lblAOverB label and display an error message when it fails.

3. The program could check to see if this directory exists. If not, it could warn the user and use another directory more likely to exist, such as C:\.

4. Since the program is creating a file that does not exist, it should open the file for Output instead of Append. Opening for Append works, but it does not reflect what the program is doing.

5. Here the code tries to save a few lines of code by saving all these values at once. Unfortunately, that places them all on the same line in the file, making the file hard to read.

6. The error handler does not close the file if it is open. It also does not describe the new error. Instead, it glosses over an important bug.

This program must cope with two main error conditions: divide by zero errors when B is 0, and conversion errors when A or B are nonnumeric. They are known errors that may be caused by the user. The program should check for those conditions and handle them specifically.

The following code is modified so it handles errors and success more gracefully.

```
' Calculate the ratio of A / B.
Private Sub cmdCalculate_Click()
Dim A As Single
Dim B As Single
Dim A_over_B As Single

    On Error GoTo RaiseErrorError

    A = CSng(txtA.Text)
    B = CSng(txtB.Text)
    A_over_B = A / B
    lblAOverB.Caption = Format$(A_over_B, "0.000")
    Exit Sub

RaiseErrorError:
    ' Blank the result.
    lblAOverB.Caption = ""

    ' See what kind of error it was.
    Select Case Err.number
        Case 11
            ' Divide by zero.
            MsgBox "B must not be zero."
            Exit Sub

        Case 13
            ' Type mismatch.
            MsgBox "Both arguments must be numeric."
            Exit Sub

        Case Else
            ' Tell the user we failed.
            MsgBox "Error calculating ratio."

            ' Save an error message.
            SaveErrorToFile _
                "Error " & Format$(Err.number) & _
```

```
                       " in FileError.cmdRaiseError_Click." & _
                    vbCrLf & Err.Description
        End Select
End Sub

' Append mail to an error log file.
Public Sub SaveErrorToFile(ByVal txt1 As String)
Const FILE_DIRECTORY = "C:\Errors"
Const BACKUP_DIRECTORY = "C:\"
Const FILE_SUFFIX = ".txt"
Dim file_prefix As String
Dim file_name As String
Dim fnum As Integer
Dim trial As Integer
Dim txt2 As String
Dim file_open As Boolean

    On Error GoTo SaveErrorToFileError

    ' See if the error directory exists.
    If Dir(FILE_DIRECTORY) <> "" Then
        file_prefix = FILE_DIRECTORY & "err"
    Else
        file_prefix = BACKUP_DIRECTORY & "err"
        txt1 = txt1 & vbCrLf & _
            "Warning: Directory " & _
            FILE_DIRECTORY & _
            " does not exist. Using " & _
            BACKUP_DIRECTORY & "."
    End If

    ' Find a file name we can use.
    trial = 1
    Do
        ' Compute the next name to try.
        file_name = file_prefix & _
            Format$(trial) & FILE_SUFFIX

        ' See if the file exists.
        If Dir(file_name) = "" Then Exit Do
        trial = trial + 1
    Loop

    ' Open the file.
    fnum = FreeFile
    Open file_name For Output As #fnum
    file_open = True

    ' Write the date and time, and the error message.
    Print #fnum, Now
    Print #fnum, txt1
    Print #fnum, "**********"
```

```
      ' Close the file.
      Close #fnum
      Exit Sub


SaveErrorToFileError:
      ' There was an error saving to the file.
      ' Just display the message.
      txt2 = "Error " & Format$(Err.number) & _
          " saving error message to file." & _
          vbCrLf & Err.Description
      MsgBox txt2 & vbCrLf & vbCrLf & txt1

      ' Close the file if it is open.
      If file_open Then Close #fnum
      Exit Sub
End Sub
```

Chapter 14

The Calc program available on the book's Web site performs black box and white box tests. You can use the Test menu's Black Box and White Box commands to run the tests.

There are two ways the user can enter values into the program: clicking on buttons and pressing keys on the keyboard. For example, to enter a + operator, the user can click the + button or press the + key. Program Calc allows you to determine which type of input to test. Select the Key or Button command from the Tests menu to tell the program which method to use. Then when you run a test, the test routine uses the appropriate input method to send inputs to the program.

The program's black box test generates random numbers and random operators. It enters the first value, the operator, and the second value. It then sends the equals character and compares the result in the display TextBox with a value the test calculates.

To look for unusual special cases, the program generates three sets of random values. These values are small, medium, and large, and are chosen from the three ranges –1 to 1, –1000000 to 1000000, and –999999999999 to 999999999999.

The white box tests do the following:

- Force an overflow
- Force an underflow
- Divide by zero

- Multiply by zero
- Subtract a number from itself
- Multiply two very small values
- Add two very small values
- Create the largest and smallest sums possible
- Create one more than the largest sum possible
- Create one less than the smallest sum possible
- Enter very long values and verify that they are truncated correctly

These tests were not scientifically generated. They were simply chosen to test unusual special cases that could make the program fail. Despite their ad hoc creation, in some of the early versions of the program these tests were very helpful in pinpointing bugs.

Chapter 15

Figure A.2 shows line timing results produced by the Visual Basic Code Profiler for program Bad15. These results show that the program spends almost 80 percent of its time in just two lines in the Crypt subroutine.

```
ch = Mid$(txtIn.Text, i, 1)
    :
txtOut.Text = txtOut.Text & ch
```

These lines are hit often, but other lines are hit just as often and they do not take a lot of time. The reason these lines are slow is that they reference a control's properties. Referencing properties is relatively slow.

Line Timing Analysis

FuncName	CodeLine	TotalTime	AvgTime	PctTime	Hits	PctHits	LineText
Crypt	3	0.0400	0	1.28%	890	10.04%	For i = 1 To Len(txtIn.Text)
cmdEncrypt_Click	2	0.0400	0.0400	1.28%	1	0.01%	txtCiphertext.Text = ""
Crypt	11	0.0500	0.0001	1.60%	890	10.04%	ch = Chr$(ch_num)
cmdEncrypt_Click	3	0.0500	0.0500	1.60%	1	0.01%	MousePointer = vbHourglass
cmdEncrypt_Click	4	0.0500	0.0500	1.60%	1	0.01%	DoEvents
Crypt	7	0.0600	0.0001	1.91%	878	9.90%	ch_num = ch_num + key - MIN_ASC
Crypt	6	0.0600	0.0001	1.91%	890	10.04%	If ch_num >= MIN_ASC And ch_num <= MAX_ASC Then
Crypt	8	0.0800	0.0001	2.55%	878	9.90%	ch_num = (ch_num Mod NUM_ASC)
Crypt	10	0.1010	0.0001	3.22%	878	9.90%	ch_num = ch_num + MIN_ASC
Crypt	4	0.5610	0.0006	17.90%	890	10.04%	ch = Mid$(txtIn.Text, i, 1)
Crypt	12	1.9110	0.0021	60.98%	890	10.04%	txtOut.Text = txtOut.Text & ch

Figure A.2　Line timing results for program Bad15.

An easy way to make this routine much faster is to store these values in string variables instead of using the object properties. When the Crypt routine begins, it stores the value txtIn.Text in a local variable and then uses that variable in the Mid$ statement. It also builds the output string in a local variable and assigns the result to txtOut.Text only when the conversion is finished.

If you are a fairly experienced Visual Basic programmer, you may have known that accessing control properties is slow and guessed that these two lines were the problem. If you did not make this guess and you did not use the code profiler, you might have assumed that the complicated mathematical statements were to blame for the poor performance. You might have wasted a lot of time tuning those lines without making much improvement. You might also have introduced a bug or two.

Making the routine store the two string values in local variables reduces its time to encrypt 1000 characters from around seven seconds to less than one second. The following code shows the two improvements. Because the crypt subroutine contains the program's only modifications, only it is shown here.

```
' Encrypt the input text.
Private Sub Crypt(ByVal txtIn As TextBox, ByVal txtOut As TextBox, _
    ByVal key As Integer)
Const MIN_ASC = 32  ' ASCII code for space.
Const MAX_ASC = 126 ' ASCII code for ~.
Const NUM_ASC = MAX_ASC - MIN_ASC + 1

Dim i As Integer
Dim ch As String
Dim ch_num As String
Dim input_text As String
Dim output_text As String

    input_text = txtIn.Text
    For i = 1 To Len(input_text)
        ch = Mid$(input_text, i, 1)
        ch_num = Asc(ch)
        ' Translate only printable characters.
        If ch_num >= MIN_ASC And ch_num <= MAX_ASC Then
            ch_num = ch_num + key - MIN_ASC
            ch_num = (ch_num Mod NUM_ASC)
            If ch_num < 0 Then ch_num = ch_num + NUM_ASC
            ch_num = ch_num + MIN_ASC
        End If
        ch = Chr$(ch_num)
        output_text = output_text & ch
    Next i
    txtOut.Text = output_text
End Sub
```

Chapter 16

If you use VBCP to run a line timing test on program Bad16, you will find that the program spends more than 95 percent of its time performing 4036 hits on the following statement in the ShadePicture subroutine.

```
picGraph.Line (0, Y)- _
    (picGraph.ScaleWidth, Y), _
    RGB(clr, clr, clr)
```

This line should not be executed so many times. The picGraph control is only a few hundred pixels tall, so the program should not be drawing more than 4000 lines on it. In fact, most computer monitors are only 600 or so pixels tall, so the program should never need to draw more than about 600 lines to completely cover the screen.

The problem with program Bad16 is that the picGraph control's ScaleMode property is initially set to vbTwips. Recall that there are 1/1440 twips per inch. The computer where I ran this test has 15 twips per pixel. That means the program draws 15 times as many lines as necessary to completely fill the PictureBox.

One solution to this problem would be to make the ShadePicture subroutine change the control's ScaleMode to vbPixels. Then subroutine ShadePicture would work as it is written. However, this solution violates the intent of the rule "Fix routines, not lines." Changing this control's ScaleMode property would make ShadePicture work, but it would break other routines.

This program's Form_Load event handler calls subroutines LoadData, ShadePicture, and DrawGraph, in that order. LoadData generates data based on the PictureBox's current size in twips. If ShadePicture changes the ScaleMode to pixels, subroutine DrawGraph will not be able to use the values saved by LoadData.

To fix the bug without introducing a new one, ShadePicture saves the control's scale properties before it shades the picture. It then restores the scale properties when it is finished. This is the approach taken in the following code. Only the ShadePicture routine needs to be changed, so only it is shown here.

```
' Shade picGraph from white at the top to
' black at the bottom.
Private Sub ShadePicture()
Const START_COLOR = 255
Const END_COLOR = 0
Dim Y As Single
Dim clr As Single
Dim d_clr As Single
```

```
Dim scale_mode As Integer
Dim scale_left As Single
Dim scale_top As Single
Dim scale_width As Single
Dim scale_height As Single

    ' Save the current scale information.
    scale_mode = picGraph.ScaleMode
    If scale_mode = vbUser Then
        scale_left = picGraph.ScaleLeft
        scale_top = picGraph.ScaleTop
        scale_width = picGraph.ScaleWidth
        scale_height = picGraph.ScaleHeight
    End If

    ' Shade using pixels.
    picGraph.ScaleMode = vbPixels

    d_clr = (END_COLOR - START_COLOR) / picGraph.ScaleHeight
    clr = START_COLOR
    For Y = 0 To picGraph.ScaleHeight
        picGraph.Line (0, Y)- _
            (picGraph.ScaleWidth, Y), _
            RGB(clr, clr, clr)
        clr = clr + d_clr
    Next Y

    ' Restore the scale information.
    If scale_mode = vbUser Then
        picGraph.Scale (scale_left, scale_top)- _
            (scale_left + scale_width, _
            scale_top + scale_height)
    Else
        picGraph.ScaleMode = scale_mode
    End If
End Sub
```

Header Comment Templates

T his appendix contains templates for header-style comments. You can add them to your files and routines, and then fill in the blanks. You can download copies of these templates from the book's Web site at www.vb-helper.com/err.htm.

Files

Remove any headings that you do not use in a particular file. For instance, if a .BAS module does not define any public variables, you should remove the public variable section.

```
' *************************************************
' File:
' Copyright:
'
' Date Created:
' Initial Author:
'
' Purpose:
'
' Entry Points:
'
' Dependencies:
'
' Issues:
'
```

```
' Method:
' ************************************************
Option Explicit

' ************************************************
' Global Definitions
' -------------------------
' Global API Declarations
' -------------------------

' -------------------------
' Global Types
' -------------------------

' -
' Global Enums and Constants
' -------------------------

' -------------------------
' Global Variables
' -------------------------

' ************************************************
' Private Definitions
' -------------------------
' Private API Declarations
' -------------------------

' -------------------------
' Private Types
' -------------------------

' -------------------------
' Private Constants and Enums
' -------------------------

' -------------------------
' Private Variables
' -------------------------
```

Routines

You may want to leave in sections in these comments even if they do not apply to a particular routine. For example, if a function takes no parameters, you may want to use the following comment to make it clear that the input section is blank and not accidentally omitted.

```
' Inputs:
'    None.
```

Some programmers place a routine's comments after its declaration and before any variable declarations. It does not matter where you place the comments, as long as you are consistent.

```
' **************************************************
' Purpose:
'
' Method:
'
' Inputs:
'
' Outputs:
'
' Errors:
'
' Asserts:
'
' Developer        Date      Comments
' ---------        --------  --------
'
' **************************************************
```

Event Handlers

Experienced programmers are familiar with the parameters of most common event handlers, so the comments do not need to explain them. A reader with questions can consult Visual Basic's online help

One exception to this rule is if the event handler has side effects. For example, if the routine updates a global variable, that information should be listed in the output section.

```
' **************************************************
' Purpose:
' Method:
'
' Outputs:
'
' Asserts:
'
' Developer        Date      Comments
' ---------        --------  --------
'
' **************************************************
```